THE GREATEST SEA SURVIVAL
STORIES EVER TOLD

THE GREATEST SEA SURVIVAL STORIES EVER TOLD

EDITED BY TOM MCCARTHY

Guilford, Connecticut

An imprint of The Rowman & Littlefield Publishing Group, Inc.
4501 Forbes Blvd., Ste. 200
Lanham, MD 20706
www.rowman.com

Distributed by NATIONAL BOOK NETWORK

Copyright © 2020 by Thomas P. McCarthy

British Library Cataloguing in Publication Information available

Library of Congress Cataloging-in-Publication Data available

ISBN 978-1-4930-4736-9 (paperback)

∞™ The paper used in this publication meets the minimum requirements of American National Standard for Information Sciences—Permanence of Paper for Printed Library Materials, ANSI/NISO Z39.48-1992.

CONTENTS

INTRODUCTION

WHAT SORT OF PERSON SURVIVES A SHIPWRECK?

What internal chemistry is required to spend five days drifting in the Pacific under a broiling sun while shipmates floating beside you are ripped apart by sharks? How does one maintain any sort of sanity? What degree of strength is needed to live for seventy days in a small boat as you watch your fellow survivors voluntarily drop into the sea to end it all? For that matter, at what point does one decide not to mourn over the body of a crewmate but rather to eat him?

Do only a rare few possess the specific alchemy to survive? Judging from the stories in this amazing collection, the answer is yes. But readers will also see that survival calls for a certain mad and perhaps blind combination of grit, luck, and pure determination. It is a unique blend that allows a certain man or woman to live while others wilt and perish.

Fear was no doubt a common experience for everyone thrust by cruel fate into the impossible situations you will read about in the following pages. For anyone sitting adrift in a small, fragile boat while a ship sinks rapidly nearby, the prospect of what lies ahead can hold only terror. Everyone who has experienced this has been afraid. In these stories, those who controlled their fear—the stronger ones who somehow used it to motivate themselves—made it to shore. Those who were overcome by fear soon enough perished.

Every one of the survivors herein seems almost to have had an insouciance toward the Grim Reaper that allowed them to move ahead as others around them wilted and died.

Readers of these inspiring and often shocking stories will quickly learn of one thing the survivors in this collection lacked, and therein is perhaps the greatest lesson: There were no handwringers among them, no neurotic worrywarts frantic and angry at the unfairness of fate and circumstances that put them in a fragile boat on a heaving sea thousands of miles from home and comfort. If there is one common theme that emerges, it is the fact that the self-absorbed and self-important sorts who put themselves first were inevitably among the first to succumb, unable to survive. In life, perhaps, they had always wanted to be at the front of the line, though not this particular line.

It is also clear that those who survived the calamities in this collection had no room for anger or resentment. Readers will learn that anger wastes the emotional and physical reservoirs necessary to live. In each of these stories, the survivors who emerged and made it back to safety had one common trait: the emotional energy to shrug off harsh reality—to ignore it, in fact—and channel their internal resources into ways to survive. These survivors did not panic. Ever.

The stories in this collection will provide a master class for readers seeking to understand the singular psychic strength that can persist under the direst of conditions. On a simpler level, these tales offer an astounding look at how one can stare down death and survive—with courage and strength and amazing patience. There is among the survivors a certain arrogance toward death.

These tales are also a resounding affirmation of the power of hope and the ingenuity it can inspire. One group of survivors built a working sextant from small metal scraps after their ship hit a reef. Others found creative ways to collect water, making their fragile crafts habitable as they gathered the courage to carry on. Certainly, luck plays a major role in these tales, but so too does the power of hope and its motivating aspect.

Read on, and you will see this for yourselves, whether you are looking for a common thread or simply for a romping and inspirational read.

One

The Loss of the *Indianapolis*

Raymond B. Lech

Five minutes past midnight on July 30, 1945, the first torpedo smashed into the starboard bow of the United States heavy cruiser *Indianapolis*, and an ear-shattering explosion rocked the ship. Three seconds later, the second torpedo found its mark directly under the bridge and blew up. The vessel lifted slightly out of the water, quivered, then promptly settled back down. At the same time, from the bridge to the bow on the starboard side, water was sent soaring into the midnight sky; flame, steam, and smoke belched out of her forward stack, and an enormous ball of fire swept through the entire forward half of the ship. Within seconds, the fire died away. Once again the *Indianapolis* was level and riding high, but now with the bow gone and two huge gaping holes in her right side.

From midships forward, the cruiser was a complete disaster; no light, no power, no communication, no pressure. Although the rear half of the vessel was untouched, the tons of water that gushed into the forward part of the cruiser sealed the fate of the *Indianapolis*.

IN THE WATER THE FIRST DAY: MONDAY, JULY 30, 1945

Quartermaster 3rd Class Vincent Allard found himself with six or seven other men, all desperately hanging onto a coiled floater net. One of them had a bared knife and was busy cutting the tangles in the net so that it would uncoil and spread out. While this was going on, Allard heard a cry for help. He quickly swam toward the sound and in a few seconds found a sailor floating on a pontoon from one of the ship's planes. He guided the man back to the group clustered around the net, but no sooner did he return when again he heard cries for help. Off he went once more and soon spotted two men holding onto a potato crate. One of the boys could swim, but the other could not and was very scared. Telling the swimmer to stick close, Allard began helping the nonswimmer to the safety of the net. On the way toward the group, he heard someone yell that he had a raft. Since it seemed that the raft was closer than the net, Allard changed course and headed for the sound. The voice called again, and Allard thought he recognized it as the *Indianapolis*'s skipper, Captain Charles Butler McVay III. Allard called out to ask if it were the captain calling, and Captain McVay replied that it was and to come aboard. They swam a short distance and reached the rafts.

The man who could swim climbed unassisted into the empty second raft, McVay and Allard helped the other sailor in, and then Allard joined McVay in his raft. The two men in the second raft had swallowed an enormous amount of water, and at first Captain McVay thought they were both dying. But after a while, they came around. Just before sunrise, they met up with five men on another raft that had a floater net tied to it. They lashed this raft to theirs, and, at first light Monday morning, the group consisted of three rafts, one net, and nine men. Captain McVay was the only officer.

An inspection of the rafts turned up two canoe paddles, a box of cigarettes, fishing gear, signaling mirrors, and a tin container that held twelve Very (star) shells and a pistol. They also found a canvas bag holding a first-aid kit and matches, but it was soaked and everything inside was useless except for some sealed tubes of ointment. During the day, a water breaker holding three gallons of water floated by. This was given to McVay to be tasted, but salt water had leaked into the archaic wooden container and the water was undrinkable. So as not to create unnecessary fear, the captain didn't pass on the bad news but told everyone it would be rationed out when he thought it was "absolutely necessary that they have a drink."

No food was found on any of the rafts, but fortunately, sometime during the day, an emergency ration can drifted by. Upon opening, they found it was dry inside, and they pulled out a number of cans of Spam and small tins of malted-milk tablets and biscuits. The skipper told the other eight men that one twelve-ounce tin of Spam would be opened daily and divided equally. In addition, everyone would daily receive two biscuits and two malted-milk tablets. Under this quota, he figured they had rations to last ten days.

When the rafts crashed into the sea, their gratings had broken. Nevertheless the men made themselves as comfortable as possible and hung on while they were tossed about by the heavy swells of the unending ocean. At one moment they would be deep in a valley of waves and the next moment on top, looking down into that same valley. While on this unwanted roller-coaster ride, resting momentarily on the crest of a wave, they spotted two other rafts also on the crest of their waves. One raft was about 1,500 yards away and appeared to have one man on it who was calling for help. The other raft was much farther away and looked like it held a group of men who seemed to be in good condition. At this time though, McVay's group was too exhausted to paddle over to the near raft, and any investigation had to be held off until the next day.

During this first day, a monstrous shark decided to investigate the raft and its edible cargo. The shark kept swimming under the raft. The dorsal fin was "almost as white as a sheet of paper," while the body was a darker color. The shark could therefore always be spotted because of the visibility of its white fin in the water. The frightened men attempted to catch the pilot fish by knocking them off with canoe paddles, but this was an exercise in futility. They also tried hitting the shark with paddles, but when they occasionally did manage to do so he swam away and returned a few minutes later. In the days to follow, this unwanted nuisance was to become a real menace.

After spotting the two distant rafts, McVay and the others assumed that they were the only survivors of the ship and, all in all, figured no more than twenty-five or thirty men, including themselves, made it off. What they didn't know at the time was that they had drifted seven to ten miles north of the main groups.

Stranded in the middle of the deep and seemingly never-ending Philippine Sea, the captain understandably became very depressed. He daydreamed about taking a bath, drinking a cocktail, and relaxing in comfort, and in the midst of such thoughts he wished to live, but soon reality broke in upon his fantasies.

He dreaded the idea of seeing again the wives of his now dead officers. While at Mare Island, he and Mrs. McVay had gotten to know these women, and now "I knew there was nothing I could say to them. . . ." His mind drifted back to Guam. He remembered the moment when he was told no escort was needed, and he cursed the people there for not having one available; if there had been an escort, it could have radioed for help and picked up survivors. His final, and unfortunately most nagging, thought was of his personal responsibility: he was the captain, like it or not.

Two hours prior to the close of their first day, a plane flew overhead, its red-and-green running lights clearly visible. McVay fired one of the star shells skyward, but it went unnoticed. The container holding the shells had sixteen fillers but only twelve shells, which was the standard issue for this type of raft. It irked McVay to see four empty slots. Why couldn't they just fill the entire thing up and be done with it?

As the day drew to an end, however, spirits were high in anticipation of the morrow's rescue. The *Indianapolis* was due in Leyte Gulf in the morning, and when the heavy cruiser didn't show up questions would be asked, a search made, and rescue would be on the way.

—◆—

After narrowly escaping from his after engine room, Lieutenant Richard Redmayne swam from the starboard side of the *Indianapolis*. Within five minutes, he found a kapok life preserver, which he put on, and for about a half hour he rested in the water alone. Then he spotted a life raft with men on it and joined them. During the remaining dark morning hours, two more rafts and two floater nets joined the group. The three rafts and two nets were lashed together, and they continued to drift, picking up water breakers, floating food containers, and other men.

Surveying the area at first light, they found the hostile sea covered with a heavy oil slick, five-inch powder cans, and an assortment of junk. Many of the men were terribly sick from swallowing sea water and oil, and the ones who had passed out in the water were being held up by their shipmates. A head count was attempted, and they discovered that their group consisted of approximately 150 men, including four officers and five chiefs. Lieutenant Redmayne, as the senior officer, took charge.

In addition to the three rafts and two nets, about 90 percent of the people in the water in this group were wearing life jackets; the ones who didn't have any held onto the side of the rafts or onto men who had jackets, or they hugged empty ammo cans. The rafts themselves were very overcrowded, each one averaging fifteen to twenty men, and the sailors who had been put on the rafts were the ones the officers and others in charge thought to be in the worst condition.

On Monday, nothing much happened. The large group floated, drifted, survived. They spotted the same two afternoon planes McVay had seen and also fired flares at the one plane that evening, with no success.

Certain early signs of insubordination surfaced. One of the men on the floater net was Petty Officer F. Giulio. Because of his particular job aboard ship, he was well known among the crew. On this first day, he kept complaining that he should be put on a raft since the life jacket kept slipping around his legs and he had a hard time keeping afloat. Giulio was the senior ranking man on that net and therefore their natural leader.

Distributed among the rafts and nets were four water casks and about nine or ten emergency tins of food, which contained malted-milk tablets, biscuits, and Spam. During the late afternoon, Giulio and some of his followers broke into the rations and began to eat. A short distance away, Chief Petty Officer Clarence Benton spotted them and immediately ordered them to stop, since all rations were to be divided equally. For the time being, Giulio and his small group obeyed the order.

During the evening Lieutenant Redmayne allowed a small amount of food to be rationed equally to all the men in the group.

At approximately 1:30 a.m., Quartermaster 1st Class Robert Gause spotted a fin. By estimating the distance between the dorsal and tail, he guessed the shark to be about twelve feet long.

Quite a few sailors in his group were critically wounded. There were a large number of severe flash burns of the face, arms, and body, and some men had compound fractures of one sort or another. There were no medical supplies of any kind for the frustrated Doctor Lewis Haynes, and many of the men with fractures and burns died from shock during the first few hours. After removing their life jackets, the dead were allowed to slip away. Before the boiling sun rose over the distant horizon on Monday morning, about fifty of the original four hundred were dead.

By daybreak, this mass of floating humanity had split into three subgroups. The largest group contained about two hundred men, the second one hundred, and the smallest about fifty. These subgroups were separated from each other by a distance of only several hundred yards, at most. Leader of the group of two hundred men was Captain Edward Parke, commanding officer of the Marine Detachment and holder of the Bronze Star for bravery on Guadalcanal. Strong and athletic, he was superb in his energy, leadership, and self-sacrifice. Dr. Haynes remembered him as the typical Marine, one who was very strict with the group and had the situation well in hand.

The main objective was for everyone to stay together. Captain Parke found a cork life ring with about one hundred feet of attached line. To prevent drifting, he strung the line out and each man grabbed a piece of it and took up the slack. In this way, they formed a long line of men which began to curl on itself, as a wagon train would circle against attack. The wounded were brought into the middle and tied to the life ring itself by the strings on their jackets. There was no confusion, and the men stayed well grouped together. If someone did drift off the line, Parke swam over to the man and herded him back in. On several occasions, he gave his jacket to a man without one and swam unsupported until he could find another preserver.

Bravery in this enormous group of "swimmers" was everywhere. Commander Lipski, the ship's gunnery officer, who had been very badly burned, was cheerfully supported all day Monday by Airman 1st Class Anthony Maday. Lieutenant Commander Coleman, who came aboard in Guam, was the leader of a group, and he worked unceasingly to keep them together. Time after time, he swam out to bring in stragglers. Ultimately, Commander Coleman became so weak that he died from exhaustion. And there was Ensign Moynelo, who organized a large group of men. For three days, he kept the group together, rounded up drifters, and took off his own jacket many times and gave it to those without until he could find another. Finally he, too, collapsed and died.

Shortly after dawn on Monday, Lieutenant Commander Moss W. Flannery, commanding officer of VPB-133 based on Tinian, climbed into his Ventura bomber and headed out over the Philippine Sea on routine antisubmarine patrol. Visibility was unlimited and in order to obtain better horizon shots for navigation, instead of flying at his normal 5,000 feet, he dropped down and flew between 1,500 and 2,000 feet. At 9:20 a.m., he flew directly over Dr. Haynes and his group of 350 men. In the water, the men saw this plane coming directly at them, the sun reflecting off its front window, and they began splashing the water with their hands and feet to draw attention. Ensign Park, one of the ship's aviators, had some green marker dye in his jacket and spread it in the water. They all firmly believed that they had been seen and estimated that within five hours seaplanes from Guam would be landing in their midst.

Flannery, however, couldn't see a thing. The best way to spot something as small as a head in the ocean is not to look out at an angle but straight down, and at a height of 500 to 800 feet, not 1,500 feet. Flannery was looking out his side window, and his biggest problem was the glassy sea.

By 10:00 a.m., the sun was reflecting so sharply off the sea that everyone began to suffer from intense photophobia, an intolerance to light. Dr. Haynes was very concerned, since he considered this far worse than snow blindness. It caused severe pain, which was relieved only when the sun went down. Closing the eyelids did not help since the sun burned right through. In order to somewhat ease the discomfort, the men ripped their clothing and blindfolded themselves. Fortunately, their bodies did not burn; they were all covered by fuel oil, which the searing rays of the sun could not penetrate.

For the remainder of the first day, there was constant change among the three subgroups. They would merge for a short time then break apart again. The wounded stayed in fairly good shape, and only a few men died. In order to determine death, Dr. Haynes would place his finger on the pupil of an eye and if there was no reflex it was assumed the man was dead. The jacket would be removed and the body allowed to drift away. In the background, some of the men would recite the Lord's Prayer.

By noontime, the sea became choppy again, with large swells. Practically everyone by this time had swallowed some of the oil-soaked water, and they were all throwing up. Thirst was beginning to get to the men, and Haynes, while trying unsuccessfully to find some first-aid supplies, visited all three groups and cautioned them against drinking salt water. For the moment, all the men agreed not to drink from the sea.

The survivors were beginning to see sharks in the area, but, so far, there were no major attacks. Giles McCoy, of the Marine Detachment, saw a shark attack a dead man. He believed that because of the dead men in the water so much food was available that the sharks were not inclined to bother with those still alive.

That, however, had been in the morning and afternoon. By the time that the merciless sun began to set, large numbers of sharks had arrived on the scene, and the men were scared. Cuts were bleeding. When a shark approached a group, everyone would kick, punch, and create a general racket. This often worked, and the predator would leave. At other times, however, the shark "would have singled out his victim and no amount of shouts or pounding of the water would turn him away. There would be a piercing scream and the water would be churned red as the shark cut his victim to ribbons."

In the Water the Second Day: Tuesday, July 31, 1945

Yesterday they had been too exhausted to paddle over to the raft holding the one lone man, and this morning he was still calling to them. Thinking him hurt, the McVay group began the tremendous task of pulling nine men on three lashed rafts and a floater net to this isolated and scared soul. Changing the two men paddling once every half hour, it took them four and a half hours to traverse the 1,600 yards separating them and their objective. Upon finally reaching the young man, they saw that, besides being lonely, there was nothing wrong with the new member, and McVay said, "As misery loves company, he wanted somebody to talk to."

There still remained the other group farther away that had been spotted the day before, but the men were now too exhausted to try to reach them. Besides, most of the men had blisters on their hands, and these were creating saltwater ulcers. The new man told the skipper he had seen no one else in the water, and the captain was convinced that his group, plus the small pack of men in the distance, were the sole survivors, even though it seemed incredible that no one else had escaped.

In the morning there was no wind, but the sea could still be described as rough. As the day wore on, the endless water calmed down. There were very long, sweeping swells, but they didn't break and no whitecaps could be seen. Considering the circumstances, the group was comfortable and in fairly good shape.

During the day, Vincent Allard took the large canvas bag that had held the matches, first-aid kits, etc., and fashioned out of the fabric a "cornucopia" cap for everyone. The men pulled the hats over their ears, and this, together with the fuel oil that covered them, saved them from the scorching rays of the sun. To further protect their hands from sunburn, they placed them under the oil-covered water sloshing around in the grating of the rafts.

The fishing kit they found on one of the rafts was a delight to any fisherman's eye, and both McVay and Allard were excellent fishermen. But it didn't help much since there were a number of sharks in the area, and the one big monster of the first day was still performing his merry-go-round act. They did manage to catch some black fish which McVay thought to be in the parrot family; although the meat was very white, he was afraid to let the men eat it. Instead, he used this flesh as bait, hoping to catch nearby schools of bonito and mackerel. However, every time they dropped the line, the shark took what they offered, and, after a while, they gave up the idea of fishing.

During this second twenty-four-hour period, two planes had been spotted; one at 1:00 a.m. and the second at 9:00 p.m. A pair of star shells were fired at both planes, but they weren't seen. The men griped about the shells, for once they reached their maximum height they burst like fireworks and then immediately died. The group wished parachutes were attached, which would float the light back and give the aviator more time to recognize the distress signal.

～～

At dawn on the second day, the isolated Redmayne group had about sixty men on rafts and another sixty to eighty in the water. Meanwhile, during the dark morning hours, some of the more seriously injured men had died.

The water breakers turned out to be a disappointment. Some of the casks were empty while the others contained either salt or cruddy black water. Lieutenant Redmayne said, "It was dirty and tasted as though the salt content was about equal to the salt content of the seawater." These casks were made of wood, and when the rafts crashed into the sea the seams on the casks split, thereby allowing fresh water to escape and salt water to seep in. The casks were large, heavy, and difficult to handle, and in the standard life raft the water would probably become salty after the first use. Once the seal was broken to pour water, it couldn't properly be resealed, thus allowing salt water to seep in. Should the cup become lost, serving fresh water from the cask resulted in great wastage.

First-aid equipment was generally useless, since the containers were not watertight. Anything in tubes remained sealed, but there weren't enough remedies to go around for burns and eye troubles caused by salt water and fuel oil. The food stayed in good condition but, here again, there was a problem since the primary staple was Spam. Not only did this increase thirst because it was salty, but Spam draws sharks. The men discovered this when they opened a can of Spam and sharks gathered all around them.

The policy of the group was to put all men on rafts who were sick, injured, or didn't have life jackets or belts. The problem with this, however, was that men with belts or jackets began taking them off and allowing them to drift away in order to qualify for the relative safety of a raft. This necessitated keeping a close watch on the men. Giulio and his small band were now beginning to start trouble. Giulio, who was still on a floater net, kept insisting that he deserved some time on a raft. This request was not granted, and he continued to complain.

During the early part of this second day, some of the men swam over to Ensign Donald Blum and reported that the food had been broken into. Blum swam back with them to take a look and saw men eating and drinking. This was immediately reported to Redmayne, who then ordered that all food and water be placed on one raft and guarded at all times by the officers and chiefs. Later in the day there were reports that Giulio was again stealing food, but it was not clear whether food was being taken from the guarded raft or all the food had not been handed in. Ensign Harlan Twible, who was on a floater net about forty feet from Giulio, yelled out in a loud, clear voice, "The first man I see eating food not rationed I will report if we ever get in." He further told them that they were acting like a bunch of recruits and not seamen. As far as can be ascertained, there were no deaths in this group during the second day, and everyone appeared to be in fairly good shape. The only problem was Giulio and his gang. The next day would be a different story.

Even though total blackness surrounded them, because of the choppy sea the men were having a very difficult time sleeping. In this inky isolation, some of the weaker members of the crew, who could not face what they thought must be ahead of them, gave up all hope; they silently slipped out of their life jackets and committed suicide by drowning. Numerous deadly fights broke out over life jackets, and about twenty-five men were killed by their shipmates. At dawn, Dr. Haynes saw that the general condition of the men was not good, and the group appeared to be smaller. Haynes later recalled that basically two factors, other than lack of water, contributed greatly to the high mortality: the heat from the tropical sun and the ingestion of salt water. The drinking of salt water in his group was generally not deliberate but occurred during bouts of delirium or from the accidental swallowing of water in the choppy sea.

The constant breaking of waves over the men's heads the first two days, particularly when they tried to rest, caused most of them to develop a mechanical sinusitis. The swallowing of small amounts of seawater and fuel oil could not be avoided, and the sun caused intense headache and photophobia. The combination of these factors resulted in many deaths.

During the latter part of the day, the sea grew calmer. The men's thirst, however, had become overpowering as the placid water became very clear. As the day wore on, the men became more and more exhausted and complained of their thirst. Dr. Haynes noticed that the younger men, largely those without families, started to drink salt water first. As the hot sun continued to beat down on them, an increasing number of survivors were becoming delirious, talking incoherently, and drinking tremendous amounts of salt water.

They started becoming maniacal, thrashing around in the water and exhibiting considerable strength and energy compared to those who were exhausted but still sane. These spells would continue until the man either drowned or went into a coma. Several brave men, wearing rubber life belts, tried to support maniacal men and also drowned, for during the struggles the belts developed punctures or rips and deflated. Haynes kept swimming from one huge huddle of sailors to another, desperately trying to help. All during this time, people were getting discouraged and calling out for help, and he would be there to reassure and calm them down.

There were sharks in the area again. The clear water allowed the men to look down and see them. It seems that during this second day, however, the sharks were going after dead men, especially the bodies that were sinking down into the deeper ocean. They didn't seem to bother the men on the surface.

Things became progressively worse from sundown on the second day. The men's stories become mixed up, and some accounts are totally incoherent, making it difficult to piece together what actually happened. Haynes remembered that shortly after sundown they all experienced severe chills, which lasted for at least an hour. These were followed by high fever, as most of the group became delirious and got out of control. The men fought with one another, thinking there were Japanese in the group, and disorganization and disintegration occurred rapidly. Captain Parke worked until he collapsed. Haynes was so exhausted that he drifted away from the group.

Some of the men attempted to help their shipmates. They swam outside the group, rounding up stragglers and towing them back in. The kapok jackets had a brass ring and also a snap on the back. At night, people who had these jackets on would form a circle and hook them all together. The rest of the men would get in the middle. The corrallers themselves were worried, however, since the jackets had lost so much buoyancy that the feeling of security they provided was rapidly ebbing.

By nightfall, more and more people were removing their preservers and throwing them away. Most of these men died. Haynes swam from one batch of crazed men to another, trying to calm them down. He would locate the groups by the screaming of the delirious men. From this night on, what happened in the water can only be described as a nightmare.

IN THE WATER THE THIRD DAY: WEDNESDAY, AUGUST 1, 1945

The captain and the men with him were continuing to fare relatively well. McVay still believed that his ship went down with all hands and that, at most, there could only be thirty survivors.

From the opening of this day, the central thought on the minds of the men was to kill the shark; it was big, it kept circling closer and closer, and they were frightened. This monster could easily rip the raft apart with one swift motion of his enormous jaws. But the only weapon they had was a knife from the fishing kit, with a one-inch blade, and there was no way they could tackle this massive creature with a blade that small. So the day passed with the men sitting and staring at the shark, annoyed that a larger weapon was not in the kit and further chafed that not one man had a sheath knife, an implement customarily carried by many of the sailors aboard ship.

Just before first light, a plane flew over, and two star shells were fired. Again at 1:00 p.m., a bomber, heading toward Leyte, passed above. They tried to attract this second plane with mirrors, yellow signal flags, and splashing, but to no avail.

Although the order had been given the day before to bring all food to the command raft, there was still a certain amount of hoarding going on. This morning, however, several more rafts handed their cached rations over to Redmayne. During the day, one cracker, a malted-milk tablet, and a few drops of precious water were allocated to each man. Some survivors tried their luck at fishing but, as with the McVay group, the numerous sharks in the area kept stealing the bait. Not everyone realized there was safety in numbers. Some men swam away. Attempts to stop them failed, and soon after leaving the security of the group these sailors were usually dragged beneath the surface by the sharks.

Toward late afternoon, some of the sailors started becoming delirious again. More and more men were drinking salt water. Chief Benton (Redmayne's assistant) attempted to talk to these half-crazed men in a calm, reassuring voice, but it wasn't much use. Fights broke out, men started swimming away, and people committed suicide by drowning themselves. A sailor yelled to Redmayne that things were getting very bad on his raft, and Ensign Eames was sent over to investigate. Upon returning, Eames reported that some of the men were making homosexual advances toward one of the other men. Upon hearing these reports, the chief engineer's reaction was to have the people around him recite the Lord's Prayer.

Giulio had been on a net for the previous two days, but this morning the pharmacist's mate decided to transfer him to a raft because Giulio complained that his eyes were bothering him. Shortly thereafter, it was noticed that Giulio and the people with him were eating and drinking. Upon checking the stored rations on the command raft, it was discovered that two of the four water breakers were missing, plus several cans of rations. The officers and chiefs ordered Giulio to return everything immediately, but he ignored them. Some of the senior people then swam over to the mutineers and tried to grab the food and water away, but they were unsuccessful since Giulio and his small band were much stronger than the tired officers. Throughout the day, he and his gang had themselves a veritable Roman feast while others suffered and died.

The early morning hours found Dr. Haynes with a large pack of swimmers headed by Captain Parke of the Marines who, through willpower, strength, and sheer determination, kept the group under control. Before dawn Haynes twice became delirious. At one point, he remembered, "The waves kept hitting me in the face, and I got the impression that people were splashing water in my face as a joke, and I pleaded with them that it wasn't funny and that I was sick. I begged them to stop and kept swimming furiously to make them stop, and then my head cleared."

Most of the men had become hysterical, and some were quickly going mad. A few of the sailors got the idea that people were trying to drown them and that there were Japanese in the group. The cry would circulate, "Get the Jap! Kill him!" Fights broke out, knives were drawn, and several men were brutally stabbed. Mass hysteria reigned.

The doctor did his best to calm them down but was unsuccessful and at one point he himself was held underwater by an insane crewman and had to fight his way back up. Captain Parke desperately tried to regain control but finally became delirious himself and eventually died. Once Parke was gone, the mass madness forced the subgroup to further dissolve, and the men scattered. They wanted to be alone, for no one trusted anyone else.

Under a cloudless sky and full moon, Haynes drifted, isolated but totally alert. A man floated by, and they instinctively backed away from each other. Everyone was crazy. Haynes hated being alone, however, and not very far away he heard the noises that the irrational members of another group were making and began swimming toward the sound. Only a few yards short of this band of men, his strength gave out, and he screamed for help. Breaking off from the pack, his chief pharmacist's mate, John Schmueck, grabbed him and towed him to the safety of their numbers.

Supported by Schmueck, who put his arm through the back of Haynes's jacket and lifted the doctor's body so that it rested on his own hip, Dr. Haynes fell asleep for a few hours. Schmueck himself was not in good shape and was having a difficult time with his rubber life ring. It was defective, and for two days—until he finally got a kapok jacket—he had had to hold his finger over the valve. When the ring would deflate too much, he would have to blow it up again and then hold his finger on it some more.

The new group was well organized and ably led by Ensign Moynelo. Someone in the group suggested using the leg straps on the kapok jackets to snap the men together. This worked very well and prevented them from drifting apart. By daybreak the sea was mirror calm, but the condition of the men was becoming critical. They had difficulty thinking clearly, and most of them talked incoherently and had hallucinations.

By this time, the kapok jackets just kept the men's heads out of the water. There was a great deal of anxiety within Moynelo's group concerning the buoyancy of the preservers since the Navy Manual stated that jackets would remain buoyant for only two days, and they were now well into their third. However, the kapok preservers maintained fair buoyancy, even after one hundred hours, and the mental distress that the men felt on this account turned out to have been uncalled for.

Preservers were, unfortunately, fairly easy to obtain. When a man died (and they were now dying en masse), Haynes would remove his jacket and add it to a pile in the middle of the group. This became their reserve when somebody's jacket went on the "fritz."

Sanity, as we know it, virtually disappeared on this third day. The few men who retained some semblance of sense tried to help their weaker shipmates, but it was a losing battle. Chief Gunner Harrison recalled that "Doctor Haynes's conduct throughout the time he was in the water was, in my opinion, above his normal call of duty. The comfort the men got from just talking to him seemed to quiet them down and relieve some of their worry."

Haynes felt that what kept him going was taking care of the men. They constantly asked him questions about whether the water was salty all the way down and when he thought the planes were coming.

Gunner Harrison remembered, "Early one morning somebody woke me up and wanted to know why we did not stop at an island that we passed. That story caused a great deal of trouble. Several of them believed that those islands were there—three islands. Lieutenant McKissick even dreamed he went to the island and there was a hotel there and they would not let him on the island. The first time I heard the story was, this kid woke me up and wanted to know why we did not stop there." All day long, small numbers of men broke off from the gathering and swam for the "island," never to be seen again.

Noticing a line of men stretching for some distance, Commander Haynes curiously swam to it and asked what was going on. He was told to be quiet for there was a hotel up ahead but it only had one room, and when it was your turn to get in you could sleep for fifteen minutes. Haynes turned and swam away from this procession of patient survivors. Stragglers were continually being rounded up and herded back to the group. Sometimes the job would take up to an hour but Haynes knew that they had to stay together in order to be found.

On this Wednesday afternoon, Ensign Moynelo disappeared with the group who were going to swim to Leyte. It all started out when some quartermaster claimed to have figured out the current and the wind, and how long it would take to swim to Leyte. Approximately twenty-five men joined him. They anticipated that it would take them a day and a half to reach the Philippines, based upon a two-knot current and swimming at one knot per hour. Once this large party disappeared from sight, it was never seen again. This was the largest single group of men lost during the days in the water. All of the strong leaders were now dead, except for Gunner Harrison and Commander Haynes. The doctor recalled that "Gunner Harrison and I were about the only ones left who were well enough to think, and he was just like the Rock of Gibraltar. He always had a smile and kept the group together. He used to say to the fellows, 'If that old broken-down Rickenbacker can stay out on the ocean for a week, we can stay for a month.'" Because of Harrison's leadership, "we managed to keep together. His morale was high, and his cheerful exhortations kept everyone united."

The doctor continued to pronounce men dead. He would remove their jackets, recite the Lord's Prayer, and release the bodies. The water was very clear, and Dr. Haynes remembered the bodies looking like small dolls sinking in the deep sea. He watched them until they faded from sight. A cloud of death hung over everyone, and rescue was no longer discussed. By early evening, all was calm—it was no longer a question of who would die, but when.

In the Water the Fourth Day: Thursday, August 2, 1945

With Lieutenant Redmayne delirious, Ensign Twible tried to command the group until he became totally exhausted and his effectiveness limited. Chief Benton was in a little better shape, however, and issued many orders on his own. During the morning, a man swam over to Twible's raft with cans of crackers and said Giulio sent them. No reason was given, and it is not known whether this was in response to a direct order or a limited act of charity.

More and more people were losing touch with their rational selves. For example, there were plenty of good kapok jackets available, but an insane sailor went up to a man wearing one of the rubber rings, ripped it off his body, and swam away. Unnecessary and foolish acts of this type were taking place throughout the groups. As Freud said, "The primitive stages can always be reestablished; the primitive mind is, in the fullest meaning of the word, imperishable."

The pharmacist's mate in this group, Harold Anthony, worked as hard as humanly possible to aid men in the water and became extremely fatigued. During the night he mentioned to one of his friends that he couldn't keep this pace up much longer and would probably be dead shortly. Twelve hours later, with the relentless Pacific sun beating down on this lonely spot of ocean, the lifeless body of the corpsman was permitted to drift away.

Doctor Haynes's group disbanded again. Small groups were continually forming and breaking up. The night had been particularly difficult, and most of the men suffered from chills, fever, and delirium. These lonely people were now dying in droves, and the helpless physician could only float and watch. By Thursday morning, August 2, the condition of most of the men was critical. Many were in coma and could be aroused only with exceptional effort. The group no longer existed, with the men drifting off and dying one by one. This isolation from the companionship of another human was cataclysmic.

At 9:00 a.m., on Thursday, August 2, securely strapped in the pilot's seat, Lieutenant (jg) Wilbur C. Gwinn pushed the throttles forward, brought the motors of his twin-engine Ventura bomber to an ear-splitting roar, and raced down the Peleliu runway. His mission was a regular day reconnaissance patrol of Sector 19V258. He was to report and attempt to sink any Japanese submarine in his area. The route for the outward leg of his journey just happened to have him flying directly over the heads of the dying men of the *Indianapolis*.

At the very rear of a Ventura is an antenna that trails behind the aircraft. It is used primarily for navigation. In order to keep the antenna from whipping around in the wind, which would make it useless, a weight (known as a "sock") is secured to the end. Once Gwinn gained enough speed to get airborne, he pulled back and the nose of the bomber pointed up toward the blue sky. At the same time, he lost the weight from his navigational antenna. With this "trailing antenna sock" gone, he had two choices: turn around and get it fixed, or continue on patrol and navigate by dead reckoning. Because the weather was excellent, Lieutenant Gwinn decided to go on, took the plane up to 3,000 feet, and over a glassy sea began looking for enemy submarines.

Dead reckoning navigation is not very accurate, and over the Pacific Ocean it is neither a very comfortable nor enviable position to be in. At 11:00 a.m., about an hour and forty-five minutes out of Peleliu, Gwinn figured that since caution is the better part of valor, the whipping antenna being pulled behind the plane should somehow be anchored down. Because the radioman was busy with something else and his co-pilot was concentrating on filling out a weather report, Gwinn resolved to repair it himself. Crawling through the after tunnel of the Ventura, he reached the narrow end and stared at the long, slender, thrashing piece of metal, wondering how to fix it. While attempting to come up with some creative solution to his problem, Gwinn happened to look down from his 3,000-foot perch into the Philippine Sea. At that precise moment, he saw it. The thin line of oil could only have come from a leaking submarine, and the startled pilot rushed back to his left-hand seat and began flying the airplane.

At 11:18 a.m., he changed his course so as to follow the snake-like slick. Not being able to see very well, he brought the bomber down to 900 feet. Mile after mile the slick continued, never seeming to reach an end. Five miles later, he suddenly saw them—thirty heads wrapped in a twenty-five-mile orbit of oil. Many were clinging to the sides of a raft, while others floated and feebly made motions to the plane. Who in the world could these people be? At 11:20 a.m., about two minutes after sighting what had looked like black balls on the water, the pilot dropped down to a wave-skimming 300 feet.

He ordered his radioman to get a message off, and at 11:25 a.m., the following transmission was sent:

SIGHTED 30 SURVIVORS
011-30 NORTH 133-30 EAST
DROPPED TRANSMITTER AND LIFEBOAT EMERGENCY
IFF ON 133-30

Now that he had positioned the thirty survivors, there was nothing more Gwinn could do so he decided to spread out his search. Following the slick on a northerly course, six miles farther on he found forty more men. Continuing on, four miles more had him pass over another fifty-five to seventy-five people—and still farther north, he found scattered groups of twos and threes. After an hour of flying and looking, Lieutenant Gwinn estimated that there were 150 men in the water.

The survivors were dispersed along a line about twenty miles long. He noticed a group so crowded on rafts that he was unable to tell the exact number of rafts they had. He could barely spot a lone oil-covered man, even at his low altitude, unless he was splashing the water.

Gwinn's antenna problem now had to be solved—quickly. The position he sent out in his first message was calculated by dead reckoning and couldn't possibly be accurate. He had to fix the whipping antenna, and once again he crawled through the dark tunnel to reach the end of the bomber. Once there, he put his hand out the tail, grabbed the long rod, and pulled it inside. Taking a rubber hose, he tied it around the tip of the antenna and pushed the length back out, hoping, while crawling back to the pilot's seat, that there would be enough weight to stop the shaking and get a decent fix. They tried, and it worked.

One hour and twenty minutes after sending his first message of thirty survivors, a second dispatch from the bomber was transmitted:

SEND RESCUE SHIP
11-15N 133-47E 150 SURVIVORS
IN LIFE BOAT AND JACKETS
DROPPED RED RAMROD

Gwinn received orders to stick around.

Dr. Haynes saw the thing and prayed it was real. Flying very low, the bomber zoomed over his head and as quickly as it came, it passed and soon was a dot on the opposite horizon. At that moment, Haynes knew he and his fellow survivors were dead men. Their last ounce of strength was giving out, and this plane was like all the others—blind to the living hell beneath it.

After scouting the area, there was no doubt in Gwinn's mind that these were American sailors below him. Turning the plane, he looked for a group which appeared to be alone and without rafts, and began dropping everything in the plane that floated.

When Dr. Haynes saw the distant dot suddenly reverse course and come back toward them, low over the water, he then knew that they had been sighted. Like a sudden tropical squall, things began falling from the sky. Two life rafts were dropped, together with cans of fresh water. The water cans ruptured on landing but the most important thing was that Gwinn saw them, and those fortunate enough to be still alive knew rescue was near.

Once there was nothing left to drop to the splashing, oil-covered men, Gwinn released dye markers and smoke bombs so as not to lose the position.

It would not be until the next day that the Navy finally discovered that these were survivors from the *Indianapolis*. By this time, the entire Pacific was curious as to who these people were. Ashore, many people thought that they had Japanese in the water and weren't in too big a rush to get things moving. A short time before, in this same area, escorts from a convoy had reported they had attacked a Japanese submarine.

However, after the second report citing "150 survivors" came in, all hell broke loose. Because submarines don't carry 150 men, Pacific Fleet knew they had a surface vessel to contend with, and if a Japanese warship had been sunk they would have known about it. It finally dawned on CinCPac that they might have an American ship down, and panic started to set in. Shortly after Gwinn's second message was received, CinCPac (now in a state of agitation) began radioing ships to report their positions.

For an hour after his second dispatch, Gwinn was all alone, attempting to comfort the dying men beneath him as best he could. Then another plane, on transport duty to the Philippines, appeared. It stayed with the Ventura for about an hour and dropped three of its rafts.

Back at Gwinn's base, the communications officer decoded the first message concerning the thirty survivors and quickly passed it on to his (and Gwinn's) boss, Lieutenant Commander George Atteberry, commanding officer of VPB-152. This was the Peleliu unit of the Search and Reconnaissance Command of Vice Admiral Murray, Commander, Marianas. The unit was under the command of Rear Admiral W. R. Greer.

Atteberry calculated the fuel supply of the lone, circling bomber and estimated that Gwinn would have to leave the scene by 3:30 p.m. in order to land with a small amount of reserve fuel. Not wanting to leave the survivors alone, Commander Atteberry started making some fast decisions.

Not far from the Ventura squadron was a squadron of seaplanes (Dumbos), and Atteberry picked up the phone and told the duty officer of VPB-23 to get a seaplane out to the area by 3:30 p.m. Not having intercepted Gwinn's message, "23" was skeptical about the whole thing and not eager to cooperate. Not liking this attitude, Atteberry drove over to their unit to ascertain the ready status personally. Once there, he decided they couldn't get a plane up in time to relieve Gwinn, so he quickly drove back to his own unit and ordered his plane and crew to get ready for takeoff. At exactly the same moment Gwinn's second message came in, Atteberry, whose call sign was "Gambler Leader," was lifting his bomber off the Peleliu runway.

During the hour-and-a-half flight out, "Leader" was in constant contact with his squadron office and was happy to hear that "23" finally had gotten airborne and on the way. At 2:15 p.m., Atteberry spotted Gwinn, together with the PBM, the large seaplane on transport duty, and immediately established voice contact with both. The commander was given a quick tour of the groups in order to size up the situation. Finally, so that the men in the water wouldn't think they were being deserted, the pilot of the PBM was ordered to circle the southwest half of the huge slick while "Gambler Leader" ranged the northeast portion.

Gwinn's fuel supply was running low, and twenty minutes after Atteberry arrived, he sent Gwinn on his way. Lieutenant Gwinn's third and final message read:

RELIEF BY 70V [Atteberry]
RETURNING TO BASE

The PBM also had to go, and for forty-five minutes Commander Atteberry was all alone, circling and comforting those below by his presence. Then out of his cockpit window, he saw the big, lumbering Dumbo waddling toward him from the distant southern horizon.

Patrol Bombing Squadron 23 was told that Atteberry and his planes were going to remain on the scene until "23" got one of their Catalinas out there. Lieutenant R. Adrian Marks happened to be the duty pilot at the time, and 1,400 gallons of gas were loaded into his seaplane. While this was taking place, Marks, together with his air combat intelligence officer, went to group operations to see if they could gather any more information than what Commander Atteberry had given them. Operations had nothing to offer and, unable to believe that there were so many men (i.e., thirty men as per Gwinn's first transmission) in the water, Marks assumed he was going out to pick up a ditched pilot. With a full tank of gas and extra air–sea rescue gear, Lieutenant Marks shoved his mammoth down the Peleliu runway and, once airborne, turned north. The time was 12:45 p.m.

On the way out, "Playmate 2" (Marks's call sign) received word that instead of thirty men in the sea there were now about 150. This was absolutely incomprehensible to Marks, and he assumed that the message must have been garbled in transmission. However, he "thought it would be a good idea to get to the scene as quickly as possible." At 3:03 p.m., he began picking up radio signals from Atteberry, and a little over three hours from takeoff, at 3:50 p.m., "Playmate 2" made visual contact and established communications with the commander.

Marks was dumbfounded—how did all these people get here? "Gambler Leader" instructed "Playmate 2" not to drop a single thing—there was much more than met the eye. For a half hour, Atteberry gave Marks the tour. Then the Dumbo dropped everything it had (saving only one small raft for itself), concentrating on those floaters who had only jackets.

With everything out of the plane, Marks wondered what he could do next. Looking down at the bobbing mass of humanity, he knew they were in horrible shape but also just as important—and maybe more so—he saw the sharks. Therefore, at "about 16:30 I decided a landing would be necessary to gather in the single ones. This decision was based partly on the number of single survivors, and the fact that they were bothered by sharks. We did observe bodies being eaten by sharks." Marks told "Gambler Leader" he was going in, and Atteberry notified his base that the Dumbo was landing and that he himself needed relief.

Preparations were made inside the Catalina for landing, while Marks looked for a spot where he thought the floating plane would do the most good. Never having made a landing at sea before, he was a little nervous. However, "at 17:15 a power stall was made into the wind. The wind was due north, swells about twelve feet high. The plane landed in three bounces, the first bounce being about fifteen feet high." "Playmate 2" was down safe—but not very sound.

The hull was intact, but rivets had sprung loose and seams ripped open from impact. While rivet holes were plugged with pencils and cotton shoved into the seams, the radio compartment was taking on water and was being bailed out at the rate of ten to twelve buckets per hour. In the meantime, the co-pilot went aft and began organizing the rescue effort. Because of the high swells, Marks couldn't see anything from his cockpit seat. Atteberry stayed in direct communication with him, however, and guided the Dumbo toward the survivors. Both pilots made the decision to stay away from men on rafts, since they appeared to be in better shape than those floating alone. There were problems, however, for although every effort was made to pick up the single ones it was necessary to avoid passing near the men on life rafts because they would jump onto the plane.

The side hatch had been opened, and the plane's ladder was hung out. Standing on the rungs was a crewman and, when they passed a swimmer, he would grab him and pull him aboard. This was very unsatisfactory though, because the people in the water were too weak to hang on. Furthermore, when a burned survivor, or one whose arm or leg was broken, was snatched, the pain was excruciating. They tried throwing out their remaining raft with a rope attached for a swimmer to grab (they were too frail to jump in). Then they would reel the raft back in. This proved to be impractical, because Marks continually kept the plane taxiing and anyone hanging on was dragged through the water. Finally, they settled on going up to a man, cutting the engines, bringing him aboard, and then starting up again and going to another swimmer. Once the engines were cut, silence enveloped the area except for the terrifying cries for help heard by the crew of "Playmate 2."

Before night fell, Marks had picked up thirty people and crammed them into the body of his leaking seaplane. All were in bad shape, and they were immediately given water and first aid. Naturally, as soon as the first man was plucked from the sea, Lieutenant Marks learned the *Indianapolis* had gone down. There was no way, however, that he was going to transmit this word in the clear and "I was too busy to code a message of this nature." So it would not be until Friday, August 3, that the U.S. Navy finally learned that one of their heavy cruisers had been sunk just after midnight on July 30.

In the sky above the drifting Dumbo, Atteberry was busy directing Marks and telling other planes coming into the area where to drop their gear in order "to obtain the best possible distribution among them." Between the first sighting and midnight, planes continually flew in, and, at one point, there were eleven aircraft on the scene.

With night upon him, it was impossible for Marks to pick up any more individual swimmers, and he therefore taxied toward a large assembly of men who had had rafts dropped to them earlier in the day. This was Commander Haynes's group. Survivors were packed like sardines inside the hull of the Dumbo, so Marks ordered these men to be laid on top of the wings, covered with parachutes, and given water. This damaged the wing fabric, and it became doubtful whether the Catalina would ever fly again.

In the black of this Pacific night, things began to settle down; the stillness was interrupted only by the occasional pained moans of the *Indianapolis* crew. Marks couldn't move the plane for fear of running people down, so they drifted and waited for rescue. Just before midnight, a searchlight on the far horizon pierced the onyx sky, and at the same time a circling plane dropped a parachute flare over "Playmate 2." The ship changed course and steered toward the beat-up PBY and her precious cargo of fifty-six former *Indianapolis* crewmen.

It was 4:55 p.m. when 1st Lieutenant Richard Alcorn, U.S. Army Air Corps, 4th Emergency Rescue Squadron, forced his Catalina into the air over Palau. Two hours and twenty minutes later, he arrived, and after quickly surveying the situation tossed three of his eleven rafts out the door. He also saw Marks's plane already on the water picking up survivors. Noticing that the swimmers didn't have enough strength to pull themselves into the rubber boats, Alcorn decided not to throw any more out. Instead he landed at 7:30 p.m., bringing his plane down two miles north of Marks.

Within minutes his crew saw the first survivor and pulled him into the aircraft. Then they taxied a few feet, stopped; taxied again, stopped—and kept this up until darkness without seeing another living soul. When Alcorn stopped and searched, they found a tremendous amount of debris in the area, most of it having fallen from the sky during the day.

They also saw bodies, dead bodies everywhere. In the dark, they floated silently with their lone passenger. Soon they heard cries for help from a group of men and sergeants Needham and Higbee volunteered to take one of the rafts, pick them up and bring them back. Alcorn agreed, but with one provision—they could only go as far as the rope attached to raft and plane would take them. Unfortunately, the umbilical cord was not long enough, and the men returned disappointed.

Overhead, planes circled all night. Marks's Dumbo was totally out of commission, but Alcorn continued to signal to the flyers and they reassuringly flashed back to the two. By the end of the day, still no one on shore knew for certain who the people in the water were.

Yet after Gwinn's second frightful message was received, one of the largest rescue operations in U.S. naval history began. The *Cecil J. Doyle* (DE 368) was heading home after an unsuccessful submarine hunt, when she suddenly received orders from the Western Carolines Sub Area to reverse course and steam north to pick up survivors. This was immediately after Gwinn's first transmission. Once the second message came in, the destroyer escort increased speed to 22.5 knots.

At 2:35 p.m., *Doyle's* radio room made voice contact with Commander Atteberry, and they were kept informed of what was going on. The ship was asked to rush but replied that there was no way they could make it to the area until after midnight.

The destroyers *Ralph Talbot* and *Madison*, both on separate patrol off Ulithi, at 4:00 p.m. turned their sleek bows northward and hastened to the scene at thirty-two knots. It was 6:56 p.m. when the *Madison* made contact with the *Doyle* and pointed out that she wouldn't be able to help until 3:00 a.m. the next morning, and the *Talbot* announced that her ETA wasn't until 4:00 a.m.

At 9:49 p.m., *Doyle's* lookouts spotted their first star shell, and from that moment on flares were always visible. An hour later, the ship's giant twenty-four-inch searchlight was switched on and pointed skyward to give the guarding planes an idea of where she was. Instead of seeking individual people in the water, the destroyer escort headed straight for Marks's Dumbo and, shortly after midnight, the first survivor from the incredibly luckless *Indianapolis* was pulled aboard a rescue ship.

It was noon when they noticed the circling plane far to the south of them. An hour later, there was another, and as the day wore on the planes swarmed over the line separating sky from sea. Frantically the men signaled, but they were too small to be seen. They ripped the kapok out of jackets, threw the silky fiber into an empty 40-mm ammo can, and set it afire, hoping the rising smoke would draw attention to their plight. It didn't work.

Captain McVay was confused and couldn't imagine what was going on. If the men in his group were the only survivors of the ill-fated cruiser, what was going on ten miles to the south of them? They began to feel discouraged, for as darkness blanketed their isolated spot of ocean the search seemed to be moving farther away. McVay was almost certain they were not going to be found and ordered all rations cut in half.

Midnight saw them staring at the tiny pinprick of *Doyle*'s light piercing the black sky, and now they were certain of other survivors. They were also certain, though, that the search area didn't extend north to their position and that it would be a long time, if ever, before they were found. No one slept, and, as the night wore on, this lonely group was very frightened.

The planes had no problem spotting the large Redmayne group and in the afternoon rafts, rations, and other emergency gear showered downward. With the security of sentinels circling above them, the men calmed down and patiently waited for rescue.

After Gwinn dropped the two rafts, they were quickly inflated, and, while the men held onto the side, Haynes was pushed in to investigate. The doctor ordered the sickest men put on the raft. He found an eleven-ounce can of water and doled it out in a plastic cup at the rate of one ounce per man. An enormous amount of equipment was dropped to this "swimmer" group, including a ten-man boat that soon had thirty people in it. But, during the day, it became so hot in the rafts that a great many men jumped back in the water to cool off.

Once the supplies were delivered, the group had almost everything they needed to keep them relatively comfortable until rescue ships arrived. Included in this bonanza were fresh water, rations, emergency medical supplies, and sun helmets. Dr. Haynes greatly appreciated the helmets for, when properly used, not only did they protect the wearer from the roasting sun but they also had a screen which dropped down in front of the face and prevented water from getting in the eyes and up the nose. As for the food, they found it impossible to eat the meat and crackers, but the malted-milk tablets and citrus candies went down easily.

Even though so much was dropped to them, the men's deteriorating physical condition made it essential that they be taken out of the water and given rudimentary first aid and medication; otherwise they wouldn't be alive when the ships came. Commander Haynes decided to swim for the plane. He told the group to stay where they were and explained what he was going to do. Then he swam toward Marks's plane and, after what seemed like two hours, finally reached it. His group still didn't have enough water, and he asked the crew of the plane to swing closer and give them some. They did so, and an emergency kit containing K-rations and a quart of water. Fresh water was still a problem, but at sundown Haynes found a saltwater converter in one of the rafts. He treated burns and administered morphine to the more seriously wounded.

When nightfall came, they were in much better shape and had enough rafts so that all but four or five were out of the water. Fresh water was still a problem, but at sundown Haynes had found a saltwater converter in one of the rafts. He spent all night trying to make fresh water out of salt water. Because he was so exhausted, the directions didn't help and the effort was a failure. He eventually made two batches of water which tasted horrible, but which the men drank. They even asked for more, but it had taken almost four hours to make the first batch and Haynes had had it. The doctor, who had worked so hard over the last four days, finally surrendered. He took the converter, flung it into the hated sea, and began to cry.

IN THE WATER THE FIFTH DAY: FRIDAY, AUGUST 3, 1945

Ten minutes after midnight, in a rough sea with a north–northwest wind blowing between eight and ten miles per hour, the *Cecil J. Doyle* lowered her heavy-motor whaleboat. It headed directly for the closer of the two Dumbos. Twenty minutes later, it returned with eighteen former crewmen of the *Indianapolis*, taken from Marks's plane. As soon as the first man was lifted aboard, he was asked, "Who are you?" Minutes later, an urgent secret dispatch was sent to the Commander of the Western Carolines:

HAVE ARRIVED AREA X
AM PICKING UP SURVIVORS
FROM U.S.S. INDIANAPOLIS
(CA 35) TORPEODED [sic]
AND SUNK LAST SUNDAY NIGHT

Between 12:30 and 4:45 a.m., *Doyle* raised from the brutal sea ninety-three men, which included all survivors aboard Marks's plane and the lone man on Alcorn's. In addition about forty men were retrieved from the water and the rafts. While the whaleboat shuttled back and forth, the mother ship slowly cruised the area, sweeping the watery expanse with her huge searchlight and following the flares dropped from the circling planes. The crew of the whaleboat, meanwhile, had a tough time removing men from the plane and bringing them aboard ship. Transfer was difficult because of the condition of the survivors, some of whom were badly burned from the fires on board the ship, one of whom had a broken leg, and all of whom were terribly weak from thirst and exposure.

At 1:10 a.m., the *Doyle* saw a searchlight to the north and soon discovered it to be the high-speed transport U.S.S. *Bassett*. Two hours later, the destroyer escort U.S.S. *Dufilho* also appeared. Until dawn, the *Doyle*, *Bassett* and *Dufilho* worked independently, hoisting men to the safety of their steel decks. Sunup brought the two destroyers *Madison* and *Ralph Talbot* on the scene.

First light allowed Marks to inspect his Catalina, and he quickly determined that it would never fly again. At 6:00 a.m., *Doyle* sent her boat over to the Dumbo and transferred the crew and all salvageable gear to the ship.

Lieutenant Alcorn was relieved of his lone survivor by *Doyle* at 4:00 a.m. and, with the sun rising over the eastern horizon, he had to decide whether or not to take off. The sea was very rough and a heavy wind was blowing, but, fortunately, his Catalina was not nearly as beat up as Marks's. He resolved to try it, and at 7:30 a.m., with no trouble at all, he powered his way down the endless runway and lifted off. At almost the same time, *Doyle* poured eighty rounds of 40-mm gunfire into Marks's abandoned plane, and she sank in the same area as the ship whose men she had so valiantly rescued.

After sinking the seaplane, *Doyle* secured from general quarters, and all of her survivors were logged in, treated, and put to bed. The crew of the *Doyle* were extremely helpful to their fellow sailors who had so recently suffered through a living hell. Men moved out of their bunks to make room for the former crewmen of the *Indianapolis* and constantly hovered around them, waiting for the slightest request that they could fill. The men were all given baths, and the oil was removed from their tired bodies. Every thirty minutes, a half glass of water, hot soup, hot coffee, and fruit were served to them, and this continued throughout the night and into the next day. The *Doyle's* doctor examined everyone and listed them all in medical condition ranging from serious to acute.

As it searched for the living, *Doyle* passed by the bodies of twenty-five to fifty dead sailors floating in life jackets. At 12:20 p.m., *Madison* ordered *Doyle* to take off for Peleliu, and this, the first ship on the scene, was now the first to leave, heading south at 22.5 knots.

All McVay and his isolated band could do was watch the distant searchlights, the falling flares, the circling planes. When the sun rose over the horizon, they were in despair. The entire morning was spent staring at the activity very far away. It did not seem to be coming closer. At 11:30 a.m., they spotted a plane making a box search. It was a very wide pattern, and on each leg it came closer. They found it extremely depressing, for the plane gave no recognition sign. Captain McVay contended that they were never spotted from the air. But they were, for this plane, flown by Marks's squadron leader, Lieutenant Commander M. V. Ricketts, saw them and reported that he sighted two rafts, with five survivors in one and four in the other. By voice radio, he directed the U.S.S. *Ringness* (APD 100) to pick them up. Like *Bassett*, *Ringness* was a high-speed transport sent by Philippine Sea Frontier, and it had just arrived. After receiving Ricketts's message, *Ringness* headed for the spot, and at 4,046 yards she picked

McVay up on radar. On the rafts, the spell of isolation and despair was suddenly broken when somebody cried, "My God, look at this! There are two destroyers bearing down on us. Why, they're almost on top of us." The two destroyers were both transports, *Ringness* and the newly arrived *Register*. *Register* turned north to pick up another small group while *Ringness* headed for McVay.

Everyone made it aboard under his own power, and all were immediately given first aid. They had lost about 14 percent of their body weight, and during the afternoon they were given ice cream, coffee, and as much water as they could drink. During the entire four and a half days on the rafts, no one in the group asked for a drink. This was surprising to McVay, since he had assumed people couldn't go that long without water—but they did.

While *Doyle* was taking care of the Haynes group, *Bassett* took care of Lieutenant Redmayne and his men. Lowering her four landing craft at 2:30 a.m., *Bassett*'s boats picked up most of Redmayne's people. A head count was taken, and a little over eighty sailors were collected from the original group of 150. *Bassett* next sent a message to Frontier Headquarters:

SURVIVORS ARE FROM USS
INDIANAPOLIS (CA 35) WHICH
WAS TORPEDOED 29 JULY [sic] X
CONTINUING TO PICK UP
SURVIVORS X MANY BADLY
INJURED

Ralph Talbot picked up twenty-four survivors and then spent most of the afternoon sinking eight rafts and a small boat with her 20-mm guns. Later she transferred her survivors to *Register*. As soon as *Madison* arrived in the area, *Bassett* reported that she had 150 survivors aboard and desperately needed a doctor. Shortly thereafter, at 5:15 a.m., *Madison*'s physician, Lieutenant (jg) H. A. Stiles, was transferred to the transport.

It was at the time the landing craft from *Bassett* came over to pick up Dr. Stiles that *Madison* first learned the survivors were from the *Indianapolis*.

During the day scouting lines were formed with the planes bird-dogging, but nothing was seen except for the dead, and they were generally left where they were. The unpleasant task of recovery and identification was postponed until the next day. The last living man plucked from the Philippine Sea was Captain McVay, who was the last man to enter it.

By the time the blazing Pacific sun reached its zenith on this day, not another living person from *Indianapolis* was to be found in that enormous ocean. She had sailed from San Francisco with 1,196 young men, was torpedoed, and about eight hundred of her crew escaped from the sinking ship. Of these eight hundred, 320 were rescued; two later died in the Philippines, and two on Peleliu. Because of complacency and carelessness, approximately five hundred U.S. sailors (no one will ever know the exact number) died in the waters of the Philippine Sea.

Two

The *Karluk*'s Last Voyage

Robert Bartlett

Introduction

"We did not all come back," wrote Robert Bartlett in his firsthand account of the ordeal of the Karluk, *the flagship of explorer Vilhjalmar Stefansson's Arctic expedition of 1913–16. When ice trapped the* Karluk, *Stefansson abandoned Captain Bartlett and the crew—eleven of whom perished—to their fate.*

During the night of New Year's Day we could hear, when we were below, a rumbling noise not unlike that which one often hears singing along the telegraph wires on a country road. The sound was inaudible from the deck. It was clear that there was tremendous pressure somewhere, though there were no visible indications of it in the vicinity of the ship. We were practically stationary. Apparently the great field of ice in which we had been zigzagging for so many months had finally brought up on the shore of Wrangell Island and was comparatively at rest, while the running ice outside this great field was still in active motion and tended to force the ice constantly in the direction of the island.

On Saturday, with a fresh north wind, in spite of which ship and ice still remained stationary, the rumbling noise could again be heard in the interior of the ship. On Sunday the fourth there was an increasing easterly wind which sent us slowly westward. Evidently we could make no movement towards the south on account of the pressure but when the wind blew us towards the west and north we could go along without undue danger. The football game was played as planned on this day until the second engineer strained a muscle in his leg kicking the ball along the ice, and the game had to stop.

The easterly gale continued for several days, sometimes with hard snowstorms, sometimes with clearer skies. The barometer was low; the temperature rose to sixteen degrees above zero. I had the engineers at work making tins of one-gallon capacity to hold kerosene for our sledges if we should have to use them. All of our oil was in five-gallon tins which were unhandy for sledging use. They also made tea-boilers out of gasoline tins, to be used with the Primus stoves; these held about a gallon of tea and were very handy. I had five with me on my subsequent sledge trip. Besides these jobs the engineers trimmed down our pickaxes so that they would weigh not over two and a half or three pounds. They put them in the portable forge in the engine room, heated the iron and beat it down, and put on the steel tips afterwards.

On the seventh and eighth the variable weather continued with occasional twilight of considerable intensity; the low barometer and high thermometer still prevailed. Our observations on the seventh, the last we were to take on shipboard, gave us our position as Lat. 72.11 N., Long. 174.86 W. The temperature dropped on the ninth; the sky, which was clear in the morning, became overcast by afternoon and the wind shifted from southeast to southwest.

We were getting nearer the land and the ice was raftering in places with the pressure, so that I felt sure that something was going to happen before long. We continued our preparations for putting emergency supplies in condition to be handled quickly, putting tea tablets in tins made by the engineers, and twenty-two calibre cartridges in similar tins. Mannlicher cartridges we put up in packages of thin canvas, fifty to a package. At five o'clock on the morning of the tenth I was awakened by a loud report like a rifle shot. Then there came a tremor all through the ship. I was soon on deck. The watchman, who for that night was Brady, had already been overboard on the ice and I met him coming up the ice gangway to tell me what he had found. There was a small crack right at the stem of the ship, he said. I went there with him at once and found that the crack ran irregularly but in general northwesterly for about two hundred yards. At first it was very slight, although it was a clean and unmistakable break; in the course of half an hour, however, it grew to a foot in width and as the day wore on widened still more until it was two feet wide on an average.

By 10 a.m. there was a narrow lane of water off both bow and stern. The ship was now entirely free on the starboard side but still frozen fast in her ice cradle on the port side; her head was pointed southwest. On account of the way in which the ice had split the ship was held in a kind of pocket; the wind, which was from the north in the earlier part of the day, hauled to the northwest towards afternoon and increased to a gale, with blinding snowdrift, and the sheet of ice on the starboard side began to move astern, only a little at a time.

The ship felt no pressure, only slight shocks, and her hull was still untouched, for the open ends of the pocket fended off the moving ice, especially at the stem. It was clear to me, however, that as soon as the moving ice should grind or break off the points of these natural fenders there was a strong probability that the moving ice sheet would draw nearer to the starboard side of the ship and, not unlike the jaws of a nutcracker, squeeze her against the sheet in which she was frozen on the port side, particularly as the wind was attaining a velocity of forty-five miles an hour.

Everything indicated, therefore, that the time was near at hand when we should have to leave the ship. We must have things ready. I gave orders to get the snow off the deck and the skylights and the outer walls of the cabin, to lighten her. Some of the men were sent over to the box-house to remove the few dogs that were still tethered there and set them free on the ice, and to get the house ready in case we had to move into it. They cleaned it up, put fresh boards on the floor and laid a fire in the stove, ready for lighting.

At about half past seven in the evening I chanced to be standing near the engine-room door. The lamps were lighted. The labors of the day were over and now, after dinner, the men were playing cards or reading or sewing, as usual. All at once I heard a splitting, crashing sound below.

I went down into the engine room and found the chief engineer there. We could hear water rushing into the hold and by lantern light could see it pouring in at different places for a distance of ten feet along the port side. As I had feared, the ice astern had broken or worn off and the sheet moving along the starboard side had swung in against the ship, heeling her over three or four feet to port; a point of ice on the port side had pierced the planking and timbers of the engine room for ten feet or more, ripping off all the pump fixtures and putting the pump out of commission. It was obvious that it would be useless to attempt to rig a temporary pump; the break was beyond repair.

I went on deck again and gave the order, "All hands abandon ship." We had all the fires except that in the galley extinguished at once and all the lamps, using hurricane lanterns to see our way around. There was no confusion. The men worked with a will, putting the emergency supplies overboard on the ice, some ten thousand pounds of pemmican, furs, clothing, rifles and cartridges. The Eskimo woman, with her children, I sent to the box-house to start the fire in the stove and keep the place warm. The steward was kept in the galley so that the men could have coffee and hot food.

By 10:45 p.m. there were eleven feet of water in the engine room. At this stage the pressure of the ice on both sides kept the ship from going down. We were less than an hour getting the supplies off the ship on to the ice; we could have saved everything on board but no attempt was made to save luxuries or souvenirs or personal belongings above the essentials, for it did not seem advisable to burden the sledges on our prospective journey over the ice with loads of material that would have to occupy space needed for indispensables.

When I was satisfied with the amount of supplies on the ice I started the men sledging the stuff over to the big floe. Here, as I have said, in addition to the box-house, we had a large snow igloo which had been completed sometime before. It had been smashed in by the wind, but the men now repaired it and made it ready for occupancy. They did a good job with their evening's work and I told them so, and said that they could turn in at the box-house and igloo and go to sleep whenever they got their sledging done.

After everyone else had left the ship I remained on board to await the end. For a time the chief engineer and Hadley stayed with me. There was a big fire in the galley and we moved the Victrola in there to while away the time. After the first sharp crash and the closing in of the ice the pressure was not heavy and all through the morning of the eleventh and well into the afternoon, the ship remained in about the same position as when she was first struck. No more water was coming in; the ice was holding her up. I would play a few records—we had a hundred and fifty or so altogether—and then I would go outside and walk around the deck, watching for any change in the ship's position. It cleared off towards noon and there was a little twilight but the snow was still blowing.

As I played the records I threw them into the stove. At last I found Chopin's Funeral March, played it over and laid it aside. I ate when I was hungry and had plenty of coffee and tea. My companions had gone over to the floe and turned in early in the morning. It was quite comfortable in the galley, for I could keep the fire going with coal from the galley locker. At times I would take a look into the engine room, being careful not to get too far from an exit; the water was nearly up to the deck.

At 3:15 p.m. the ice opened and the ship began to get lower in the water. Then the ice closed up again for a while and supported her by the bowsprit and both quarters. About half past three she began to settle in earnest and as the minutes went by the decks were nearly awash. Putting Chopin's Funeral March on the Victrola, I started the machine and when the water came running along the deck and poured down the hatches, I stood up on the rail and as she took a header with the rail level with the ice I stepped off. It was at 4 p.m. on January 11, 1914, with the blue Canadian Government ensign at her main-topmast-head, blowing out straight and cutting the water as it disappeared, and the Victrola in the galley sending out the strains of Chopin's Funeral March, that the *Karluk* sank, going down by the head in thirty-eight fathoms of water. As she took the final plunge, I bared my head and said, "Adios, *Karluk*." It was light enough to see and the rest of the party came out of the camp to watch the end. As she went down the yards lodged on the ice and broke off; in such a narrow lane of water did she disappear.

As soon as the *Karluk* sank, I turned in at the igloo to have a good sleep, for I had been awake since five o'clock on the morning of the tenth, and it was now late in the afternoon of the eleventh. It was nearly noon of the next day before I awoke. The sky was clear overhead but the fresh northwest wind kept the snow spinning over the ice and there was still only a brief twilight in the middle of the day.

We conducted our lives according to a regular routine similar to that which we had followed on shipboard during the last few months of our drift. We kept our records of wind and weather, of soundings and of temperature, which remained in the minus thirties for a good many days. We did not bother with latitude as we had the land in view some sixty to eighty miles away, not distinctly visible but plain enough on a clear day when the light was fairly good. The light of course came from the south and the land, being in that direction, was set off by the twilight glow, and the sun was getting nearer and nearer to the horizon as the days went by.

We saved a chronometer from the ship but it got somewhat banged about in the transfer from the ship to the camp, so that we could not depend upon it. I had a watch which I have carried for a number of years and which I was careful never to allow to run down. Each house had a watchman, every man taking his turn. It was his duty to keep the fires going. At 6 a.m. the watchman would call the cook; our meal hours were the same as those which we had observed during the past few months on the ship. Lights were out at 10 p.m. and all hands turned in.

We had a stove in the centre of the room in each house and around the stove on three sides, built out from the walls, were the bed platforms, which came close to the stove and were on a somewhat higher level. Here we slept warmly and comfortably on the mattresses we had saved from the ship.

On January 17 I decided that before long I would send a party of four men to the land to look out for game, see whether any driftwood was to be found on Wrangell Island, report on ice conditions and blaze a trail over the ice. This expedition would make an end to the men's enforced inactivity and the natural uneasiness of some of them, which I was unwilling to prolong if I could avoid doing so, and would, besides, be valuable in determining our subsequent movements. I did not like to take the whole party to the island without previously transporting supplies that would be sure to last them for at least four months.

Furthermore, the men had been living for a long time on shipboard and were not inured to the cold or yet in condition to withstand the privations they would have to undergo. None of them had had any experience in travelling over the Arctic ice during the brief and meagre light and in the low temperatures which would be our portion for another month, and the sledging of supplies towards the island would afford them the necessary practice. Travelling over the sea ice at any time is altogether different from land travelling. On the sea ice you have to spend a great deal of time looking about for good places to make the road for the sledging of supplies, for the ice is continually cracking and shifting and piling up in fantastic ridges from the pressure when the fissures close up, especially as near the land as we were, and its surface is so much rougher than the crystal levels of the lakes and ponds on which the landsman goes skating that there can hardly be said to be any comparison.

For the past week or so, I had noticed that our drift was slow, and I felt that as the daylight lengthened we should have ample time, long before we could drift away from the land, to sledge enough supplies ashore to last the party until the birds returned and the ice broke up. If we could start the men in small parties to relay supplies to the island we could get a shore camp established where the men could dry out their footgear for their journey back over the ice to Shipwreck Camp for more supplies, especially if we should find plenty of driftwood on Wrangell Island, as I hoped and expected; we had fuel enough at the camp to last a year.

The men could erect permanent snow igloos along the way, for relay stations, and once the road to the island was made, there would be little difficulty in keeping it open and by continuing the relays any faults that might come in the trail could be easily repaired. In these preliminary journeys, as I have said, the men would get accustomed to ice travel and finally the whole party, with its supplies, would be safe ashore. We were of course handicapped by lack of sufficient dogs, and in ice travel and in fact in any polar work, dogs are the prime requisites for success; manpower for hauling the sledgeloads of supplies puts a double burden on the men.

Those assigned for the first shoregoing party were First Mate Anderson, Second Mate Barker and Sailors King and Brady. They were to go to the island with three sledges and eighteen dogs, with Mamen and the two Eskimo men, as a supporting party, to come back with the dogs and two of the sledges after they had landed the mate's party on the island.

The eighteenth was another bad day, with a strong northeast gale and blinding snowdrift. Some of the men were at work loading the three sledges for the mate's party. Of the others, those that could be spared I sent out with pickaxes to make a trail towards the land, so that the shoregoing party might have a good start, but the weather was so bad that they had to return to camp after they had gone two or three miles. They reported seeing bear tracks on the ice and seal in open leads which they came to. We had plenty of seal meat so no attempt was made to do any shooting at this time.

The next day, Wednesday the twenty-first, conditions were more favorable and the party started. In addition to oral instructions about ice conditions and about returning to camp in case he met with open water, I gave the mate the following written orders:

SHIPWRECK CAMP, ARCTIC OCEAN,
January 20, 1914.
My dear Mr. Anderson: You will leave to-morrow morning with Mamen, three sledges, 18 dogs, Mr. Barker, Sailors King and Brady and the two Eskimo. The sledges are loaded with pemmican, biscuit and oil. You will find list of articles attached to this. When you reach Berry Point, Wrangell Island, you will be in charge of supplies. Kindly pay special attention to the uses of them. The rations are: 1 lb. pemmican, 1 lb. biscuits, with tea, per day. One gallon of oil will last you ten days. Mamen will leave one sledge and the tent, taking back with him enough supplies to carry him to Shipwreck. Whilst on the island you will endeavor to find game. Be sure and bring it to your camp. Also collect all the driftwood you can find. Very sincerely,
R. A. BARTLETT.

To Mamen I gave a brief letter of instructions, concluding with this paragraph: "Should you miss the trail and fail to connect with our camp, after a reasonable time has been spent in looking it up, you will go back to Wrangell Island and await my arriving there."

The party got away at 9:30 a.m., accompanied for about five miles by other members of the expedition to give them a good start. There was a strong east wind, with drifting snow, but the weather cleared later in the day and it grew calm in the evening. There were about four hours' light a day now good for travelling.

On the twenty-second I sent Chafe and Williams out to begin marking the landward trail with empty pemmican tins. Pemmican has been the staple article of food for polar expeditions for many years and contains, in small compass, the essentials adequate to support life. It is put up by various packinghouses, expressly for such needs as ours. I have lived for a hundred and twenty days on pemmican, biscuit and tea and found it amply sufficient. We had two kinds of pemmican; one, for ourselves, consisting of beef, raisins, sugar and suet, all cooked together and pressed, was packed in blue tins; the other, for the dogs, without the raisins and sugar, in red tins. I remember once, after a talk which I was giving on the North Pole trip, a lady came up to me and inquired what pemmican was, which I had mentioned several times. I explained what it was made of and what it was used for. She thought for a moment and then said, "Well, what I don't understand is how you shoot them."

January 25 was a day of rejoicing, because it marked the return of the sun, after seventy-one days. The sun was only rather indistinctly visible, half a disc above the ice, to the south, at noon, but from now on every day would be a little longer than the day before. It was the fourth time I had seen the sun come back in the Arctic and this time was the one which gave me the greatest satisfaction, because so much depended on our getting good daylight.

We celebrated by a little feast and some good singing in the evening. We had had a couple of cases of canned oysters on deck when the *Karluk* was struck and while I was waiting for the ship to go down on the eleventh I had found two tins of these oysters in the galley; the cook had brought them in to thaw them out. I threw the cases overboard on the ice where they broke and scattered tins of oysters around. We dug in the drifting snow and found this treasure trove and we had the oysters in soup and otherwise, and then had a "sing."

Every day we progressed in our preparations to make the landward journey. On the twenty-sixth, for instance, in addition to the constant round of packing and repacking, weighing this and measuring that, we tested a couple of bell tents, which had been made on shipboard, to see if they were alright for use later on. Each had a pole going up through the middle; we found they were quite satisfactory and the men used them afterwards to live in on Wrangell Island.

On the twenty-seventh we got a view of the whole sun above the horizon and a good look at the land. In the half-light of the previous days it had varied in size from time to time like a mirage and we could not tell whether it was Wrangell Island or not; now it seemed certain that it was not Wrangell so it must be Herald, according to the chart, a surmise which turned out to be correct.

I sent three men out on the twenty-eighth to see how the trail made by the mate's and Mamen's parties was lasting; they returned late in the day and reported an alteration and said that they had been unable to pick up the trail again beyond the break. So the next day I sent them out again, with Mr. Hadley. They succeeded in picking up the trail and went as far as Mamen's first outward camp, about twelve miles from our main camp. I had told Mamen before he left that when it came near the time when I should be expecting him back I would build a big bonfire near Shipwreck Camp to guide him, one an hour before dark and another an hour after dark. We now carried out this programme, using altogether thirteen sacks of coal, a whaleboat and ten tins of gasoline. It gave out a big smoke. At night we opened a drum of alcohol and burned the canoe, besides three cases of gasoline.

January 30 was a beautiful day with little or no wind and a temperature not much below zero. Chafe, Williams and Maurer walked to Mamen's second camp and an hour and a half beyond it, returning about half past four to report that there were no alterations in the trail and that the going was good. They put up a flag at the point where they turned back. When the men went out on these short journeys over the ice they carried some supplies with them to cache along the trail for future use.

THE RETURN OF MAMEN AND THE DEPARTURE OF THE DOCTOR'S PARTY

February 8 dawned fine and clear. There were a few narrow leads of water near Shipwreck Camp; the ice was constantly cracking here and there around us as the wind veered and changed in velocity and as we were still drifting we heard many a crashing or grinding sound. Our own floe was intact, but wherever the ice opened beyond the edges of the floe the open water would make young ice again and this was not always heavy enough to withstand the constantly recurring pressure.

At half past eight Chafe and Williams left with a Peary sledge, four dogs and the following supplies, to leave at Mamen's fourth camp: eight tins of Hudson's Bay pemmican, one case of Underwood dog pemmican, two cases of biscuits, one case of coal oil, together with seventy days' food for themselves and the dogs, a camping outfit, empty pemmican tins and flags, to place on the ice rafters.

All day long we kept a lookout for Mamen and his two Eskimo. About thirty yards away from the camp was a high rafter which we used as an observatory; every now and then while it was light, I was in the habit of going up there. Keruk, who was naturally anxious for the return of her husband, used to go up there, too, and as she had good eyesight I often asked her to go up and take a look.

Just before dark—that is, about four o'clock—when we were most of us indoors, sewing or getting ready for dinner, Breddy came in and said that he believed Mamen was coming. We all rushed out. Keruk was up on the rafter but it was already too dark to see far. I could hear the dogs barking, however, and the voice of Kataktovick shouting to them. It was glorious. I ran down the trail and met the returning party coming along at a good pace. "Well done, Norway!" I shouted, shaking Mamen's hand and patting him on the back.

They came in to the camp, greeted with cheers, and we rushed them in and filled them up with hot coffee and biscuit. It was about dinnertime and we put off dinner for about half an hour. The dogs, too, were hungry but I was ready for them with some pemmican and seal meat all cut up the day before and I fed them myself.

Nothing was said of their trip until after the men had had their dinner; then Mamen related his experiences. They had made eleven marches going in, until they were stopped by open water three miles from land. He described the land which they saw and I made up my mind that it was not Wrangell Island but Herald Island, a conjecture which proved to be correct. They had had pretty good going, without the trouble with open leads and raftered ice which we had when we made our main journey later on.

They had reached the edge of the open water January 31 without untoward incident, though one of their dogs had run away and King had frozen his heel. Mamen and the Eskimo had stayed with the shore party a day and had left on February 1 for their return to Shipwreck Camp. The mate, he said, had decided to land as soon as the lead closed up; this worried me a good deal because the mate and his party were not familiar with travel over the young ice and, besides that, Herald Island is no place for a party to land upon, for it is inaccessible, owing to its precipitous sides, and, according to American government reports, has no driftwood on its shores. In fact it has practically no shore to speak of, excepting one short stretch; it is simply a rocky islet.

Up to the time when Mamen left there was no chance to land on the island and Mamen hardly thought that the mate's party would be able to land there. I hoped that they would keep on to Wrangell Island and carry out their instructions.

Mamen's journey back to camp was much faster than the shoreward journey, because they had more light and could sleep in the igloos they had built going in. The last day back they had made a wonderful march, leaving their igloo at the earliest twilight and coming all day; they had not even stopped to eat since they had broken camp. They had relieved each other at driving the dogs.

Sunday, the eighth, I took stock of our pemmican and found that we had 4,982 pounds left in camp; we had used up and sledged along the trail some 5,000 pounds. We ate no pemmican in camp, and fed the dogs mostly on seal meat excepting when on the march. Most of the dogs were now out and we had in camp only those which were crippled or otherwise incapacitated.

We had a northeast gale on the seventeenth which continued for many days. On the seventeenth and eighteenth we had all hands hard at work, drying out clothing and getting sledges and equipment ready for the march. There was a pronounced drift westerly so that on the eighteenth Herald Island bore southeast by south, half south.

On the morning of February 19, I called the cook at four o'clock, so that we had an early breakfast for the start of the advance guard. There were two parties, each with a sledge and four dogs. In the first party were Malloch, Hadley, Williamson and Breddy; in the second Munro, Maurer, Williams and Chafe. Each party would have man-harness to help out the dogs when necessary.

Every man had a new suit of Jaeger underwear given him. The parties were to pick up supplies along the trail so that they would thus be replacing supplies used on the march, and take full loads with them in to the land. For this march was to take these eight men clear through to Wrangell Island and they were saying good-by to Shipwreck Camp for good. The men shook hands all around and got away about eight o'clock in the morning.

On one of the sledges they had a passenger. While we were fitting out the ship at the navy yard at Esquimault, someone presented us with a cat, as black as the ace of spades. She was kept in the forecastle at first; after a while she got aft and Mr. Hadley became greatly interested in her, training her to do tricks. When the ship was crushed and we were working to get things out of her before she sank I told the men to be sure not to forget the cat, but to put her in a basket and place her in the box-house. There she became very much at home. Early in her residence she got into difficulties with a dog that had wandered through the entrance, by landing suddenly like an animated bunch of porcupine quills on the dog's nose. The dog shook her off and tried to take his revenge.

We saved the cat just in time. After that she never bothered the dogs again. When the advance party now started for the land Hadley and

Maurer made a deerskin bag to carry the cat and she rode on a sledge in state. Her food consisted chiefly of pemmican scraps.

We fed the dogs seal meat, for we had several seal left, and also pemmican, for we still had plenty of that, and I was feeding the dogs all they would eat, to get them in as good condition as possible for the final march. This would be continuous travel with little sleep and now, on account of the storm, hard going and extra work in locating the trail. The Eskimo occupied some of their time in camp fitting up harpoons and spears to save ammunition.

They also put our snowshoes in good condition and spliced hatchet handles onto the handles of the snow knives so that they could wield them better in cutting out snowblocks for igloos.

On the twenty-third the storm was breaking at last. Huge banks of snow were piled high around the camp; we were all snowed in. The two crippled dogs were in the box-house with us; the other dogs were in the snow igloo, which had been occupied by the men who had now gone to the land. It took us nearly all day on the twenty-third to dig our way through the snow from the box-house to the igloo in order to feed the dogs. We dug the supply tent out and busied ourselves getting ready for our departure. In fact we stayed up all night, giving the final touches to our clothing.

At 4 a.m. on February 24 we had coffee and began loading our sledges. As soon as Kerdrillo's sledge, a remodeled Nome sledge, was loaded I started him off. With him went his wife and their two children, and Templeman, the cook. Keruk carried her baby, Mugpi, on her back all the way to Wrangell Island; the older girl covered the entire distance on foot, sometimes even helping her father with the sledge.

The rest of us had two sledges, one with three dogs, driven by Kataktovick, the other with four dogs, driven by myself.

We had to leave a Peary sledge in camp because there were not dogs enough to make a team to haul it. As it was, our three sledges, with their four-hundred-pound loads, were heavily burdened for the dogs we had, with some of them in a half-crippled condition. At about noon we finally got away—Kataktovick, McKinlay, Mamen and I. McKinlay, wearing man-harness, helped pull my sledge, while I guided and drove the dogs.

On account of his dislocated kneecap, which bothered him constantly and once on the march got out of place and had to be put back, with strenuous efforts on my part and much silent suffering on his, Mamen could not help pull Kataktovick's sledge but had to limp alongside and make his way as best he could. He chafed very much over his temporary uselessness and I had to cheer him up as well as I could by telling him constantly what wonderful work he had already accomplished.

We placed a record in a copper tank on the ice, telling where the ship was lost and when we left camp, with the names of the members of the various parties as they had left. In camp and on the ice we left behind us two transits, about 8,000 pounds of pemmican, 80 cases of biscuit, 200 sacks of coal, ten cases of gasoline, two drums of coal oil, with various odds and ends; over the camp we left the British ensign flying. I had my charts with me.

We had reached a point beyond the second camp by nightfall. Here we stopped. We had intended to make the third camp, but it was getting very dark, we had been up all the previous night, had worked hard all day and were very tired, so we were forced to pitch our tents and had to spend a miserable night under canvas. The tent was not large enough for us, yet all four of us occupied it and our breathing filled it with condensation. Our dogs, too, were rather sluggish the first day out, for they had been well stuffed with food during the time of our enforced delay in camp.

We welcomed daylight the next morning and turned out at four o'clock, and after our standard ration of tea, biscuit and pemmican, were soon on the march. All hands were glad to be off and the dogs, too, worked better than on the first day, so we made good progress.

At the fourth camp I found a note from Munro saying that they had been held up there by open water and a heavy gale, the same, evidently, which had detained us at Shipwreck Camp, and that they had shot a polar bear nearby. This I knew even before I read the note for I found a big piece of bear meat that they had left in the igloo for us. They had been unable to take all the pemmican at the cache here along with them; we picked up a few tins of it but could not take any more, for we were already overburdened.

Munro's note further said that the trail beyond was badly smashed but we went on as fast as we could, for we wanted to catch up with Kerdrillo and I was anxious to know that the advance party was continuing to get along well. At quarter past four we reached the sixth igloo. These camps were from four to ten miles apart. We found at this camp five gallons of oil, which the advance party left, three cases of pemmican, four cases of biscuit and some alcohol.

There should have been another cache nearby but the ice had raftered under pressure of the recent storm and destroyed it, thereby losing us a lot of biscuit and pemmican, and, what was just then even more valuable, perhaps, twelve gallons of oil.

At half past four we finally came up with Kerdrillo and his party. We had made the thirty miles from Shipwreck Camp to the sixth camp in two days, going twelve the first day and eighteen the second. Kerdrillo and his family were already occupying the igloo at this camp so we built another for ourselves.

We were not ordinarily troubled with insomnia, but sometimes, like a peaceful community the night before the Fourth, we were kept awake in spite of ourselves. Between ten and eleven on the night of the twenty-fifth, for instance, the ice began to crack in the vicinity of our camp and from time to time we in our igloo would feel severe shocks, as of an earthquake. Through the snow walls I could hear the Eskimo out on the ice. Kataktovick went out to see what was up and came back at once to tell me that a crack two or three feet wide had opened through the middle of Kerdrillo's igloo, which was about five yards away from ours, and that they had nearly lost their little baby but fortunately had got out before anything happened to them.

The ice continued to crack about us all through the night. There was no crack in our igloo so I gave it to Keruk and her children for the rest of the night and we walked back and forth, waiting for daylight. It was not very dark for the stars were shining brilliantly. The temperature was about forty below zero. All around us the ice was breaking and at times we were on a floating island. As soon as daylight came I sent McKinlay and Kataktovick, with all the dogs and an empty sledge, back to Shipwreck

Camp for about thirty gallons of the oil that we had left there. They had all the dogs from the three sledges and could make good progress.

While McKinlay and Kataktovick were gone Kerdrillo and I went on a scouting tour ahead for a way to see how the road looked. We found that the storm had destroyed the old trail and that the trail newly made by the Munro-Radley party was already changed somewhat, though as yet not very much. While we were on this scout Kerdrillo caught a glimpse, through our binoculars, of two men of the advance party, just visible against the skyline on a high rafter eight or ten miles away. When we came back to camp, I had Kerdrillo build another igloo for his party. During the day the ice had all closed up again.

About half past three the next afternoon, McKinlay and Kataktovick returned from Shipwreck Camp, with thirty gallons of oil, two tins of alcohol, twelve sealskins, a few fawnskins and 6,000 tea tablets. They said that both ways they had found our trail unaltered; apparently the only movement of the ice had been at the sixth camp, where we were.

THROUGH THE PRESSURE RIDGE

At dawn the next morning, February 28, leaving at this sixth camp some cases of biscuits, with alcohol and coal oil, we started again landward, going over the trail made by the advance party. At 1 p.m. we came up with them. They were halted by a huge conglomeration of raftered ice tossed up by the storm which had delayed us at Shipwreck Camp. The rafters were from twenty-five to a hundred feet high and ran directly across our path, parallel to the land, and extending in either direction as far as the eye could reach.

Viewed from an ice pinnacle high enough to give a clear sight across in the direction of the land the mass of broken ice looked to be at least three miles wide. To get around it was clearly out of the question; an attempt to do so might lead us no one knew whither. Clearly it was a case for hard labor, to build a road across it practicable for sledging; I had seen similar apparently impassible ice on our polar trips but never anything worse. At three o'clock, therefore, I told all hands to set to work building igloos and said that tomorrow we would begin with pickaxes to make a road across the rafters. While they were building the igloos I made a reconnaissance ahead for some distance, returning about dark.

We had no thermometer, so that we could not tell the exact temperature, but from the condition of the coal oil, which was very thick and viscid, it must have been between forty-five and fifty-five below zero. It was excellent weather for sledging, fine, clear and calm, if the going had only been good.

March 1, at daylight, I sent back Chafe and Mamen, with an empty sledge and ten dogs, to bring up all the oil, biscuit and alcohol that remained at the sixth camp. They returned with a well-laden sledge, late in the afternoon. I discovered during the day that Malloch and Maurer had frozen their feet, a thing which caused them a good deal of suffering and me a good deal of anxiety. Men with frozen feet are seriously handicapped and make the progress of all difficult until they recover. Fortunately in the present instance the men made known their predicament soon enough to be relieved before dangerously frostbitten.

At daylight the next morning I sent McKinlay, Hadley and Chafe back over the trail again, to go clear through to Shipwreck Camp with an empty sledge and fourteen dogs. They were to bring back the Peary sledge that we had left there and full loads of pemmican, biscuit and tea.

March 4, at about 4 p.m., we finished working through the rafter and came out on the smoother ice on its landward side. Mamen, Kataktovick and I spent the day sledging supplies across from the camp on the farther side and when the road was finished we all went back for the last load. It was not until 8 p.m. that we had all our supplies at the new camp and we had to do the last of the work in the dark; the Eskimo had built three igloos while we were sledging. It had taken us four days to get across a distance of three miles.

Our progress in to the island was retarded by the necessity of keeping along with us as large a quantity of supplies as possible. This meant relaying supplies, because the going was bad and made sledging difficult, with the small number of dogs we had. On the sixth, as soon as the first streak of light appeared, I sent Munro and his party back again to meet the McKinlay party, while I took Kataktovick and Kerdrillo and went ahead towards the island, roadmaking with our pickaxes.

At half past four the McKinlay party came in, convoyed by Munro and his party. McKinlay and his companions had gone clear back to Shipwreck Camp and brought in six cases of dog pemmican, sixteen cases of Hudson's Bay pemmican, thirty gallons of gasoline, and some hatchets and snow knives. They had left at the first camp from Shipwreck Camp four cases of Underwood dog pemmican and ten tins of Hudson's Bay pemmican, for they already had too heavy loads to bring them.

They said that the day before, as the darkness was coming on, they had come to the conclusion that they would be unable to reach the big camp near the raftered ice before night, so they had decided to stop where they were and build an igloo, while there was still light enough to see. They were busily at work, cutting out snowblocks and piling them up, when suddenly three bears came upon them, evidently the same ones whose tracks we had seen on our march.

One of the bears got between them and the sledge which bore their rifles. They made noise enough, however, to frighten this bear and start all three running away; then they sprang for their rifles and shot the bears on the run.

———

March 12 we got away again at dawn. McKinlay, Mamen, Kataktovick, Kerdrillo and his family and I went ahead of the others, with lightly loaded sledges, and, on account of improved ice conditions, made such good progress that at 1 p.m. we landed on Icy Spit, on the northeast side of Wrangell Island. It is perhaps easier to imagine than to describe our feelings of relief at being once again on terra firma, after two months of drifting and travelling on the ice.

We had had a hard road to travel much of the way from Shipwreck Camp, but fortunately, since the big storm in the days following the departure of the advance party, we had had continuously fine weather, with good daylight and exhilarating temperatures in the minus forties and fifties.

As soon as we landed we began building an igloo. There was plenty of driftwood scattered all about and Keruk gathered up a lot of it and built a fire, so that by the time the first of our three igloos was built she had some tea for us and the rest of the party who, coming along easily with light loads over our trail, arrived an hour and a half after we did. We were overjoyed to find the driftwood for, although we were pretty sure of finding it, we were a little dubious and it was a great relief to my mind to know that fuel was assured.

The northeast side of the island, on which we now were, sent several low sandy spits out from the land, thus forming lagoons which of course were covered with ice. Near the coast were low mountains and valleys, with higher peaks in the interior beyond. Here and there on the beach were dead trees that had drifted ashore, with the roots sticking up into the air; we also found planks and other lumber. Everything was snowclad and white, only a degree less cheerless than the frozen ocean itself.

The next day Munro, Chafe, Breddy and Williams went back with all the dogs and sledges to the last camp on the ice, fifteen miles from our landing place, and brought in all the supplies we had left there. While they were gone I sent Kerdrillo nine miles across the lagoon to Berry Spit, to see if he could find any traces of the mate's party or the McKinlay party. He took his rifle with him to look for game. When he came back at nightfall, he reported that he had seen no traces of either party and only one bear track and one fox track.

This was an indication that there was small chance of getting a bear on or near the island, because there were no seal holes within twenty-five miles from land; we had seen some near the big rafter, about forty miles out. Later in the season, as the ice broke up nearer the land, the seal would work in shore and of course the bears would follow. I asked Kerdrillo what he thought the chances were of there being any caribou or reindeer on the island.

The next day, I sent him out again, giving him tea and pemmican, so that he could have a full day's march and make a reconnaissance into the interior. About dark he returned and reported that he had seen no traces of caribou, reindeer or hare and very few signs of foxes. Later on, however, he thought ptarmigan would visit the island. He had seen one bear track, which he thought was about three days old, probably of the bear whose tracks he had seen on the previous day.

We now made a snow shelter and started in on the fourteenth to dry out our boots and stockings; we had plenty of firewood. Keruk looked after this work. Maurer's and Malloch's feet still troubled them and Mamen's knee was a constant cause of suffering, so that I was glad that they could now have an opportunity to rest. From the moment of our departure from Shipwreck Camp we had been constantly on the move during every minute of the daylight.

The weather, though cold, had been exceptionally fine and clear; in fact we had not lost an hour on account of bad weather and had been inconvenienced for only one night by open water. As a consequence all hands were in need of a little rest. The dogs, too, were in a reduced condition, for though they had had plenty to eat they had worked very hard and I wanted them to get what rest they could.

For the plan I had been evolving to make my way across Long Strait from Wrangell Island to the coast of Siberia and seeking an opportunity of getting help for the party here on the island was now about to be put to the test. We were on land but were a long way from civilization; we need not drown but we might starve or freeze to death if we could not get help within a reasonable time. With the decline of the whaling industry there was no chance that any ship would come so far out from the mainland so that the only way to expect help to reach the party was to go after it.

I would take only Kataktovick with me. He was sufficiently experienced in ice travel and inured to the hardships of life in the Arctic to know how to take care of himself in the constantly recurring emergencies that menace the traveller on the ever-shifting surface of the sea ice. On my trips with Peary I had had plenty of leads of open water to negotiate at this time of year but that was twelve or fifteen degrees north of where we now were.

The weather continued fine and clear nearly all day on the fourteenth, as it had been for so many days past, but towards night clouds began to come up from the south and I felt that some change in the weather was likely to take place. The wind began to blow and by the next morning had become a gale. We devoted the time to drying out our clothes, mending them and making what alterations might be necessary.

On March 16 a howling northwest gale sprang up in the early morning, continuing all day long, with blinding snowdrift. On account of the storm, the party for Shipwreck Camp was unable to leave. The next morning, however, the wind had died down to a gentle breeze and at 8 a.m. the men got away. We parted for journeys in opposite directions, for I planned to leave on the following day for Siberia and would have gone on the seventeenth only that I wanted to see the others safely off. Munro, Breddy and Williams, with sixteen dogs and one sledge, were the ones chosen for the work. They were to go out over the trail to Shipwreck Camp and sledge supplies in two trips across the big pressure ridge in to the still ice about twenty-five miles from land and thence to the shore itself, their first load to consist chiefly of biscuit and their second of pemmican.

After my departure Munro would be in general charge of the men on Wrangell Island, as, in the absence of the mate, he was by rank second in command and was, moreover, well fitted for the post. On seeing him off I went over my instructions to him, which I told him I would also write out and leave with McKinlay when I got away the next day. I had had McKinlay make an inventory of the supplies and apportion them among the party, each to be responsible for his own share.

There would be eighty days' full rations apiece, even if they got no game or any further supplies from the caches along the trail and at Shipwreck Camp. During my absence I directed that the party be divided into three detachments, living far enough apart from one another to ensure as wide a hunting area as possible for each.

SHORE CAMP, ICY SPIT, WRANGELL ISLAND,
March 18th, 1914.
My dear Mr. Munro:
I am leaving this morning with seven dogs, one sledge and Kataktovick to get the news of our disaster before the authorities at Ottawa. During my absence you will be in charge. I have already allocated supplies to the different parties. McKinley [sic] has four men, Hadley is with the Eskimo Kerdrillo which makes four people, Mr. Williamson three men and yourself three men. McKinlay kindly made out a list for me and I will ask him to give a copy to you when you get back from your

trip to Shipwreck Camp. You will make a trip to Herald Island to search for traces of mate's party. On my way I will cover the coast as far as Rodgers Harbor. The great thing of course is the procuring of game. In this Kerdrillo will be of great assistance. Let him have his dogs and the two others so he can cover a good deal of ground; and our own parties, scatter them around so that they will be able to hunt and while away the time. Give each party enough dogs, if you can spare them so that they can better cover the ground. As we talked about distributing supplies that you bring back; give each one their proportional share. As it stands now there are 80 days' pemmican and oil for each person. Please do all you can to promote good feeling in camp. You will assemble at Rodgers Harbor about the middle of July where I hope to meet you with a ship.

Sincerely yours,

R. A. BARTLETT,

Captain, C. G. S.

THREE

The Savage Sea

Dougal Robertson

THE BLACK VOLCANIC MOUNTAIN OF FERNANDINA, THE MOST WESTERLY of the Galapagos Islands, towered high above the tall masts of the schooner *Lucette* as she lay at anchor, rolling gently in the remnants of the long Pacific swell which surged round the rocky headland of Cape Espinosa, and sent searching fingers of white surf curling into the sheltered waters of the anchorage.

We were on the eve of our departure for the Marquesas Islands, three thousand miles to the west, and now, as the wind swung to the east under a grey mantle of rain cloud, I felt anxious to be gone, for if we left now we would be out from under the lee of the island by morning. Lyn protested vehemently at the thought of starting our journey on June the thirteenth, even when I pointed out that the most superstitious of seafarers didn't mind so long as it wasn't a Friday as well, but Douglas and Robin both now joined with my feelings of anxiety to be gone, and after a short spell of intense activity, we stowed and lashed the dinghy and secured all movables on deck and below.

By five o'clock in the afternoon we were ready for sea, and with mainsail and jibs set we heaved the anchor home, reached past the headland into the strait, then altering course to the west ran free towards the Pacific, a thousand square feet of sail billowing above *Lucette* as she moved easily along the ragged black coastline of Fernandina towards the largest stretch of ocean in the world.

By the morning of the fourteenth, the Galapagos Islands were receding into the distance astern, merging with the clouds of the overcast sky above as *Lucette,* now rolling and pitching in the heavy swell and rough seas of the Pacific trades, made steady progress west by south towards the Marquesas Islands.

In spite of the fact that we had been sailing for over a year, our stomachs still took a little time to adjust from the quietness of sheltered waters to the lively movement of the yacht in the open sea and so throughout the day those of us not actively engaged in steering and sailing *Lucette* rested as best we could in the bunks below, supplied at intervals with hot soup or coffee from Lyn's indomitable labours at the stove. Unused to the sea, Robin had been sick most of the way from Panama to the Galapagos, but he now seemed better adjusted to the physical discomfort of the constant heave of the hull. He was able to steer a fairly accurate course by compass, and although the principles of sailing were still something of a closed book to him, he could help Douglas and me with the night watches whilst Lyn and the twins helped with the watches during the day.

The wind moderated a little during the following night and breaks in the cloud enabled us to catch glimpses of stars in the predawn sky; on the morning of the fifteenth we had our first glimpse of the sun since leaving the Galapagos and with the slackening of wind and speed *Lucette* settled to a more comfortable movement in the diminishing seas.

The morning sun shone fitfully from the thinning cloud, and as I balanced myself against the surge of *Lucette*'s deck, sextant glued to my eye, I watched for the right moment when the image of the sun's rim would tip the true horizon, no easy combination when both deck and horizon are in constant motion. Douglas and Sandy were in the cockpit, one steering and the other tending the fishing line, while Robin, finding it difficult to sleep in his own bunk on the port side of the main cabin, had nipped quietly into Sandy's bunk on the starboard side of the fo'c'stle to rest after his spell on the four to eight morning watch. Neil was reading a book in his own bunk on the port side of the fo'c'stle, and Lyn had just started to clean up the usual chaos which results from a rough stretch of sailing. At last the sun, the horizon and the deck cooperated to give me a fairly accurate reading, and noting the local time by my watch at 09h 54m

45s, I collected my logarithm tables and Nautical Almanac from the chart table and retired below to the relative comfort of the after cabin to work out our longitude; it was my first position sight since leaving the islands.

With my sextant carefully replaced in its box I had turned to my books to work up a reasonably accurate dead-reckoning position when sledgehammer blows of incredible force struck the hull beneath my feet, hurling me against the bunk, the noise of the impact almost deafening my ears to the roar of inrushing water. I heard Lyn call out, and almost at the same time heard the cry of 'Whales!' from the cockpit. My senses still reeled as I dropped to my knees and tore up the floorboards to gaze in horror at the blue Pacific through the large splintered hole punched up through the hull planking between two of the grown oak frames. Water was pouring up through the hole with torrential force and although Lyn called out that it was no use, that the water was pouring in from another hole under the WC flooring as well, I jammed my foot on the broken strakes and shouted to her to give me large cloths, anything to stem the flood. She threw me a pillow and I jammed it down on top of the broken planking, rammed the floorboard on top and stood on it; the roar of the incoming water scarcely diminished, it was already above the level of the floorboards as I heard Douglas cry from the deck 'Are we sinking, Dad?' 'Yes! Abandon ship!'; my voice felt remote as numbly I watched the water rise rapidly up the engine casing; it was lapping my knees as I turned to follow Lyn, already urging Neil and Robin on deck. Wading past the galley stove, my eye glimpsed the sharp vegetable knife, and grabbing it in passing I leapt for the companionway; the water, now up to my thighs, was already lapping the top of the batteries in the engine room; it was my last glimpse of *Lucette's* interior, our home for nearly eighteen months. Lyn was tying the twins' lifejackets on with rapid efficiency as I slashed at the lashings holding the bow of the dinghy to the mainmast; Douglas struggled to free the self-inflatable raft from under the dinghy and I ran forward to cut the remaining lashings holding the stern of the dinghy to the foremast, lifting the dinghy and freeing the raft at the same time. Lyn shouted for the knife to free the water containers and I threw it towards her; Douglas again shouted to me if he should throw the raft over, disbelieving that we were really sinking. 'Yes, get on with it!'

I yelled, indicating to Robin, who now had his lifejacket on, to help him. Grasping the handles at the stern of the dinghy, I twisted it over from its inverted stowed position and slid it towards the rail, noting that the water was now nearly level with *Lucette*'s deck as she wallowed sluggishly in the seaway.

Douglas ran from the after deck with the oars and thrust them under the thwarts as I slid the dinghy seawards across the coach roof, then he took hold of the stern from me and slid the dinghy the rest of the way into the sea, Robin holding on to the painter to keep it from floating away. The raft, to our relief, our great and lasting relief, had gone off with a bang and was already half inflated, and Lyn, having severed the lashings on the water containers and flares, was carrying them to the dinghy. I caught up the knife and again shouted 'Abandon ship!' for I feared *Lucette*'s rigging might catch one of us as she went down, then cut the lashings on a bag of onions, which I gave to Sandy, instructing him to make for the raft, a bag of oranges which I threw into the dinghy and a small bag of lemons to follow. It was now too dangerous to stay aboard, and noting that Douglas, Robin and Sandy had already gone and that Neil was still sitting in the dinghy which was three-quarters full of water, I shouted that he also should make for the raft. He jumped back on *Lucette*, clutching his teddy bears, then plunged into the sea, swimming strongly for the raft. Lyn struggled through the rails into the water, still without a lifejacket, and I walked into the sea, first throwing the knife into the dinghy, the waters closing over *Lucette*'s scuppers as we left her.

I feared that the whales would now attack us and urged everyone into the raft, which was fully inflated and exhausting surplus gas noisily. After helping Lyn into the raft I swam back to the dinghy, now completely swamped, with oranges floating around it from the bag which had burst, and standing inside it to protect myself from attack, threw all the oranges and lemons within reach into the raft. The water containers had already floated away or had sunk, as had the box of flares, and since the dinghy was now three feet under the water, having only enough flotation to support itself, I made my way back to the raft again, grabbing a floating tin of petrol as I went. On leaving the dinghy I caught a last glimpse of *Lucette*, the water level with her spreaders and only the tops of her sails showing. Slowly she curtsied below the waves, a lady to the last; she was gone when I looked again.

I climbed wearily into the yellow inflatable, a sense of unreality flooding through me, feeling sure that soon I would waken and find the dream gone. I looked at my watch; it was one minute to ten. 'Killer whales,' said Douglas. 'All sizes, about twenty of them. Sandy saw one with a big V in its head. I think three of them hit us at once.' My mind refused to take in the implications of the attack; I gazed at the huge genoa sail lying on the raft floor where Lyn was sitting with the twins. 'How the hell did that get there?' I asked stupidly. Douglas grinned. 'I saw the fishing line spool floating on the surface unwinding itself,' he said, 'so I grabbed it and pulled it in, the sail was hooked in the other end!'

Three killer whales; I remembered the one in captivity in Miami Seaquarium weighed three tons and that they swam at about thirty knots into an attack; no wonder the holes in *Lucette*! The others had probably eaten the injured one with the V in its head, which must have split its skull when it hit *Lucette's* three-ton lead keel. She had served us well to the very end, and now she was gone.

Lyn gazed numbly at me, quietly reassuring the twins who had started crying, and, apart from the noise of the sea round us, we gazed in silent disbelief at our strange surroundings.

CASTAWAYS

We sat on the salvaged pieces of flotsam lying on the raft floor, our faces a pale bilious colour under the bright yellow canopy, and stared at each other, the shock of the last few minutes gradually seeping through to our consciousness. Neil, his teddy bears gone, sobbed in accompaniment to Sandy's hiccup cry, while Lyn repeated the Lord's Prayer, then, comforting them, sang the hymn 'For those in peril on the Sea.' Douglas and Robin watched at the doors of the canopy to retrieve any useful pieces of debris which might float within reach and gazed with dumb longing at the distant five-gallon water container, bobbing its polystyrene lightness ever farther away from us in the steady trade wind.

The dinghy *Ednamair* wallowed, swamped, nearby with a line attached to it from the raft and our eyes travelled over and beyond to the heaving undulations of the horizon, already searching for a rescue ship even while knowing there would not be one. Our eyes travelled fruitlessly across the limitless waste of sea and sky, then once more ranged over the scattering debris. Of the killer whales which had so recently shattered our very existence, there was no sign. Lyn's sewing basket floated close and it was brought aboard followed by a couple of empty boxes, the canvas raft cover, and a plastic cup. I leaned across to Neil and put my arm round him, 'It's alright now, son, we're safe and the whales have gone.' He looked at me reproachfully. 'We're not crying 'cos we're frightened,' he sobbed, 'we're crying 'cos Lucy's gone.' Lyn gazed at me over their heads, her eyes filling with tears. 'Me too,' she said, and after a moment added, 'I suppose we'd better find out how we stand.'

I looked at Douglas, he had grown to manhood in our eighteen months at sea together; the twins, previously shy, introspective farm lads, had become interested in the different peoples we had met and their various ways of life, and were now keen to learn more; I tried to ease my conscience with the thought that they had derived much benefit from their voyage and that our sinking was as unforeseeable as an earthquake, or an aeroplane crash, or anything to ease my conscience.

We cleared a space on the floor and opened the survival kit, which was part of the raft's equipment, and was contained in a three-foot-long polythene cylinder; slowly we took stock: Vitamin-fortified bread and glucose for ten men for two days. Eighteen pints of water, eight flares. One bailer, two large fishhooks, two small, one spinner and trace and a twenty-five-pound breaking strain fishing line. A patent knife which would not puncture the raft (or anything else for that matter), a signal mirror, torch [flashlight], first-aid box, two sea anchors, instruction book, bellows, and three paddles.

In addition to this there was the bag of a dozen onions which I had given to Sandy, to which Lyn had added a one-pound tin of biscuits and a bottle containing about half a pound of glucose sweets, ten oranges and six lemons. How long would this have to last us? As I looked round our meagre stores my heart sank and it must have shown on my face for Lyn put her hand on mine; 'We must get these boys to land,' she said quietly. 'If we do nothing else with our lives, we must get them to land!' I looked at her and nodded, 'Of course, we'll make it!' The answer came from my heart but my head was telling me a different story.

We were over two hundred miles down wind and current from the Galapagos Islands. To try to row the small dinghy into two hundred miles of rough ocean weather was an impossible journey even if it was tried by only two of us in an attempt to seek help for the others left behind in the raft. The fact that the current was against us as well only put the seal of hopelessness on the idea. There was no way back.

The Marquesas Islands lay two thousand eight hundred miles to the west but we had no compass or means of finding our position; if, by some miraculous feat of endurance, one of us made the distance the chances of striking an island were remote. The coast of Central America, more than a thousand miles to the northeast, lay on the other side of the windless Doldrums, that dread area of calms and squalls which had inspired Coleridge's

Water, water, everywhere,
And all the boards did shrink;
Water, water, everywhere,
Nor any drop to drink.

I was a Master Mariner, I thought ruefully, not an ancient one, and could count on no ghostly crew to get me out of this dilemma!

What were our chances if we followed the textbook answer, 'Stay put and wait for rescue'? In the first place we wouldn't be missed for at least five weeks and if a search was made, where would they start looking in three thousand miles of ocean? In the second place the chance of seeing a passing vessel in this area was extremely remote and could be discounted completely, for of the two possible shipping routes from Panama to Tahiti and New Zealand, one lay four hundred miles to the south and the other three hundred miles to the north.

Looking at the food, I estimated that six of us might live for ten days and since we could expect no rain in this area for at least six months, apart from an odd shower, our chances of survival beyond ten days were doubtful indeed.

My struggle to reach a decision, gloomy whichever way I looked at it, showed on my face, and Lyn leaned forward. 'Tell us how we stand,' she said, looking round, 'we want to know the truth.' They all nodded, 'What chance have we?' I could not tell them I thought they were going to die so I slowly spelled out the alternatives, and then suddenly I knew there was only one course open to us; we must sail with the trade winds to the Doldrums four hundred miles to the north. We stood a thin chance of reaching land but the only possible shipping route lay in that direction, our only possible chance of rainwater in any quantity lay in that direction even if it was four hundred miles away, and our only possible chance of reaching land lay in that direction, however small that chance might be.

We would work and fight for our lives at least; better than dying in idleness! 'We must get these boys to land,' Lyn had said. I felt the reality of the decision lifting the hopelessness from my shoulders and looked around; five pairs of eyes watched me as I spoke, Lyn once again with her arms round the twins, Douglas and Robin each at their lookout posts watching for any useful debris that might come within reach. 'We have no alternative,' I said, 'we'll stay here for twenty-four hours to see if any other wreckage appears, then we must head north and hope to find rain in the Doldrums.'

—◆—

I peeped round the canopy of the raft at the dinghy; the *Ednamair* lay disconsolately awash at the end of her painter, her white gunwale just visible above the surface of the water. She was helping the sea anchor, I supposed, but we'd have to bail her out first thing in the morning, for the wooden thwarts, which contained the polystyrene flotation reserve, would loosen and come adrift if they became waterlogged.

The water exploded as a thirty-pound dorado leapt high in the air after a flying fish, landing with a slap on its side in a shower of luminescence. I glanced down to where several large fish swam under the raft, constantly rising to skim the underside of the raft's edge, sometimes hitting it a heavy blow with their high jutting foreheads.

I looked across at Lyn, rubbing the cramp out of the twins' legs. 'We'll see to the *Ednamair* after breakfast'; I looked hopefully at the water jar, but it was nearly empty. We had emptied the glucose sweets out of their glass jar so that it could be used to hold drinking water as it was decanted from the tin, for although we had discussed the issue of equal rations of water (there wasn't enough to do that) we had decided simply to pass the jar round, each person limiting him or herself to the minimum needed to carry on; at the same time, the visible water level in the jar enabled everyone to see there was no cheating. Breakfast consisted of one quarter-ounce biscuit, a piece of onion and a sip of water, except for Robin and Neil who could not eat and were with difficulty persuaded to take some extra water with a seasick pill. We had used two pints of water in one day between six, hardly a maintenance ration under a tropic sun, which I remembered had been placed as high as two pints per person per day! We ate slowly, savouring each taste of onion and biscuit with a new appreciation and, although we hardly felt as if we had breakfasted on bacon and eggs, we were still sufficiently shocked at our altered circumstances not to feel hunger.

Breakfast over, Lyn, with Sandy helping, sorted out the various pieces of sail which were to be used for bedding, chatting quietly all the while to Neil and Robin. Douglas and I went to the door of the raft and, pulling the dinghy alongside, first attempted to bail it out as it lay swamped, but the waves filled it as fast as we bailed. We turned its stern towards us and, lifting slowly, allowed the bow to submerge, then when we could lift it no higher, I called 'Let go!' The dinghy flopped back in the water with three inches of freeboard, we bailed desperately with small bailers, then Douglas took one of the wooden boxes and with massive scoops bailed enough water out to allow him to board the dinghy and bail it dry. We were all cheered by the sight of little *Ednamair* afloat again, and with a cry of delight Douglas held up his Timex watch; it had been lying in the bottom of the dinghy all this time and was still going! He also found what was to prove our most valuable possession, the stainless-steel kitchen knife which I had thrown in after the fruit.

After a segment of orange each for elevenses we loaded the oars, a paddle, the empty boxes, the petrol can, the hundredfoot raft painter, and the piece of the genoa designated for the dinghy sail, then climbing into the dinghy started work on the jury rig that was to turn the *Ednamair* into a tugboat for our first stage of the journey north. Douglas, in the meantime, helped Lyn to reorganise the inside of the raft now that there was much more room, and topped up the flotation chambers with air.

I rigged one oar in the mast step with appropriate fore and back stays, then cutting notches in the raft paddle, bent the head of the sail onto it to form a square sail. The paddle was made fast to the top of the oar, and the sail foot secured to the two ends of the other oar, placed athwartships across the rowlock sockets. A violent jerk sent me sprawling into the bottom of the boat and I realised that we were operational.

I climbed back aboard the raft for a lunch of a small piece of fortified bread, of which there was about a pound and a half in the emergency rations, along with eight ounces of glucose and a mouthful of water; I felt very thirsty after my exertions in the raft. *Ednamair* was now straining at the leash so I called to Douglas to trip the sea anchor and haul it aboard; the time was two o'clock in the afternoon and we had started our voyage to the Doldrums, and, I shuddered at the thought of the alternative, rain. I estimated our position at Latitude 1° South and Longitude 94°40' West or, more accurately, two hundred miles west of Cape Espinosa.

The white plastic-covered luff wire was now snapping taut with considerable force as *Ednamair* yawed at the end of her towrope, so having little use for the petrol I lashed the can to the centre of the towing wire to act as a tension buffer which it did quite effectively. We now turned our attention to the flotation chambers of the raft to see if we could find any leaks. The double canopy alone was worth a gallon of water a day to us in keeping out the heat of the sun, and its emergency rations were available to us now only because they were already stowed inside the raft.

We examined the raft's flotation chambers as well as we could, pouring water over all the exposed surface areas, but could find no leaks, although there were one or two repair patches, and finally put down the loss of air to seepage through the treated fabric of the raft. We arranged a regular routine of topping up on each watch to keep the raft as rigid as possible, for the continuous flexing of the softened chambers by the waves was bound to cause wear.

I lay down to think in the long hours of the night of how long it would take us to reach the Doldrums and of our chances of finding rain there; an exercise that was to occupy my nights with increasing urgency as our meagre store of water cans gradually dwindled. Robin had puffed rather ineffectually at the inflating tube before he went off watch, but the raft was still pretty soft, so I stuck the end in my mouth and gave it a good blow at both ends; Robin would get better at it as he got used to the idea.

DAY THREE

My watch, in the dawn hours of the morning, started with a clear sky, but, as the sun tinted the clouds, the wind freshened again from the south and the tall flowery cumulus, pink peaked with grey bases, seemed heavy enough to give rain. As soon it was light I pulled in the dinghy and climbed aboard to inspect the sail fastenings and stays, one of which had worked loose in the night. While I was securing the stay I caught sight of a small black shape under the wooden box by the thwart; I stooped and lifted our first contribution from the sea, a flying fish of about eight inches. I gutted and descaled it, then passed it over to Lyn, now awake, for her to marinate it in a squeeze of lemon juice, which acted as a cooking agent. We breakfasted at seven, an hour later, each savouring our tiny piece of fish done to a turn in the lemon juice, followed by a crunchy piece of onion and a mouthful of water. The raft had begun pitching heavily again, surging on the crests of the breaking sea and dropping steeply into the troughs. To our disappointment, both Neil and Robin started being seasick again and though we offered them seasick pills they decided to do without and try to get used to the motion of the raft instead.

The waves began to break over the stern of the raft, and with swells of up to twenty feet high, it looked as if we were in for a bad day. *Ednamair* yawed violently as the wind gusted in her sail and she pulled hard on the towrope, lifting it clear of the water at times. I decided to take a reef in the sail to ease the strain on the towing straps of the raft, so Douglas hauled the dinghy alongside the raft and held her while I balanced precariously on the seat. To reef her, I simply tied a rope around the belly of the sail, giving it an hourglass effect and reducing its effective pulling power by half. I had just completed the operation and was standing up again to return when a large breaker surged round the raft and caught the dinghy broadside. As she tilted, I lost balance and fell, grabbing at the mast to prevent myself falling into the sea; *Ednamair* tilted sharply with the increased leverage and the sea rushed in over the gunwale in a wave. Before I could let go the mast and drop to the floor of the dinghy, it was swamped. Luckily we retained about three inches of freeboard and before the next wave could complete the damage, I dived through the door of the canopy into the raft, and the dinghy, relieved of my weight, floated a little higher. We bailed desperately for several minutes from the raft and then, gaining on the influx of water slopping over the gunwale, we finally got enough freeboard to allow me to return to the *Ednamair* and bail it dry again. In the night, I had thought of the possibility of us taking to the dinghy altogether and leaving the raft, but this incident served to highlight the difficulty of any such move; the subject of trim with a very small freeboard would be of paramount importance and now I doubted if the dinghy could take the six of us and remain afloat in the open sea.

After our exhausting morning, we rested awhile, lunching on a mouthful of water and a few 'crumbs' of a type of fortified bread which, although made up in tablet form, disintegrated at the first touch and made the conveyance of the crumbs from container to mouth an operation that required great care to avoid spilling and usually resulted in some waste, even when we licked the stray crumbs off our clothes. This was followed by a piece of orange.

The clouds thickened as the day advanced and the high cumulus began to drop rain in isolated showers. The wind freshened still further and with the surf of breaking waves slopping through the canopy door at the rear of the raft, we closed the drawstrings on the flaps as much as was possible without cutting off all ventilation. With the large blanket pin I punched bigger holes in the empty water cans and made plugs to fit them in case a shower should cross us and give us water, while Douglas blew lustily into the pipe to make the raft as rigid as possible in the heavy seas. *Ednamair* bounced around at the end of her towrope like a pup on a leash and I was considering taking the sail down altogether when the patter of raindrops on the canopy warned us that we were about to get rain. A pipe led down from the centre of the rain catchment area on the roof and, pulling this to form a depression in the roof, we prepared to gather our first rainwater. With fascinated eyes we gazed at the mouth of the pipe, at the liquid that dribbled from the end, bright yellow, and saltier than the sea. As soon as the salt had been washed off the roof, we managed to collect half a pint of yellowish rubbery-tasting liquid before the shower passed over. I looked at the jar of fluid (one could hardly call it water) sadly; we would need to do a lot better than that if we were to survive.

The raft, now pitching heavily, required blowing up every hour to keep it rigid, and the undulations and jerks did nothing to ease the spasms of seasickness which Neil and Robin were suffering; they both looked drawn and pale, refusing even water in spite of Lyn's pleading. As the raft slid up the twenty-foot swells to the breaking combers at the top, Lyn prayed desperately for calm weather and for rain, urging that the rest of us should join her in prayer with such insistence that I had to remind her that freedom of thought and religion was a matter of individual choice and no one should be coerced.

I passed the water jar around for 'sippers' before our meagre ration of biscuit, reminding everyone that our supplies were now very low and that only minimal amounts should be taken. 'We must try to drink less than two pints per day between us,' I said. 'We have only twelve tins left and we still have over three hundred miles to go.' A quart of water each for the next three hundred miles, it didn't sound much.

As darkness closed in and the first watchkeeper settled to his two-hour vigil, I could feel the bump and bite of the dorado fish through the bottom of the raft and resolved to try to catch one in the morning. Neil and Sandy were sleeping soundly after helping to blow up the raft and mop up the water which was now coming through the floor at a greater rate than before. They looked so vulnerable that my heart turned over at the prospect of what lay ahead for them; death by thirst, or starvation, or just a slow deterioration into exhaustion. I heard Lyn's voice many times that night, in my mind: 'We must get these boys to land,' and sleep would not come to ease the burden of my conscience.

DAY TEN

As soon as daylight had faded the stars from the clearing skies, we tripped and housed the sea anchor, shook the reef out of the sail and continued on our way to the Doldrums. We had paid lip service to the standard practices of rescue by remaining in the shipping lane for as long as we could, but I felt that our present circumstances called for more than standard practice and was anxious that no more time should be wasted, for we were still some distance from the rain area and our stocks of water were dwindling once more.

As soon as we were moving again I dumped the offal and bailed the blood out of the dinghy; dozens of scavenger fish appeared from nowhere, the sea swirling as they fought to devour the scraps of coagulated turtle blood. In a few minutes, the now familiar fins of four sharks were seen as they cruised around looking for the source of the blood. The sea boiled as one of them attacked a dorado, the shark leaping its full ten-foot length clear of the water in a tremendous strike. Although they were our constant reminders of what lay in store for us if we failed, we could not help admiring the beautiful streamlined shape of these white-tipped sharks as they cruised in smooth unhurried serenity with their attendant bevies of pilot fish close to the raft. Our admiration did not deter me from thumping one of them with a paddle when it came too close (it beat a hasty retreat) and as if they had taken the hint we weren't troubled by any of the others, but from then onwards we were never without at least one shark in attendance.

At 3°30' North and 250 miles west of Cape Espinosa, our noon position confirmed that the Doldrums, a mere ninety miles now, were well within striking distance and that our first leg of the journey was nearly over. High cirrus clouds moved contrary to the trade winds, their unsubstantial vapours conveying little to the searcher for weather signs, and I turned my attention to the dinghy, scraping out the turtle shell and collecting all the pieces of bone from the flippers. The half-cured meat had turned a deep brown colour under the heat of the sun and I took a little of it back to the raft, to spin out our luncheon of flipper bones and eggs.

During the afternoon the plug in the bottom of the raft was dislodged and water flooded into the forward compartment through a now much enlarged hole. We plugged it eventually by ramming an aircraft dinghy instruction book, made of waterproof material, into the hole, a creditable use for it, and while Robin bailed the compartment dry again, I wondered how long it would be before the raft became untenable altogether and we became dependent on *Ednamair* for our lives. There was no doubt in my mind that we should have to do this eventually, but the prospect of the six of us fitting into, and living in, the confined limits of the nine-foot-six-inch boat along with our food and water supplies and other items of equipment appalled me, for the slightest imbalance would bring the sea flooding in over the small freeboard.

The life belts, which were filled with kapok, had been used as pillows, and for keeping our bodies from lying in the pools of water which collected in the raft during the night, but now they had become so saturated that I took them over to the dinghy and placed them between the thwarts to dry out. In the meanwhile, we again searched for leaks, for there was one, as yet unlocated, in the after section which was causing us much bodily discomfort. I decided we would have to rip the side screens out of the raft to find the leak which was coming from under them and set about doing this before darkness fell, using the blunt-nosed raft knife for the purpose to avoid cutting into any of the flotation chambers.

The continuous contact with the salt water had aggravated our skin eruptions and we all suffered from an increasing number of saltwater boils on our arms and legs, shoulders and buttocks; they were extremely painful when brought in contact with the terylene sail and other rough objects, and would soon present an additional health hazard unless we could keep out of the seawater and stop the eruptions spreading.

We were still examining the raft inch by inch when daylight faded and we settled down to another comfortless night, the constant plying of the bailing cup broken only when the watchkeeper stopped to blow up the flotation chambers.

Day Eighteen

A new arrival in the way of bird life came on this, our first morning in the dinghy; a blue-footed booby circled us curiously and landed in the sea not far away. It preened its feathers and surveyed us with the rather comical expression peculiar to these birds. I caught my breath, then shouted as I saw a shark nosing upwards towards the bird; the booby looked at me curiously, then sensing the presence of danger, stuck its head under the water. The shark, now only a few feet away, moved swiftly towards it, but to my surprise the booby, instead of taking off, pecked at that shark's nose three or four times, then as the shark turned away, spread its wings and flew off. The shark was young and perhaps just curious, but I wondered how the booby would have fared if it had been an older and hungrier shark.

It had been cold in the night without the shelter from the canopy and we were grateful for the warming sun. After sorting out the meat, discarding the slimy pieces (even the scavenger fish were not interested in them!), we pulled the sea anchor aboard and set the sail, sheeted to the bow. The light southerly breeze allowed us to steer northeast, using the steering oar to hold the dinghy on course; we were on our way again, and with six hundred miles to go, we were nearly halfway to the coast!

Douglas and I had changed places with Lyn and Robin, a precarious business involving much bad language on my part and fearful reaction on theirs, the tiny dinghy tipping dangerously as frantic yells of 'Trim!' rent the Pacific air. The change was necessary to allow Douglas and me to steer, for neither Lyn nor Robin could use the steering oar or find the direction in which to steer, and although Douglas could scull expertly this was the first time he had used the oar as a rudder.

As we settled down again, the dinghy only making half a knot in the slight breeze, we talked of the North Staffordshire countryside where Lyn and the children had been born, of rolling hills and valleys in the Peak district. It was at this time that we started talking of the thing that was eventually to become our main topic of conversation: a kitchen-type restaurant in the North Staffordshire town of Leek, to be called Dougal's Kitchen. It was a wonderful opportunity to talk about food.

Our estimated noon position was 5°30' North, 245 miles west of Cape Espinosa; we had made our first easting since *Lucette* had sunk and I felt that we were now far enough north to allow some set and drift for the countercurrent which runs east through the Doldrums; we really were on our way home! The sores and boils on our limbs had already begun to dry and while they were still badly inflamed and septic, the surrounding skin felt much better and there was no further extension of the infected areas. Our clothes had begun to disintegrate rapidly now, and our principal concern was to avoid being sunburned on hitherto unexposed parts of our bodies (my contortions to avoid putting pressure on my blistered posterior were sufficient warning to the others); it was the warmth these clothes afforded us at night that concerned us, far more than any moral aspect. Indeed our absence of clothing was never discussed in terms of morality and while the capes that had been cut from the doors of the raft saved us many a night of misery by containing a little of our body warmth, we never wore them during the day unless it rained, our singlets or shirts affording adequate cover from the sun while we exposed the various parts of our distressed anatomy to the dry fresh air. We steered a steady northeasterly course all day and then towards evening the wind freshened a little, building the waves big enough to slop in over the square stern of the dinghy, so with much manoeuvring to maintain an even keel, the steering oar was lashed across the stern, the sail brought aft and sheeted to the two ends of the oar.

This move allowed the dinghy to ride bow onto the waves again and we proceeded more slowly, stern first, but the danger of being swamped by a wave was much lessened. Steering in this position was done by means of pulling the sail down on the side the stern was required to move towards, and we were able to angle the dinghy across the wind by as much as forty-five degrees, if the sea was not too rough, by this method. The fore and aft trim was of much importance now, for if the bow was too light it tended to fall away from the wind, bringing the dinghy broadside to the waves, a most vulnerable position; so I streamed the sea anchor from the bow and left it half-tripped so that it would not hinder our progress too much while keeping the bow pointed to the waves. We also moved the two persons from the back seat into the bottom of the dinghy to give it more forward trim.

With the sea anchor streamed we found we could lash the sail in position, making *Ednamair* self-steering and allowing us to continue watches as before, but now Lyn insisted that I be spared the necessity of taking a watch at all, for I was liable to be called out at all times and the heavy work of tending rigging and turtle dressing was most onerous in my exhausted condition. (Douglas was quite eager to take his share in dressing turtles but he is heavy handed and I dared not risk breaking the knife again.)

The night closed in on *Ednamair*, a lonely speck in the vast reaches of the ocean, and as we arranged and rearranged our comfortless limbs we felt that we had conquered a major obstacle to our survival. We could manage to live in the dinghy.

DAY THIRTY

The gentle breeze fell calm during the night and at dawn the promise of another dry day was reflected in the sunrise. The limpid blue of the sea flashed as the dorado sped under and around *Ednamair*, then the cry of 'Turtle!' from Sandy made us move hastily to our positions, clearing the dinghy for action.

A large stag turtle nosed curiously at a trailing rope, and with a swift grab we secured first one then both back flippers. A wild struggle ensued, for this was a tough one and with painful lacerations to our hands, we finally landed him, lashing out wildly with clawed flippers in the bottom of the dinghy. We secured him, Douglas holding one flipper and snapping beak, Neil and Robin a back flipper each, and myself a front flipper under my knee to have both hands free for the coup de grâce. The tough hide made difficult work of it and we all sustained bruises and cuts to our legs before the deed was done and the turtle lay quiet.

It was well past noon by the time the meat was hanging and the shells and offal dumped. It had been tough work, but the meat was a good deep red and tastier than usual. Neil had helped to collect the fat and Douglas had done his stuff on the flipper bones. Robin had finally been persuaded to help Neil collect the fat but he didn't seem to have much liking for the job. We nursed our wounds and cut the meat into small pieces for drying in the hot sunshine. The shark was still occupying the rigging, so since there was no wind, the sail was taken down and the small pieces of meat spread out across the stern seat and the centre thwart while we all crouched in the bottom of the dinghy, limbs overlapping in the cramped space.

We lunched well on shark and fresh turtle meat, nibbling at turtle fat afterwards and crunching the bones to extract the rich marrow from the centre. We were all blessed with fairly strong teeth and although the rest of our anatomy suffered in many degrees from the privations we had undergone, our teeth remained clean and unfurred without any external assistance from brushes. The diet obviously suited them!

The sun shone all day, but we suffered it gladly for the drying meat and fish needed every minute of it. The quicker it dried the better it cured so we poured cups of salt water over each other to keep cool and turned the meat over at regular intervals.

It was only when I was making up the log for the day and was about to enter up the small change in our position since noon the day before, that Neil leaned across to me and whispered, 'Hey, Dad, put this in your log. On the thirtieth day Neil had a shit.' I looked to see if he was serious; he grinned an impish smile and said, 'It's right,' so I put it in. It was, after all, a fairly remarkable incident and that's what logs are for, as well as the routine remarks.

While our skin problems were generally improving in a slow sort of way, my hands had become a mass of hacks and cuts. Every time we caught a turtle I usually collected one or two cuts to mark the occasion and this, aggravated with sticking fishhooks into myself, brought the combination of cuts and old boil scars to a pitch where I looked like the victim of some ancient torture. Yet after the initial hurt of these cuts they gave me very little pain and I wondered if the salt water anaesthetised them in some way.

Evening threw quiet shadows over the sea as we packed the drying food under cover for the night. The small pieces of turtle were placed in one section of Lyn's bamboo sewing basket, while the shark strips, now smelling pretty strongly, were placed in a separate piece of sail. The sea was almost mirror calm and loud splashes broke the unaccustomed silence as dorado leapt after flying fish. A louder splash made the sea foam, as a larger predator, probably a shark, attacked a dorado which leapt desperately to escape. The fins of the larger sharks were never far away but we ignored them now as long as they left us alone.

Day Thirty-Six

Slowly the wind rose from the south. At first it was a fine gentle breeze, then blew with increasing force until the breaking tips of the waves gleamed in the darkness.

As *Ednamair* pitched and yawed, shipping more and more water over the midships section, I set Douglas steering her into the waves while I opened the sea anchor out and adjusted the trim of the dinghy to keep a high, weather side. The squalls strengthened and Douglas and I stood watch on watch, helping the tiny boat through the violence of the rising seas. Lyn and Robin were still unable to steer so that they took over the bailing when necessary. I felt uncomfortable without the assurance of the flotation collar and prepared a strangle cord on the water sleeve to enable me to make it into an airtight float very swiftly if an emergency arose.

The squalls brought rain, intermittent and of moderate precipitation, to make the night cold and uncomfortable. We bailed and sang songs to keep warm, the memory of drought too recent for us to feel churlish with the weather. Collecting rainwater became difficult in the strong wind but we managed to gather enough to rinse the salt out of the sleeve and put a half gallon of good fresh water into it before the rain finally tailed off into a drizzle. The wind eased with the rain, and dawn found us shivering and huddled together, eating dried turtle and shark to comfort our sodden skins. The turtle of yesterday was forgotten in the discomfort of the new day.

Each day had now acquired a built-in objective in that we had to try to gain as much as possible over our reserves of stores and water until there would be enough in stock to get us to the coast. I looked upon each turtle as the last, each fish as the one before I lost the hook, by an error in strike. It only needed a six-inch mistake to make the difference between a dynamic pull of about eighty pounds and one of a hundred and eighty with the consequent breaking of the unevenly tensioned lines, and I knew that sooner or later it had to happen.

Lyn washed and mended our clothes, which now had the appearance of some aboriginal garb. Douglas had only his shirt left (Lyn was trying to sew his shredded undershorts together in some attempt to make him presentable when we reached land); Lyn's housecoat, now in ribbons, was more ornament than use, and my tattered underpants and vest were stiff with turtle blood and fat. Robin and the twins were in rather better garb, for their labours made less demands on their clothing. I suppose we would have been thought a most indecent lot in civilised society. (On second thoughts, I've seen some weird products of modern society whose appearance was rather similar so that perhaps we would merely have been thought a little avant-garde.) Robin and I had beards with unkempt moustaches which hung over our upper lips; saltwater boils and scars covered our arms, legs and buttocks and were scattered on other parts of our anatomy, intermingled with clawmarks from turtles, as well as cuts and scratches from other sources. The adults were not desperately thin but the twins, Neil in particular, had become very emaciated.

Knee cramps troubled us from time to time, but generally speaking, apart from Sandy who had a slight bronchial cough which Lyn's expert ear had detected the day previously (for she had a constant fear of a static pneumonia developing in our cramped situation), we were in better physical condition than when we had abandoned the raft. Many of our sores had healed and our bodies were functioning again. We were eating and drinking more, and our ability to gnaw bones and suck nutrition from them increased with our knowledge of the easiest ways to attack them.

We were no longer just surviving, but were improving in our physical condition. As I looked around at our little company, only Neil gave me cause for worry, for his thin physique made it difficult to determine whether he was improving or not, and though he was a most imaginative child, he seldom complained unless in real physical pain. Lyn was careful to see that his supplementary diet was kept as high as possible, and I scraped bone marrow to add to the twins' turtle 'soup' (a mixture of pieces of dried turtle, meat juice, water, eggs when available, and fresh or dried fish).

Our thirty-sixth day ended much as it had started; wet, cold and windy, seas slopping into *Ednamair* as she bounced in the steep short waves, the bailer's familiar scrape and splash, and the helmsman hunched on the stern and peering at each wave to determine its potential danger to our craft. Robin, trying to snatch forty winks in his 'off' time, suddenly sat up with a cry of distress. 'There's no meat on my bone!' he shouted. Then looking at his thumb (which he had been sucking) with a puzzled expression on his face, he lay down to sleep again.

The twins chortled in the bows for an hour afterwards. Late that evening Sandy said he thought he must have 'done it' accidentally for there was diarrhoea all over his clothes. I passed Sandy over to Lyn while I cleaned up the sheets, moving Neil around to get the muck cleaned off the dinghy, when Lyn said 'You'd better send Neil along when I've finished with this one, Sandy hasn't done anything at all!' Neil's voice full of injured innocence came from the bow, 'Well, how was I to know?' We chortled for half an hour over that one!

Day Thirty-Eight

After breakfast of some raw steak and the flesh of a scavenger fish (which I speared on the end of the knife) marinated in the meat juice collected overnight, we felt more able to see through the day. It hadn't rained much, and I had a good-sized lump on my head where the shark had left its mark.

A small shower, followed by some drizzle, had increased our water reserves by a pint and the overcast sky gave little prospect of a good drying day, but we hung out the meat in small strips to make the most of it. A large white-tipped shark cruised nearby, reminding me of my lump, and the escort of eight pilot fish in perfect formation across its back lent it the appearance of an underwater aeroplane.

I prepared the gaff while Lyn and Robin sorted out the turtle meat for drying and the twins readjusted the canopy and handed out some strips of dried dorado which needed airing for an hour. We now checked over our considerable amount of dry stores every morning to ensure that it kept in good condition. The fish strips quickly went damp and soggy in the humid atmosphere and the small pieces of turtle meat, if they were allowed to become compacted, warmed up as if affected by spontaneous combustion.

The dorado were reluctant to come near the *Ednamair* with the shark still cruising around, but after we had made one or two swipes at it with the paddle, it went away. I planned to land another two dorado that morning, one for eating immediately, to save the turtle steak for drying, and the other to increase our already good stocks of dried fish. I angled the gaff towards two likely bull dorado of rather a large size, then a large female shot close above the hook; I struck swiftly and missed, but at that instant a small bull of about fifteen pounds followed the female's track and my hook sank into it in a perfect strike! The fish flew into the dinghy with unerring precision and it was secured and killed in the space of seconds.

Feeling very pleased with ourselves, we admired the high forehead of the bull while I made some adjustments to the nylon lines which weren't taking the strain evenly, then I told Douglas to gut it and keep the offal. I had noticed that although the dorado didn't eat the offal, they gathered round curiously as the scavenger fish fought over it. I had the idea a good fish could be taken unawares at this time, so I had Robin throw some offal over just ahead of the gaff. The scavenger fish rushed in, a boil of foam as they fought over the scraps, while the dorado swooped close by. I chose a twenty-five-pound female dorado and struck.

The hook gave, then with a ripping sound the lines snapped one after the other, and the gaff went light. I looked swiftly at Douglas but he was pulling in the reserve line slowly. 'Didn't feel a thing,' he said. My initial reaction was one of extreme dejection; that fish had gone with our last big hook, no more fresh dorado. The nylon must have been cracked and I failed to notice; the tensions of the lines had been different too or they would have broken together; the disturbed water had probably distorted my aim, but it was no use being wise now, there wasn't another hook to be wise with. My spirits picked up a little as I realised that our stocks of dorado exceeded those of turtle meat and we had enough of both now to get us to the coast, even if we caught no more fresh turtle to supplement our rations. I still had another small hook to use for inshore fishing if that should be necessary, and if we felt like a taste of fresh fish I could always try a stab at another scavenger fish; we had been fattening them up for a while now, with our regular dumpings of turtle and fish offal.

Noon position 8°21' North and 85 miles west of Espinosa, twelve miles nearer land, was not a great boost to our morale but I pointed out that throughout all the time we had been adrift we had either been becalmed or the wind had been favourable. There hadn't been a day yet when I had had to record an adverse run. The calming seas also indicated that we might soon be able to row although the heavy cross swell would have to diminish a little too before that would be possible.

Lyn bathed the twins that afternoon and after their daily exercises and a half hour apiece on the centre thwart to move around a bit, they retreated under the canopy again as a heavy shower threatened. The dorado, caught in the morning, now hung in wet strips from the forestay while the drying turtle meat festooned the stays and cross lines which had been rigged to carry the extra load of meat from two turtles. We worked a little on the thole pins, binding canvas on them to save wear on the rope, then realising that we were neglecting the most important job of making a flotation piece, took the unused piece of sleeve and started to bind one end with fishing line. The clouds grew thicker as the afternoon advanced; it was going to be a wet night again and perhaps we would be able to fill the water sleeve. Seven gallons of water seemed like wealth beyond measure in our altered sense of values.

I chopped up some dried turtle meat for tea, and Lyn put it with a little wet fish to soak in meat juice. She spread the dry sheets for the twins under the canopy, then prepared their little supper as we started to talk of Dougal's Kitchen and if it should have a wine license. As we pondered the delights of Gaelic coffee, my eye, looking past the sail, caught sight of something that wasn't sea. I stopped talking and stared; the others all looked at me. 'A ship,' I said. 'There's a ship and it's coming towards us!' I could hardly believe it but it seemed solid enough. 'Keep still now!' In the sudden surge of excitement, everyone wanted to see. 'Trim her! We mustn't capsize now!' All sank back to their places.

I felt my voice tremble as I told them that I was going to stand on the thwart and hold a flare above the sail. They trimmed the dinghy as I stood on the thwart. 'Right, hand me a flare, and remember what happened with the last ship we saw!' They suddenly fell silent in memory of that terrible despondency when our signals had been unnoticed. 'Oh God!' prayed Lyn. 'Please let them see us.'

I could see the ship quite clearly now, a Japanese tunny fisher. Her grey and white paint stood out clearly against the dark cross swell. 'Like a great white bird,' Lyn said to the twins, and she would pass within about a mile of us at her nearest approach. I relayed the information as they listened excitedly, the tension of not knowing, of imminent rescue, building like a tangible, touchable, unbearable unreality around me. My eye caught the outlines of two large sharks, a hundred yards to starboard. 'Watch the trim,' I warned. 'We have two man-eating sharks waiting if we capsize!' Then, 'I'm going to light the flare now, have the torch ready in case it doesn't work.'

I ripped the caps off, pulled out the striker and struck the primer. The flare smoked then sparked into life, the red glare illuminating *Ednamair* and the sea around us in the twilight. I could feel my index finger roasting under the heat of the flare and waved it to and fro to escape the searing heat radiating outwards in the calm air, then unable to bear the heat any longer, I dropped my arm, nearly scorching Lyn's face, and threw the flare high in the air. It curved in a brilliant arc and dropped into the sea. 'Hand me another, I think she's altered course!' My voice was hoarse with pain and excitement and I felt sick with apprehension that it might only be the ship corkscrewing in the swell, for she had made no signal that she had seen us. The second flare didn't work. I cursed it in frustrated anguish as the priming substance chipped off instead of lighting. 'The torch!' I shouted, but it wasn't needed, she had seen us, and was coming towards us.

I flopped down on the thwart. 'Our ordeal is over,' I said quietly. Lyn and the twins were crying with happiness; Douglas, with tears of joy in his eyes, hugged his mother. Robin laughed and cried at the same time, slapped me on the back and shouted, 'Wonderful! We've done it. Oh! Wonderful!' I put my arms about Lyn, feeling the tears stinging my own eyes: 'We'll get these boys to land after all.' As we shared our happiness and watched the fishing boat close with us, death could have taken me quite easily just then, for I knew that I would never experience another such pinnacle of contentment.

FOUR

Loss of the Whaleship *Essex*

Owen Chase

THE SHIP *ESSEX*, COMMANDED BY CAPTAIN GEORGE POLLARD, JUNIOR, was fitted out at Nantucket, and sailed on the 12th day of August, 1819, for the Pacific Ocean, on a whaling voyage. Of this ship I was first mate. She had lately undergone a thorough repair in her upper works, and was at that time, in all respects, a sound, substantial vessel: she had a crew of twenty-one men, and was victualled and provided for two years and a half.

I have not been able to recur to the scenes which are now to become the subject of description, although a considerable time has elapsed, without feeling a mingled emotion of horror and astonishment at the almost incredible destiny that has preserved me and my surviving companions from a terrible death.

Frequently, in my reflections on the subject, even after this lapse of time, I find myself shedding tears of gratitude for our deliverance, and blessing God, by whose divine aid and protection we were conducted through a series of unparalleled suffering and distress, and restored to the bosoms of our families and friends.

On the 20th of November (cruising in latitude 0° 40' S., longitude 119° 0' W.) a shoal of whales was discovered off the lee-bow. The weather at this time was extremely fine and clear, and it was about eight o'clock in the morning that the man at the masthead gave the usual cry of "there she blows." The ship was immediately put away, and we ran down in the direction for them. When we had got within half a mile of the place where they were observed, all our boats were lowered down, manned, and we started in pursuit of them.

The captain and the second mate, in the other two boats, kept up the pursuit, and soon struck another whale. They being at this time a considerable distance to leeward, I went forward, braced around the mainyard, and put the ship off in a direction for them.

I observed a very large spermaceti whale, as well as I could judge about eighty-five feet in length; he broke water about twenty rods off our weather-bow, and was lying quietly, with his head in a direction for the ship. He spouted two or three times, and then disappeared. In less than two or three seconds he came up again, about the length of the ship off, and made directly for us, at the rate of about three knots. The ship was then going with about the same velocity. His appearance and attitude gave us at first no alarm; but while I stood watching his movements, and observing him but a ship's length off, coming down for us with great celerity, I involuntarily ordered the boy at the helm to put it hard up; intending to sheer off and avoid him. The words were scarcely out of my mouth, before he came down upon us with full speed, and struck the ship with his head, just forward of the fore-chains; he gave us such an appalling and tremendous jar, as nearly threw us all on our faces.

The ship brought up as suddenly and violently as if she had struck a rock, and trembled for a few seconds like a leaf. We looked at each other with perfect amazement, deprived almost of the power of speech. Many minutes elapsed before we were able to realize the dreadful accident; during which time he passed under the ship, grazing her keel as he went along, came up alongside of her to leeward, and lay on the top of the water (apparently stunned with the violence of the blow) for the space of a minute; he then suddenly started off, in a direction to leeward. After a few moments' reflection, and recovering, in some measure, from the sudden consternation that had seized us, I of course concluded that he had stove a hole in the ship, and that it would be necessary to set the pumps going.

Accordingly they were rigged, but had not been in operation more than one minute before I perceived the head of the ship to be gradually settling down in the water; I then ordered the signal to be set for the other boats, which, scarcely had I despatched, before I again discovered the whale, apparently in convulsions, on the top of the water, about one hundred rods to leeward. He was enveloped in the foam of the sea, that his continual and violent thrashing about in the water had created around him, and I could distinctly see him smite his jaws together, as if distracted with rage and fury. He remained a short time in this situation, and then started off with great velocity, across the bows of the ship, to windward. By this time the ship had settled down a considerable distance in the water, and I gave her up for lost. I, however, ordered the pumps to be kept constantly going, and endeavoured to collect my thoughts for the occasion. I turned to the boats, two of which we then had with the ship, with an intention of clearing them away, and getting all things ready to embark in them, if there should be no other resource left; and while my attention was thus engaged for a moment, I was aroused with the cry of a man at the hatch way, "here he is—he is making for us again."

I turned around, and saw him about one hundred rods directly ahead of us, coming down apparently with twice his ordinary speed, and to me at that moment, it appeared with tenfold fury and vengeance in his aspect. The surf flew in all directions about him, and his course towards us was marked by a white foam of a rod in width, which he made with the continual violent thrashing of his tail; his head was about half out of water, and in that way he came upon, and again struck the ship. I was in hopes when I descried him making for us, that by a dexterous movement of putting the ship away immediately, I should be able to cross the line of his approach, before he could get up to us, and thus avoid what I knew, if he should strike us again, would prove our inevitable destruction.

I bawled out to the helmsman, "hard up!" but she had not fallen off more than a point, before we took the second shock. I should judge the speed of the ship to have been at this time about three knots, and that of the whale about six. He struck her to windward, directly under the cathead, and completely stove in her bows. He passed under the ship again, went off to leeward, and we saw no more of him.

Not a moment, however, was to be lost in endeavouring to provide for the extremity to which it was now certain we were reduced. We were more than a thousand miles from the nearest land, and with nothing but a light open boat, as the resource of safety for myself and companions. I ordered the men to cease pumping, and everyone to provide for himself; seizing a hatchet at the same time, I cut away the lashings of the spare boat, which lay bottom-up across two spars directly over the quarter deck, and cried out to those near me to take her as she came down.

From the time we were first attacked by the whale, to the period of the fall of the ship, and of our leaving her in the boat, more than ten minutes could not certainly have elapsed! God only knows in what way, or by what means, we were enabled to accomplish in that short time what we did; the cutting away and transporting the boat from where she was deposited would of itself, in ordinary circumstances, have consumed as much time as that, if the whole ship's crew had been employed in it. My companions had not saved a single article but what they had on their backs; but to me it was a source of infinite satisfaction, if any such could be gathered from the horrors of our gloomy situation, that we had been fortunate enough to have preserved our compasses, navigators, and quadrants.

After the first shock of my feelings was over, I enthusiastically contemplated them as the probable instruments of our salvation; without them all would have been dark and hopeless. Gracious God! what a picture of distress and suffering now presented itself to my imagination. The crew of the ship were saved, consisting of twenty human souls. All that remained to conduct these twenty beings through the stormy terrors of the ocean, perhaps many thousand miles, were three open light boats. The prospect of obtaining any provisions or water from the ship, to subsist upon during the time, was at least now doubtful. How many long and watchful nights, thought I, are to be passed?

We lay at this time in our boat, about two ship lengths off from the wreck, in perfect silence, calmly contemplating her situation, and absorbed in our own melancholy reflections, when the other boats were discovered rowing up to us. They had but shortly before discovered that some accident had befallen us, but of the nature of which they were entirely ignorant. The sudden and mysterious disappearance of the ship was first discovered by the boat-steerer in the captain's boat, and with a horror-struck countenance and voice, he suddenly exclaimed, "Oh, my God!

where is the ship?" Their operations upon this were instantly suspended, and a general cry of horror and despair burst from the lips of every man, as their looks were directed for her, in vain, over every part of the ocean.

They immediately made all haste towards us. The captain's boat was the first that reached us. He stopped about a boat's length off, but had no power to utter a single syllable: he was so completely overpowered with the spectacle before him that he sat down in his boat, pale and speechless. I could scarcely recognise his countenance, he appeared to be so much altered, awed, and overcome with the oppression of his feelings, and the dreadful reality that lay before him. He was in a short time however enabled to address the inquiry to me, "My God, Mr. Chase, what is the matter?"

I answered, "We have been stove by a whale."

After a few moments' reflection he observed that we must cut away her masts, and endeavour to get something out of her to eat. Our thoughts were now all accordingly bent on endeavours to save from the wreck whatever we might possibly want, and for this purpose we rowed up and got onto her. Search was made for every means of gaining access to her hold; and for this purpose the lanyards were cut loose, and with our hatchets we commenced to cut away the masts, that she might right up again, and enable us to scuttle her decks. In doing which we were occupied about three quarters of an hour, owing to our having no axes, nor indeed any other instruments, but the small hatchets belonging to the boats.

After her masts were gone she came up about two-thirds of the way upon an even keel. While we were employed about the masts the captain took his quadrant, shoved off from the ship, and got an observation. We now commenced to cut a hole through the planks, directly above two large casks of bread, which most fortunately were between decks, in the waist of the ship, and which being in the upper side, when she upset, we had strong hopes was not wet. It turned out according to our wishes, and from these casks we obtained six hundred pounds of hard bread. Other parts of the deck were then scuttled, and we got without difficulty as much fresh water as we dared to take in the boats, so that each was supplied with about sixty-five gallons; we got also from one of the lockers a musket, a small canister of powder, a couple of files, two rasps, about two pounds of boat nails, and a few turtle.

In the afternoon the wind came on to blow a strong breeze; and having obtained everything that occurred to us could then be got out, we began to make arrangements for our safety during the night. A boat's line was made fast to the ship, and to the other end of it one of the boats was moored, at about fifty fathoms to leeward; another boat was then attached to the first one, about eight fathoms astern; and the third boat, the like distance astern of her.

Night came on just as we had finished our operations; and such a night as it was to us! so full of feverish and distracting inquietude, that we were deprived entirely of rest. The wreck was constantly before my eyes. I could not, by any effort, chase away the horrors of the preceding day from my mind.

November 21st

The morning dawned upon our wretched company. The weather was fine, but the wind blew a strong breeze from the SE. and the sea was very rugged. Watches had been kept up during the night, in our respective boats, to see that none of the spars or other articles (which continued to float out of the wreck) should be thrown by the surf against, and injure the boats. At sunrise, we began to think of doing something; what, we did not know: we cast loose our boats, and visited the wreck, to see if anything more of consequence could be preserved, but everything looked cheerless and desolate, and we made a long and vain search for any useful article; nothing could be found but a few turtle; of these we had enough already; or at least, as many as could be safely stowed in the boats, and we wandered around in every part of the ship in a sort of vacant idleness for the greater part of the morning.

We were presently aroused to a perfect sense of our destitute and forlorn condition, by thoughts of the means which we had for our subsistence, the necessity of not wasting our time, and of endeavouring to seek some relief wherever God might direct us. Our thoughts, indeed, hung about the ship, wrecked and sunken as she was, and we could scarcely discard from our minds the idea of her continuing protection.

Some great efforts in our situation were necessary, and a great deal of calculation important, as it concerned the means by which our existence was to be supported during, perhaps, a very long period, and a provision for our eventual deliverance. Accordingly, by agreement, all set to work in stripping off the light sails of the ship, for sails to our boats; and the day was consumed in making them up and fitting them. We furnished ourselves with masts and other light spars that were necessary, from the wreck. Each boat was rigged with two masts, to carry a flying-jib and two sprit-sails; the sprit-sails were made so that two reefs could be taken in them, in case of heavy blows.

We continued to watch the wreck for any serviceable articles that might float from her, and kept one man during the day, on the stump of her foremast, on the lookout for vessels. Our work was very much impeded by the increase of the wind and sea, and the surf breaking almost continually into the boats gave us many fears that we should not be able to prevent our provisions from getting wet; and above all served to increase the constant apprehensions that we had of the insufficiency of the boats themselves during the rough weather that we should necessarily experience.

In order to provide as much as possible against this, and withal to strengthen the slight materials of which the boats were constructed, we procured from the wreck some light cedar boards (intended to repair boats in cases of accidents) with which we built up additional sides, about six inches above the gunwale; these, we afterwards found, were of infinite service for the purpose for which they were intended; in truth, I am satisfied we could never have been preserved without them.

I got an observation today, by which I found we were in latitude 0° 6' S., longitude 119° 30' W., having been driven by the winds a distance of forty-nine miles the last twenty-four hours; by this it would appear that there must have been a strong current, setting us to the N.W. during the whole time.

The captain, after visiting the wreck, called a council, consisting of himself and the first and second mates, who all repaired to his boat, to interchange with the variable winds, and then, endeavour to get eastward to the coast of Chile or Peru. Accordingly, preparations were made for our immediate departure; the boat which it was my fortune, or rather misfortune to have, was the worst of the three, she was old and patched up, having been stove a number of times during the cruise. At best, a whaleboat is an extremely frail thing; the most so of any other kind of boat; they are what is called clinker built, and constructed of the lightest materials, for the purpose of being rowed with the greatest possible celerity according to the necessities of the business for which they are intended.

In consideration of my having the weakest boat, six men were allotted to it; while those of the captain and second mate took seven each, and at half past twelve we left the wreck, steering our course, with nearly all sail set, S.SE. At four o'clock in the afternoon we lost sight of her entirely. Many were the lingering and sorrowful looks we cast behind us.

The wind was strong all day; and the sea ran very high, our boat taking in water from her leaks continually, so that we were as that depended, most especially, on a reasonable calculation, and on our own labours, we conceived that our provision and water, on a small allowance, would last us sixty days; that with the trade wind, on the course we were then lying, we should be able to average the distance of a degree a day, which, in twenty-six days, would enable us to attain the region of the variable winds, and then, in thirty more, at the very utmost, should there be any favor in the elements, we might reach the coast.

Our allowance of provision at first consisted of bread, one biscuit, weighing about one pound three ounces, and half a pint of water a day, for each man. This small quantity (less than one third which is required by an ordinary person), small as it was, we however took without murmuring, and, on many occasions afterwards, blest God that even this pittance was allowed to us in our misery. The darkness of another night overtook us; and after having for the first time partook of our allowance of bread and water, we laid our weary bodies down in the boat, and endeavoured to get some repose.

November 23rd

In my chest, which I was fortunate enough to preserve, I had several small articles which we found of great service to us; among the rest, some eight or ten sheets of writing paper, a lead pencil, a suit of clothes, three small fishhooks, a jackknife, a whetstone, and a cake of soap. I commenced to keep a sort of journal with the little paper and pencil which I had; and the knife, besides other useful purposes, served us as a razor. It was with much difficulty, however, that I could keep any sort of record, owing to the incessant rocking and unsteadiness of the boat, and the continual dashing of the spray of the sea over us.

The boat contained, in addition to the articles enumerated, a lantern, tinder box, and two or three candles, which belonged to her, and with which they are kept always supplied while engaged in taking whale. In addition to all which, the captain had saved a musket, two pistols, and a canister containing about two pounds of gunpowder; the latter he distributed in equal proportions between the three boats, and gave the second mate and myself each a pistol.

When morning came we found ourselves quite near together, and the wind had considerably increased since the day before; we were consequently obliged to reef our sails; and although we did not apprehend any very great danger from the then-violence of the wind, yet it grew to be very uncomfortable in the boats from the repeated dashing of the waves that kept our bodies constantly wet with the salt spray. We, however, stood along our course until twelve o'clock, when we got an observation, as well as we were able to obtain one, while the water flew all over us, and the sea kept the boat extremely unsteady. We found ourselves this day in latitude 0° 58' S. having repassed the equator.

We abandoned the idea altogether of keeping any correct longitudinal reckoning, having no glass, nor log-line. The wind moderated in the course of the afternoon a little, but at night came on to blow again almost a gale. We began now to tremble for our little barque; she was so ill calculated, in point of strength, to withstand the racking of the sea, while it required the constant labours of one man to keep her free of water. We were surrounded in the afternoon with porpoises that kept playing about us in great numbers, and continued to follow us during the night.

November 26th

Our sufferings, heaven knows, were now sufficiently increased, and we looked forward, not without an extreme dread, and anxiety, to the gloomy and disheartening prospect before us. We experienced a little abatement of wind and rough weather today, and took the opportunity of drying the bread that had been wet the day previously; to our great joy and satisfaction also, the wind hauled out to E.NE. and enabled us to hold a much more favorable course; with these exceptions, no circumstance of any considerable interest occurred in the course of this day.

November 30th

This was a remarkably fine day; the weather not exceeded by any that we had experienced since we left the wreck. At one o'clock, I proposed to our boat's crew to kill one of the turtle; two of which we had in our possession. I need not say that the proposition was hailed with the utmost enthusiasm; hunger had set its ravenous gnawings upon our stomachs, and we waited with impatience to suck the warm flowing blood of the animal. A small fire was kindled in the shell of the turtle, and after dividing the blood (of which there was about a gill) among those of us who felt disposed to drink it, we cooked the remainder, entrails and all, and enjoyed from it an unspeakably fine repast. The stomachs of two or three revolted at the sight of the blood, and refused to partake of it; not even the outrageous thirst that was upon them could induce them to taste it; for myself, I took it like a medicine, to relieve the extreme dryness of my palate, and stopped not to inquire whether it was anything else than a liquid. After this, I may say exquisite banquet, our bodies were considerably recruited, and I felt my spirits now much higher than they had been at any time before. By observation, this day we found ourselves in latitude 7° 53' S. Our distance from the wreck, as nearly as we could calculate, was then about four hundred and eighty miles.

December 3rd

With great joy we hailed the last crumb of our damaged bread, and commenced this day to take our allowance of healthy provisions. The salutary and agreeable effects of this change were felt at first in so slight a degree as to give us no great satisfaction; but gradually, as we partook of our small allowance of water, the moisture began to collect in our mouths, and the parching fever of the palate imperceptibly left it.

An accident here happened to us which gave us a great momentary spell of uneasiness. The night was dark, and the sky was completely overcast, so that we could scarcely discern each other's boats, when at about ten o'clock, that of the second mate was suddenly missing. I felt for a moment considerable alarm at her unexpected disappearance; but after a little reflection I immediately hove to, struck a light as expeditiously as possible, and hoisted it at the masthead, in a lantern. Our eyes were now directed over every part of the ocean, in search of her, when, to our great joy, we discerned an answering light, about a quarter of a mile to leeward of us; we ran down to it, and it proved to be the lost boat.

Strange as the extraordinary interest which we felt in each other's company may appear, and much as our repugnance to separation may seem to imply of weakness, it was the subject of our continual hopes and fears. It is truly remarked that misfortune more than anything else serves to endear us to our companions.

Hard, indeed, would the case have been for all, and much as I have since reflected on the subject, I have not been able to realize, had it so happened, that a sense of our necessities would have allowed us to give so magnanimous and devoted a character to our feelings. I can only speak of the impressions which I recollect I had at the time. Subsequently, however, as our situation became more straitened and desperate, our conversation on this subject took a different turn; and it appeared to be an universal sentiment that such a course of conduct was calculated to weaken the chances of a final deliverance for some, and might be the only means of consigning every soul of us to a horrid death of starvation.

There is no question but that an immediate separation, therefore, was the most politic measure that could be adopted, and that every boat should take its own separate chance: while we remained together, should any accident happen of the nature alluded to, no other course could be adopted than that of taking the survivors into the other boats, and giving up voluntarily what we were satisfied could alone prolong our hopes and multiply the chances of our safety, or unconcernedly witness their struggles in death, perhaps beat them from our boats, with weapons, back into the ocean.

December 8th

In the afternoon of this day the wind set in E.SE. and began to blow much harder than we had yet experienced it; by twelve o'clock at night it had increased to a perfect gale, with heavy showers of rain, and we now began, from these dreadful indications, to prepare ourselves for destruction. We continued to take in sail by degrees, as the tempest gradually increased, until at last we were obliged to take down our masts. At this juncture we gave up entirely to the mercy of the waves. The sea and rain had wet us to the skin, and we sat down, silently, and with sullen resignation, awaiting our fate. We made an effort to catch some fresh water by spreading one of the sails, but after having spent a long time, and obtained but a small quantity in a bucket, it proved to be quite as salty as that from the ocean: this we attributed to its having passed through the sail which had been so often wet by the sea, and upon which, after drying so frequently in the sun, concretions of salt had been formed. It was a dreadful night— cut off from any imaginary relief—nothing remained but to await the approaching issue with firmness and resignation.

The appearance of the heavens was dark and dreary, and the blackness that was spread over the face of the waters dismal beyond description. The heavy squalls, that followed each other in quick succession, were preceded by sharp flashes of lightning, that appeared to wrap our little barge in flames. The sea rose to a fearful height, and every wave that came looked as if it must be the last that would be necessary for our destruction. To an overruling Providence alone must be attributed our salvation from the horrors of that terrible night. It can be accounted for in no other way: that a speck of substance, like that which we were, before the driving terrors of the tempest, could have been conducted safely through it. At twelve o'clock it began to abate a little in intervals of two or three minutes, during which we would venture to raise up our heads and look to windward.

Our boat was completely unmanageable; without sails, mast, or rudder, and had been driven, in the course of the afternoon and night, we knew not whither, nor how far. When the gale had in some measure subsided we made efforts to get a little sail upon her, and put her head towards the course we had been steering. My companions had not slept any during the whole night, and were dispirited and broken down to such a degree as to appear to want some more powerful stimulus than the fears of death to enable them to do their duty. By great exertions, however, towards morning we again set a double-reefed mainsail and jib upon her, and began to make tolerable progress on the voyage. An unaccountable good fortune had kept the boats together during all the troubles of the night: and the sun rose and showed the disconsolate faces of our companions once more to each other.

DECEMBER 10TH–13TH

I have omitted to notice the gradual advances which hunger and thirst for the last six days, had made upon us. As the time had lengthened since our departure from the wreck, and the allowance of provision, making the demands of the appetite daily more and more importunate, they had created in us an almost uncontrollable temptation to violate our resolution, and satisfy, for once, the hard yearnings of nature from our stock; but a little reflection served to convince us of the imprudence and unmanliness of the measure, and it was abandoned with a sort of melancholy effort of satisfaction.

I had taken into custody, by common consent, all the provisions and water belonging to the boat, and was determined that no encroachments should be made upon it with my consent; nay, I felt myself bound, by every consideration of duty, by every dictate of sense, of prudence, and discretion, without which, in my situation, all other exertions would have been folly itself, to protect them, at the hazard of my life. For this purpose I locked up in my chest the whole quantity, and never, for a single moment, closed my eyes without placing some part of my person in contact with the chest; and having loaded my pistol, kept it constantly about me. I should not certainly have put any threats in execution as long as the most distant hopes of reconciliation existed; and was determined, in case the least refractory disposition should be manifested (a thing which I contemplated not unlikely to happen, with a set of starving wretches like ourselves) that I would immediately divide our subsistence into equal proportions, and give each man's share into his own keeping.

Then, should any attempt be made upon mine, which I intended to mete out to myself according to exigencies, I was resolved to make the consequences of it fatal. There was, however, the most upright and obedient behaviour in this respect manifested by every man in the boat, and I never had the least opportunity of proving what my conduct would have been on such an occasion.

While standing on our course this day we came across a small shoal of flying fish: four of which, in their efforts to avoid us, flew against the mainsail, and dropped into the boat; one having fallen near me, I eagerly snatched up and devoured; the other three were immediately taken by the rest, and eaten alive.

For the first time I, on this occasion, felt a disposition to laugh, upon witnessing the ludicrous and almost desperate efforts of my five companions, who each sought to get a fish. They were very small of the kind, and constituted but an extremely delicate mouthful, scales, wings, and all, for hungry stomachs like ours.

From the eleventh to the thirteenth of December inclusive, our progress was very slow, owing to light winds and calms; and nothing transpired of any moment, except that on the eleventh we killed the only remaining turtle, and enjoyed another luxuriant repast, that invigorated our bodies, and gave a fresh flow to our spirits. The weather was extremely hot, and we were exposed to the full force of a meridian sun, without any covering to shield us from its burning influence, or the least breath of air to cool its parching rays.

December 15th–16th

Our boat continued to take in water so fast from her leaks, and the weather proving so moderate, we concluded to search out the bad places, and endeavour to mend them as well as we should be able. After a considerable search, and, removing the ceiling near the bows, we found the principal opening was occasioned by the starting of a plank or streak in the bottom of the boat, next to the keel. To remedy this, it was now absolutely necessary to have access to the bottom. The means of doing which did not immediately occur to our minds. After a moment's reflection, however, one of the crew, Benjamin Lawrence, offered to tie a rope around his body, take a boat's hatchet in his hand, and thus go under the water, and hold the hatchet against a nail, to be driven through from the inside, for the purpose of clenching it. This was, accordingly, all effected, with some little trouble, and answered the purpose much beyond our expectations. Our latitude was this day 21° 42' S.

The oppression of the weather still continuing through the sixteenth, bore upon our health and spirits with an amazing force and severity. The most disagreeable excitements were produced by it, which, added to the disconsolate endurance of the calm, called loudly for some mitigating expedient—some sort of relief to our prolonged sufferings. By our observations today we found, in addition to our other calamities, that we had been urged back from our progress, by the heave of the sea, a distance of ten miles; and were still without any prospect of wind.

December 20th

This was a day of great happiness and joy. After having experienced one of the most distressing nights in the whole catalogue of our sufferings, we awoke to a morning of comparative luxury and pleasure. About seven o'clock, while we were sitting dispirited, silent, and dejected, in our boats, one of our companions suddenly and loudly called out, "There is land!"

We were all aroused in an instant, as if electrified, and casting our eyes to leeward, there indeed, was the blessed vision before us, "as plain and palpable" as could be wished for. A new and extraordinary impulse now took possession of us. We shook off the lethargy of our senses, and seemed to take another, and a fresh existence.

One or two of my companions, whose lagging spirits and worn-out frames had begun to inspire them with an utter indifference to their fate, now immediately brightened up, and manifested a surprising alacrity and earnestness to gain, without delay, the much wished for shore. It appeared at first a low, white beach, and lay like a basking paradise before our longing eyes. It was discovered nearly at the same time by the other boats, and a general burst of joy and congratulation now passed between us. It is not within the scope of human calculation, by a mere listener to the story, to divine what the feelings of our hearts were on this occasion. Alternate expectation, fear, gratitude, surprise, and exultation, each swayed our minds, and quickened our exertions.

We ran down for it, and at eleven o'clock, a.m., we were within a quarter of a mile of the shore. It was an island, to all appearance, as nearly as we could determine it, about six miles long and three broad; with a very high, rugged shore, and surrounded by rocks; the sides of the mountains were bare, but on the tops it looked fresh and green with vegetation. Upon examining our navigators, we found it was Ducie's Island, lying in latitude 24° 40' S., longitude 124° 40' W.

A short moment sufficed for reflection, and we made immediate arrangements to land. None of us knew whether the island was inhabited or not, nor what it afforded, if anything; if inhabited, it was uncertain whether by beasts or savages; and a momentary suspense was created by the dangers which might possibly arise by proceeding without due preparation and care. Hunger and thirst, however, soon determined us, and having taken the musket and pistols, I, with three others, effected a landing upon some sunken rocks, and waded thence to the shore. Upon arriving at the beach, it was necessary to take a little breath, and we laid down for a few minutes to rest our weak bodies before we could proceed. Let the reader judge, if he can, what must have been our feelings now! Bereft of all comfortable hopes of life, for the space of thirty days of terrible suffering; our bodies wasted to mere skeletons, by hunger and thirst, and death itself staring us in the face; to be suddenly and unexpectedly conducted to a rich banquet of food and drink, which subsequently we enjoyed for a few days, to our full satisfaction; and he will have but a faint idea of the happiness that here fell to our lot. We now, after a few minutes, separated, and went different directions in search of water; the want of which had been our principal privation, and called for immediate relief.

I had not proceeded far in my excursion, before I discovered a fish, about a foot and a half in length, swimming along in the water close to the shore. I commenced an attack upon him with the breach of my gun, and struck him, I believe, once and he ran under a small rock, that lay near the shore, from whence I took him with the aid of my ramrod, and brought him up on the beach, and immediately fell to eating. My companions soon joined in the repast; and in less than ten minutes, the whole was consumed, bones, and skin, and scales, and all. With full stomachs, we imagined we could now attempt the mountains, where, if in any part of the island, we considered water would be most probably obtained.

I accordingly clambered, with excessive labour, suffering, and pain, up amongst the bushes, roots, and underwood, of one of the crags, looking in all directions in vain, for every appearance of water that might present itself. There was no indication of the least moisture to be found, within the distance to which I had ascended, although my strength did not enable me to get them, which only served to whet my appetite, and from which nothing like the least satisfaction had proceeded.

I immediately resolved in my own mind, upon this information, to advise remaining until morning, to endeavour to make a more thorough search the next day, and with our hatchets to pick away the rock which had been discovered, with the view of increasing, if possible, the run of the water. We all repaired again to our boats, and there found that the captain had the same impressions as to the propriety of our delay until morning. We therefore landed; and having hauled our boats up on the beach, laid down in them that night, free from all the anxieties of watching and labour, and amid all our sufferings, gave ourselves up to an unreserved forgetfulness and peace of mind, that seemed so well to accord with the pleasing anticipations that this day had brought forth.

It was but a short space, however, until the morning broke upon us; and sense, and feeling, and gnawing hunger, and the raging fever of thirst then redoubled my wishes and efforts to explore the island again. We had obtained, that night, a few crabs, by traversing the shore a considerable distance, and a few very small fish; but waited until the next day, for the labours of which, we considered a night of refreshing and undisturbed repose would better qualify us.

December 21st

We had still reserved our common allowance, but it was entirely inadequate for the purpose of supplying the raging demands of the palate; and such an excessive and cruel thirst was created, as almost to deprive us of the power of speech. The lips became cracked and swollen, and a sort of glutinous saliva collected in the mouth, disagreeable to the taste, and intolerable beyond expression. Our bodies had wasted away to almost skin and bone, and possessed so little strength as often to require each other's assistance in performing some of its weakest functions. Relief, we now felt, must come soon, or nature would sink. The most perfect discipline was still maintained in respect to our provisions; and it now became our whole object, if we should not be able to replenish our subsistence from the island, to obtain, by some means or other, a sufficient refreshment to enable us to prosecute our voyage.

Our search for water accordingly again commenced with the morning; each of us took a different direction, and prosecuted the examination of every place where there was the least indication of it; the small leaves of the shrubbery, affording a temporary alleviation, by being chewed in the mouth, and but for the peculiarly bitter taste which those of the island possessed, would have been an extremely grateful substitute. In the course of our rambles too, along the sides of the mountain, we would now and then meet with tropic birds, of a beautiful figure and plumage, occupying small holes in the sides of it, from which we plucked them without the least difficulty. Upon our approaching them they made no attempts to fly, nor did they appear to notice us at all. These birds served us for a fine repast; numbers of which were caught in the course of the day, cooked by fires which we made on the shore, and eaten with the utmost avidity. We found also a plant, in taste not unlike the peppergrass, growing in considerable abundance in the crevices of the rocks, and which proved to us a very agreeable food, by being chewed with the meat of the birds. These, with birds' nests, some of them full of young, and others of eggs, a few of which we found in the course of the day, served us for food, and supplied the place of our bread; from the use of which, during our stay here, we had restricted ourselves.

But water, the great object of all our anxieties and exertions, was nowhere to be found, and we began to despair of meeting with it on the island. Our state of extreme weakness, and many of us without shoes or any covering for the feet, prevented us from exploring any great distance; lest by some sudden faintness, or overexertion, we should not be able to return, and at night be exposed to attacks of wild beasts, which might inhabit the island, and be alike incapable of resistance, as beyond the reach of the feeble assistance that otherwise could be afforded to each.

The whole day was thus consumed in picking up whatever had the least shape or quality of sustenance, and another night of misery was before us, to be passed without a drop of water to cool our parching tongues. In this state of affairs, we could not reconcile it to ourselves to remain at this place; a day, an hour, lost to us unnecessarily here, might cost us our preservation. A drop of the water that we then had in our possession might prove, in the last stages of our debility, the very cordial of life. I addressed the substance of these few reflections to the captain, who agreed with me in opinion, upon the necessity of taking some decisive steps in our water. My principal hope was founded upon my success in picking the rocks where the moisture had been discovered the day before, and thither I hastened as soon as my strength would enable me to get there.

Upon examining the place from whence we had obtained this miraculous and unexpected succour, we were equally astonished and delighted with the discovery. It was on the shore, above which the sea flowed to the depth of nearly six feet; and we could procure the water, therefore, from it only when the tide was down. The crevice from which it rose was in a flat rock, large surfaces of which were spread around, and composed the face of the beach. We filled our two kegs before the tide rose, and went back again to our boats. The remainder of this day was spent in seeking for fish, crabs, birds, and sufficiently known whether it would be advisable to make any arrangements for a more permanent abode.

DECEMBER 23RD

At eleven o'clock, a.m., we again visited our spring: the tide had fallen to about a foot below it, and we were able to procure, before it rose again, about twenty gallons of water. It was at first a little brackish, but soon became fresh, from the constant supply from the rock and the departure of the sea. Our observations this morning tended to give us every confidence in its quantity and quality, and we, therefore, rested perfectly easy in our minds on the subject, and commenced to make further discoveries about the island. Each man sought for his own daily living, on whatsoever the mountains, the shore, or the sea, could furnish him with; and every day, during our stay there, the whole time was employed in roving about for food.

There was no one thing on the island upon which we could in the least degree rely, except the peppergrass, and of that the supply was precarious, and not much relished without some other food. Our situation here, therefore, now became worse than it would have been in our boats on the ocean; because, in the latter case, we should be still making some progress towards the land, while our provisions lasted, and the chance of falling in with some vessel be considerably increased. It was certain that we ought not to remain here unless upon the strongest assurances in our own minds, of sufficient sustenance, and that, too, in regular supplies, that might be depended upon.

After much conversation amongst us on this subject, and again examining our navigators, it was finally concluded to set sail for Easter Island, which we found to be E.SE. from us in latitude 27° 9' S., longitude 109° 35' W. All we knew of this island was that it existed as laid down in the books; but of its extent, productions, or inhabitants, if any, we were entirely ignorant; at any rate, it was nearer by eight hundred and fifty miles to the coast, and could not be worse in its productions than the one we were about leaving.

December 26th

The day was wholly employed in preparations for our departure; our boats were hauled down to the vicinity of the spring, and our casks, and everything else that would contain it, filled with water.

There had been considerable talk between three of our companions about their remaining on this island, and taking their chance both for a living, and an escape from it; and as the time drew near at which we were to leave, they made up their minds to stay behind. The rest of us could make no objection to their plan, as it lessened the load of our boats, allowed us their share of the provisions, and the probability of their being able to sustain themselves on the island was much stronger than that of our reaching the mainland. Should we, however, ever arrive safely, it would become our duty, and we so assured them, to give information of their situation, and make every effort to procure their removal from thence; which we accordingly afterwards did.

Their names were William Wright of Barnstable, Massachusetts, Thomas Chapple of Plymouth, England, and Seth Weeks of the former place. They had begun, before we came away, to construct a sort of habitation, composed of the branches of trees, and we left with them every little article that could be spared from the boats. It was their intention to build a considerable dwelling, that would protect them from the rains, as soon as time and materials could be provided.

The captain wrote letters, to be left on the island, giving information of the fate of the ship, and that of our own; and stating that we had set out to reach Easter Island, with further particulars, intended to give notice (should our fellow sufferers die there, and the place be ever visited by any vessel) of our misfortunes. These letters were put in a tin case, enclosed in a small wooden box, and nailed to a tree, on the west side of the island, near our landing place. We had observed, some days previously, the name of a ship, *The Elizabeth*, cut out in the bark of this tree, which rendered it indubitable that one of that name had once touched here. There was, however, no date to it, or anything else, by which any further particulars could be made out.

December 27th

I went, before we set sail this morning, and procured for each boat a flat stone, and two armfuls of wood, with which to make a fire in our boats, should it become afterwards necessary in the further prosecution of our voyage; as we calculated we might catch a fish, or a bird, and in that case be provided with the means of cooking it; otherwise, from the intense heat of the weather, we knew they could not be preserved from spoiling. At ten o'clock, a.m., the tide having risen far enough to allow our boats to float over the rocks, we made all sail, and steered around the island, for the purpose of making a little further observation, which would not detain us any time, and might be productive of some unexpected good fortune. Before we started we missed our three companions, and found they had not come down, either to assist us to get off, nor to take any kind of leave of us. I walked up the beach towards their rude dwelling, and informed them that we were then about to set sail, and should probably never see them more.

They seemed to be very much affected, and one of them shed tears. They wished us to write to their relations, should Providence safely direct us again to our homes, and said but little else. They had every confidence in being able to procure a subsistence there as long as they remained: and, finding them ill at heart about taking any leave of us, I hastily bid them "goodbye," hoped they would do well, and came away. They followed me with their eyes until I was out of sight, and I never saw more of them.

January 10th

Matthew P. Joy, the second mate, had suffered from debility, and the privations we had experienced, much beyond any of the rest of us, and was on the eighth removed to the captain's boat, under the impression that he would be more comfortable there, and more attention and pains be bestowed in nursing and endeavouring to comfort him. This day being calm, he manifested a desire to be taken back again; but at four o'clock in the afternoon, after having been, according to his wishes, placed in his own boat, he died very suddenly after his removal. On the eleventh, at six o'clock in the morning, we sewed him up in his clothes, tied a large stone to his feet, and, having brought all the boats to, consigned him in a solemn manner to the ocean. This man did not die of absolute starvation, although his end was no doubt very much hastened by his sufferings. He had a weak and sickly constitution, and complained of being unwell the whole voyage.

It was an incident, however, which threw a gloom over our feelings for many days. In consequence of his death, one man from the captain's boat was placed in that from which he died, to supply his place, and we stood away again on our course.

January 14th

We had now been nineteen days from the island, and had only made a distance of about nine hundred miles: necessity began to whisper to us, that a still further reduction of our allowance must take place, or we must abandon altogether the hopes of reaching the land, and rely wholly on the chance of being taken up by a vessel. But how to reduce the daily quantity of food, with any regard to life itself, was a question of the utmost consequence. Upon our first leaving the wreck, the demands of the stomach had been circumscribed to the smallest possible compass; and subsequently before reaching the island, a diminution had taken place of nearly one half and it was now, from a reasonable calculation, become necessary even to curtail that at least one half; which must, in a short time, reduce us to mere skeletons again. We had a full allowance of water, but it only served to contribute to our debility; our bodies deriving but the scanty support which an ounce and a half of bread for each man afforded. It required a great effort to bring matters to this dreadful alternative, either to feed our bodies and our hopes a little longer, or in the agonies of hunger to seize upon and devour our provisions, and coolly await the approach of death.

I had almost determined upon this occurrence to divide our provisions, and give to each man his share of the whole stock; and should have done so in the height of my resentment had it not been for the reflection that some might, by imprudence, be tempted to go beyond the daily allowance, or consume it all at once, and bring on a premature weakness or starvation: this would of course disable them for the duties of the boat, and reduce our chances of safety and deliverance.

JANUARY 15TH

A very large shark was observed swimming about us in a most ravenous manner, making attempts every now and then upon different parts of the boat, as if he would devour the very wood with hunger; he came several times and snapped at the steering oar, and even the stern-post. We tried in vain to stab him with a lance, but we were so weak as not to be able to make any impression upon his hard skin; he was so much larger than an ordinary one, and manifested such a fearless malignity, as to make us afraid of him; and our utmost efforts, which were at first directed to kill him for prey, became in the end self-defense. Baffled however in all his hungry attempts upon us, he shortly made off.

JANUARY 20TH

Richard Peterson manifested today symptoms of a speedy dissolution; he had been lying between the seats in the boat, utterly dispirited and broken down, without being able to do the least duty, or hardly to place his hand to his head for the last three days, and had this morning made up his mind to die rather than endure further misery: he refused his allowance; said he was sensible of his approaching end, and was perfectly ready to die: in a few minutes he became speechless, the breath appeared to be leaving his body without producing the least pain, and at four o'clock he was gone.

To add to our calamities, biles began to break out upon us, and our imaginations shortly became as diseased as our bodies. I laid down at night to catch a few moments of oblivious sleep, and immediately my starving fancy was at work. I dreamt of being placed near a splendid and rich repast, where there was everything that the most dainty appetite could desire; and of contemplating the moment in which we were to commence to eat with enraptured feelings of delight; and just as I was about to partake of it, I suddenly awoke to the cold realities of my miserable situation.

Nothing could have oppressed me so much. It set such a longing frenzy for victuals in my mind, that I felt as if I could have wished the dream to continue forever, that I never might have awoke from it. I cast a sort of vacant stare about the boat, until my eyes rested upon a bit of tough cowhide, which was fastened to one of the oars; I eagerly seized and commenced to chew it, but there was no substance in it, and it only served to fatigue my weak jaws, and add to my bodily pains.

My fellow sufferers murmured very much the whole time, and continued to press me continually with questions upon the probability of our reaching land again. I kept constantly rallying my spirits to enable me to afford them comfort. I encouraged them to bear up against all evils, and if we must perish, to die in our own cause, and not weakly distrust the providence of the Almighty by giving ourselves up to despair. I reasoned with them, and told them that we would not die sooner by keeping up our hopes; that the dreadful sacrifices and privations we endured were to preserve us from death, and were not to be put in competition with the price which we set upon our lives, and their value to our families: it was, besides, unmanly to repine at what neither admitted of alleviation nor cure; and withal, that it was our solemn duty to recognise in our calamities an overruling divinity, by whose mercy we might be suddenly snatched from peril, and to rely upon him alone, "Who tempers the wind to the shorn lamb."

January 28th

Our spirits this morning were hardly sufficient to allow of our enjoying a change of the wind, which took place to the westward. It had nearly become indifferent to us, from what quarter it blew: nothing but the slight chance of meeting a vessel remained to us now: it was this narrow comfort alone that prevented me from lying down at once to die. But fourteen days' stinted allowance of provisions remained, and it was absolutely necessary to increase the quantity to enable us to live five days longer: we therefore partook of it, as pinching necessity demanded, and gave ourselves wholly up to the guidance and disposal of our Creator.

February 8th

Our sufferings were now drawing to a close; a terrible death appeared shortly to await us; hunger became violent and outrageous, and we prepared for a speedy release from our troubles; our speech and reason were both considerably impaired, and we were reduced to be at this time, certainly the most helpless and wretched of the whole human race. Isaac Cole, one of our crew, had the day before this, in a fit of despair, thrown himself down in the boat, and was determined there calmly to wait for death. It was obvious that he had no chance; all was dark he said in his mind, not a single ray of hope was left for him to dwell upon; and it was folly and madness to be struggling against what appeared so palpably to be our fixed and settled destiny. I remonstrated with him as effectually as the weakness both of my body and understanding would allow of; and what I said appeared for a moment to have a considerable effect: he made a powerful and sudden effort, half rose up, crawled forward and hoisted the jib, and firmly and loudly cried that he would not give up; that he would live as long as the rest of us—but alas! this effort was but the hectic fever of the moment, and he shortly again relapsed into a state of melancholy and despair.

This day his reason was attacked, and he became about nine o'clock in the morning a most miserable spectacle of madness: he spoke incoherently about everything, calling loudly for a napkin and water, and then lying stupidly and senselessly down in the boat again, would close his hollow eyes, as if in death. About ten o'clock, we suddenly perceived that he became speechless; we got him as well as we were able upon a board, placed on one of the seats of the boat, and covering him up with some old clothes, left him to his fate. He lay in the greatest pain and apparent misery, groaning piteously until four o'clock, when he died, in the most horrid and frightful convulsions I ever witnessed.

We kept his corpse all night, and in the morning my two companions began as a course to make preparations to dispose of it in the sea; when after reflecting on the subject all night, I addressed them on the painful subject of keeping the body for food!! Our provisions could not possibly last us beyond three days, within which time, it was not in any degree probable that we should find relief from our present sufferings, and that hunger would at last drive us to the necessity of casting lots. It was without any objection agreed to, and we set to work as fast as we were able to prepare it so as to prevent its spoiling. We separated his limbs from his body, and cut all the flesh from the bones; after which, we opened the body, took out the heart, and then closed it again—sewed it up as decently as we could, and committed it to the sea. We now first commenced to satisfy the immediate cravings of nature from the heart, which we eagerly devoured, and then ate sparingly of a few pieces of the flesh; after which we hung up the remainder, cut in thin strips about the boat, to dry in the sun: we made a fire and roasted some of it, to serve us during the next day. In this manner did we dispose of our fellow sufferer; the painful recollection of which brings to mind at this moment, some of the most disagreeable and revolting ideas that it is capable of conceiving.

We knew not then to whose lot it would fall next, either to die or be shot, and eaten like the poor wretch we had just dispatched. Humanity must shudder at the dreadful recital. I have no language to paint the anguish of our souls in this dreadful dilemma.

February 10th

We found that the flesh had become tainted, and had turned a greenish colour upon which we concluded to make a fire and cook it at once, to prevent its becoming so putrid as not to be eaten at all: we accordingly did so, and by that means preserved it for six or seven days longer; our bread during the time remained untouched; as that would not be liable to spoil, we placed it carefully aside for the last moments of our trial. About three o'clock this afternoon a strong breeze set in from the N.W. and we made very good progress, considering that we were compelled to steer the boat by management of the sails alone: this wind continued until the thirteenth, when it changed again ahead.

We contrived to keep soul and body together by sparingly partaking of our flesh, cut up in small pieces and eaten with salt water. By the fourteenth, our bodies became so far recruited, as to enable us to make a few attempts at guiding our boat again with the oar; by each taking his turn, we managed to effect it, and to make a tolerable good course. On the fifteenth, our flesh was all consumed, and we were driven to the last morsel of bread, consisting of two cakes; our limbs had for the last two days swelled very much, and now began to pain us most excessively. We were still, as near as we could judge, three hundred miles from the land, and but three days of our allowance on hand.

February 16th

At night, full of the horrible reflections of our situation, and panting with weakness, I laid down to sleep, almost indifferent whether I should ever see the light again. I had not lain long, before I dreamt I saw a ship at some distance off from us, and strained every nerve to get to her, but could not. I awoke almost overpowered with the frenzy I had caught in my slumbers, and stung with the cruelties of a diseased and disappointed imagination.

February 17th

In the afternoon, a heavy cloud appeared to be settling down in an E. by N. direction from us, which in my view, indicated the vicinity of some land, which I took for the island of Massafuera. I concluded it could be no other; and immediately upon this reflection, the life blood began to flow again briskly in my veins. I told my companions that I was well convinced it was land, and if so, in all probability we should reach it before two days more. My words appeared to comfort them much; and by repeated assurances of the favourable appearance of things, their spirits acquired even a degree of elasticity that was truly astonishing. The dark features of our distress began now to diminish a little, and the countenance, even amid the gloomy bodings of our hard lot, to assume a much fresher hue.

FEBRUARY 18TH

Before daylight, Thomas Nicholson, a boy about seventeen years of age, one of my two companions who had thus far survived with me, after having bailed the boat, laid down, drew a piece of canvas over him, and cried out that he then wished to die immediately. I saw that he had given up, and I attempted to speak a few words of comfort and encouragement to him, and endeavoured to persuade him that it was a great weakness and even wickedness to abandon a reliance upon the Almighty, while the least hope, and a breath of life remained; but he felt unwilling to listen to any of the consolatory suggestions which I made to him; and, notwithstanding the extreme probability which I stated there was of our gaining the land before the end of two days more, he insisted upon lying down and giving himself up to despair.

A fixed look of settled and forsaken despondency came over his face: he lay for some time silent, sullen, and sorrowful—and I felt at once satisfied that the coldness of death was fast gathering upon him: there was a sudden and unaccountable earnestness in his manner that alarmed me, and made me fear that I myself might unexpectedly be overtaken by a like weakness, or dizziness of nature, that would bereave me at once of both reason and life; but Providence willed it otherwise.

At about seven o'clock this morning, while I was lying asleep, my companion who was steering, suddenly and loudly called out, "There's a sail!" I know not what was the first movement I made upon hearing such an unexpected cry: the earliest of my recollections are that immediately I stood up, gazing in a state of abstraction and ecstasy upon the blessed vision of a vessel about seven miles off from us; she was standing in the same direction with us, and the only sensation I felt at the moment was, that of a violent and unaccountable impulse to fly directly towards her.

I do not believe it is possible to form a just conception of the pure, strong feelings, and the unmingled emotions of joy and gratitude, that took possession of my mind on this occasion: the boy, too, took a sudden and animated start from his despondency, and stood up to witness the probable instrument of his salvation. Our only fear was now that she would not discover us, or that we might not be able to intercept her course: we, however, put our boat immediately, as well as we were able, in a direction to cut her off; and found, to our great joy, that we sailed faster than she did. Upon observing us, she shortened sail, and allowed us to come up to her.

The captain hailed us, and asked who we were. I told him we were from a wreck, and he cried out immediately for us to come alongside the ship. I made an effort to assist myself along to the side, for the purpose of getting up, but strength failed me altogether, and I found it impossible to move a step further without help. We must have formed at that moment, in the eyes of the captain and his crew, a most deplorable and affecting picture of suffering and misery. Our cadaverous countenances, sunken eyes, and bones just starting through the skin, with the ragged remnants of clothes stuck about our sunburnt bodies, must have produced an appearance to him affecting and revolting in the highest degree.

The sailors commenced to remove us from our boat, and we were taken to the cabin, and comfortably provided for in every respect. In a few minutes we were permitted to taste of a little thin food, made from tapioca, and in a few days, with prudent management, we were considerably recruited. This vessel proved to be the brig *Indian*, Captain William Crozier, of London; to whom we are indebted for every polite, friendly, and attentive disposition towards us, that can possibly characterize a man of humanity and feeling.

FEBRUARY 25TH

We arrived at Valparaiso in utter distress and poverty. Our wants were promptly relieved there.

The captain and the survivors of his boat's crew, were taken up by the American whale-ship, the *Dauphin*, Captain Zimri Coffin, of Nantucket, and arrived at Valparaiso on the seventeenth of March following.

The third boat got separated from him on the twenty-eighth of January, and has not been heard of since.

The names of all the survivors, are as follows: Captain George Pollard, Jr., Charles Ramsdale, Owen Chase, Benjamin Lawrence, and Thomas Nicholson, all of Nantucket. There died in the captain's boat, the following: Brazilla Ray of Nantucket, Owen Coffin of the same place, who was shot, and Samuel Reed.

The captain relates, that after being separated, as herein before stated, they continued to make what progress they could towards the island of Juan Fernandez, as was agreed upon; but contrary winds and the extreme debility of the crew prevailed against their united exertions. He was with us equally surprised and concerned at the separation that took place between us; but continued on his course, almost confident of meeting with us again. On the fourteenth, the whole stock of provisions belonging to the second mate's boat was entirely exhausted, and on the twenty-fifth, Lawson Thomas died, and was eaten by his surviving companions.

On the twenty-first, the captain and his crew were in the like dreadful situation with respect to their provisions; and on the twenty-third, another man, Charles Shorter, died out of the same boat, and his body was shared for food between the crews of both boats. On the twenty-seventh, another, Isaac Shepherd, died in the third boat; and on the twenty-eighth, another man, named Samuel Reed, died out of the captain's boat. The bodies of these men constituted their only food while it lasted; and on the twenty-ninth, owing to the darkness of the night and want of sufficient power to manage their boats, those of the captain and second mate separated in latitude 35° S., longitude 100° W. On the first of February, having consumed the last morsel, the captain and the three other men that remained with him were reduced to the necessity of casting lots. It fell upon Owen Coffin to die, who with great fortitude and resignation submitted to his fate.

They drew lots to see who should shoot him: he placed himself firmly to receive his death, and was immediately shot by Charles Ramsdale, whose hard fortune it was to become his executioner. On the eleventh Brazilla Ray died; and on these two bodies the captain and Charles Ramsdale, the only two that were then left, subsisted until the morning of the twenty-third, when they fell in with the *Dauphin*.

On the eleventh of June following I arrived at Nantucket in the whale-ship the *Eagle*, Captain William H. Coffin. My family had received the most distressing account of our shipwreck, and had given me up for lost. My unexpected appearance was welcomed with the most grateful obligations and acknowledgements to a beneficent Creator, who had guided me through darkness, trouble, and death, once more to the bosom of my country and friends.

FIVE

The Shetland Bus

David Howarth

During the German occupation of Norway, from 1940 to 1945, every Norwegian knew that small boats were constantly sailing from the Shetland Isles to Norway to land weapons and supplies and to rescue refugees. The Norwegians who stayed in Norway and struggled there against the invaders were fortified by this knowledge, and gave the small boats the familiar name which is used for the title of this book: 'to take the Shetland bus' became a synonym in Norway for escape when danger was overwhelming. This record of the adventures of the Norwegian sailors who manned the boats is offered as a tribute from an English colleague to Norwegian seamanship, and as a humble memorial to those who lost their lives.

~~~

On 17 March Larsen left Scalloway to carry out the last trip of the season to Traena. By the end of the month, when he was due back, it would be too light up there to visit the district again till September.

Bergholm was faster than the smaller boats, and they made good time to Traena in fine weather, arriving off the islands in three and a half days. Larsen sighted the coast and fixed his position in daylight, and when darkness fell he closed in and felt his way in among the skerries. He reached one of the sounds between the islands, where the rocks rose steeply from the water, and laid the *Bergholm* alongside them. One of the passengers jumped ashore and climbed over the steep hills to some houses on the other side of the island.

When he came back he brought with him a man who had volunteered to come with them to another very small island, where a single family lived who he thought could take charge of the passengers and cargo until the small local boats were able to ferry them across to the mainland. Larsen took *Bergholm* through the sounds to this little island and moored her to the quay there. The owner of the island had a boathouse on the quay, in which were two dinghies and a lot of nets. They woke him up, and found he was quite willing to keep the cargo in the boathouse and to take care of the passengers. Most of the rest of the night was spent in taking out the boats and nets, packing in the cargo, and arranging the boats and nets on top of it.

By the time this was finished it was too late to put to sea again that morning, and as it was a good place to lie, sheltered from observation on all sides but one, Larsen stayed there till the following evening. All day, from the island, they watched a German patrol boat steaming up and down its beat nearby, and there were several alarms when it seemed to be approaching a point from which its crew could have seen the *Bergholm*. Had it done so they would have had to fight their way out, so they cleared away the guns and started the engine. It was only an armed Norwegian Arctic whaler, and they could probably have sunk it, but the aftereffects of a fight on the passengers who had been landed and the local people who had helped them would have been disastrous, and Traena would have been finished as a landing place. So it was lucky that its beat seemed to stop just short of the point from which the quay would have been visible, and that each time discovery seemed imminent it turned back on its tracks. As darkness approached it steamed off towards the mainland, and at eight in the evening *Bergholm* left for home. It was still very fine and clear.

At two o'clock the next afternoon they were steaming on their homeward course, parallel to the coast and about seventy-five miles off it, when a twin-engined plane approached them from astern and flew round them, very low and about three hundred yards away. As they expected the plane to attack at a moment's notice, and as they were much farther offshore than an innocent fishing boat had any right to be, they dropped their camouflage and manned the guns. But it did not attack; it flew off towards the coast.

The crew of the plane had certainly seen their guns, and it seemed sure that when it reached the coast and their position was reported, a real attack would be made. Larsen altered course to the westward; but after a bit he reflected that in such perfectly clear weather, at eight knots, he had no chance whatever of evading a search, so he returned to the course he had set for Shetland. The crew tested all their weapons and brought all the ammunition on deck. They had a single .5 Colt machine gun mounted forward and a twin one aft, two twin Lewis guns amidships, and two unmounted Brens.

About six o'clock the attack came. Two twin-engined seaplanes approached the boat from the port beam and circled it at a height of two hundred feet. Then, diving to mast height, they flew across her bow, firing with cannon. *Bergholm* returned the fire with all her guns. Not much damage was done to the boat, but for a few seconds the decks were swept with cannon shell splinters, and Klausen, on the port Lewis mounting, received so many wounds that Larsen sent him below.

The planes stood off and circled for about five minutes. Perhaps the fire put up by *Bergholm* was more than they had expected, and they were discussing it on their shortwave radio. After a time they swooped again, both attacking from the starboard side. As they approached, Larsen at the wheel tried to turn the boat to bring all the guns to bear. Another storm of shells and splinters hit her. The Colt and Lewis tracers were seen hitting the planes. Enoksen, at the twin Colt, staggered away from his guns with his face and hands hidden with blood. When they went to help him they found he was riddled with shell splinters from head to foot, and he could not see, so he also had to be sent below. Kalve, at the bow Colt, was hit in one hand and one foot. As the planes roared by he swung his gun round and aimed it with his remaining hand, then jammed his other elbow onto the trigger. Faeroy and Vika, the two engineers, were firing the two Bren guns. Hansen had gone below to try to send a radio signal to us, but the aerial was shot away. By then the boat was badly damaged, but she was still underway, and they knew they had damaged the planes. Suddenly as they watched for the next attack, one plane broke away and flew off low towards the coast.

The other one went on circling round, then dived again. Faeroy and Noreiger had taken over the Colts. Enoksen was trying to get up the ladder again from the cabin, but he was hit again and fell back down the hatch. Faeroy was also wounded, but he was able to stay at the gun.

On its next attack the plane dropped a stick of six bombs. None of them fell near the boat, but its cannon fire was still accurate, and Faeroy was wounded again and could not do any more.

Then there was nobody left to man the Lewis guns or Brens. Noreiger was still at one Colt, and Vika took over the other. Larsen was still at the wheel in what remained of the wheelhouse, manoeuvring the boat to meet each attack.

In the next run another stick of bombs came down, and the last of them fell a few feet from the stern. It shook the boat badly. Noreiger and Vika both shot accurately, and Larsen saw strikes on the plane. But as it receded once more Vika fell, and when Larsen ran to help him he found his foot was shot off above the ankle. Five of the eight men aboard were out of action. Hansen had come up from below and reported that the radio was dead and the boat was leaking. Larsen, wondering how to dispose his remaining men to meet the next attack, looked up at the plane. It was disappearing to the eastward, smoking.

The whole fight had lasted just over half an hour. This short time had wrought a terrible difference on *Bergholm* and her crew; but dusk was falling, and they could be sure that the night would give them respite. Larsen, Noreiger and Hansen, who were not wounded, first went to attend to the other five men. Vika was the most seriously hurt. Someone had already put a tourniquet on his leg, but they knew he was dying, and they thought he knew it too. He was conscious, and sometimes smiled, but he did not speak or complain. Faeroy, Enoksen, and Klausen were in great pain from the number of steel splinters in their hands and heads and bodies, and they could not move. Enoksen, however, was not blinded, as they had thought at first, it was only blood which had run into his eyes, and the shock of a shell which exploded in front of his face, which had made him unable to see. Kalve, who only had one leg and one hand out of action, was able to move and to give some help with the work that had to be done. They disinfected the men's wounds and bandaged them, then turned their attention to the boat.

The engine was still running, and with the wheel lashed she was holding nearly to her course; but the water in the bilges was rising, and the two pumps on the engine could not hold it in check. Kalve and Noreiger manned the hand pump, but still the water rose, and in spite of all they could do, at about eight o'clock it reached the air intakes of the engine, and the engine stopped.

In the meantime Larsen had inspected the rest of the boat. The decks were full of holes and covered with blood and empty cartridge cases. The masts were still standing, but a lot of the rigging was shot away, and wire and rope were swinging from side to side as the boat rolled. The wheelhouse, in which Larsen had stood unscratched through the whole engagement, was literally shot to pieces. The windows were all gone and the inside was littered with broken glass. All the doors were shot away, and the wooden walls and roof were smashed by exploding shells, so that nothing but the broken framework remained.

Most important of all was the lifeboat, which was stowed on top of a deckhouse on the port side of the wheelhouse. Most of its gunwale was split off, and it had seven shell holes in its bottom. Larsen and Noreiger set to work to patch the holes with canvas and sheets cut from bully beef tins. Hansen collected food and water and navigating instruments, and the lifeboat's mast and sail and oars. By midnight they had made the boat tight enough to be kept afloat, and they launched it and stowed the essential stores aboard. Larsen tore up his marked charts and ciphers and threw them overboard. Then came a grievous struggle to get the wounded men up the steep companionway from the cabin and into the boat without hurting them too much. At last they got Vika laid in the bows, on the floor of the boat, and Enoksen and Faeroy amidships. Klausen and Kalve had to sit up in the stern, as the boat was only sixteen feet long and there was no room for them to lie down. The three who were not wounded arranged to take turns at rowing, two at a time, each rowing for four hours and resting for two. At one in the morning they abandoned the *Bergholm*. It was dead calm.

The first thing they had to do was to get as far away as possible before dawn, when the Germans would very likely send out a plane to see what had happened to the wreck. She might still be floating; a wooden ship will often float with gunwales awash. If so, there was a chance that the Germans, seeing no life aboard, would assume that they had all been killed; but it was more likely that they would see that the lifeboat was gone, and would make a search for it.

But apart from getting away from the scene of the fight, Larsen had to decide where to make for. They were seventy-five miles from the nearest point on the Norwegian coast, and three hundred fifty miles from Shetland. After thinking it over, he decided that it was very unlikely that they could reach Shetland in the lifeboat. It was heavily laden, and with most of its top plank on each side shot away it had very little freeboard, so that a very moderate sea would have swamped it. Besides, with the best of luck it would take them, say, ten days to get there, and none of the wounded men could be expected to survive so long in an open boat. On the other hand, he did not like to take the shortest route to Norway, partly because he thought it was what the Germans would expect him to do, and partly because it led to a part of the coast, near Trondheim, where he had no friends he could rely on, and he thought that even if they got there safely it would be difficult to get away again.

So he made up his mind to steer for Ålesund, a hundred and fifty miles away, twice as far as the Trondheim coast. Larsen was a seaman by nature, and the prospect of towing so far in a leaky boat did not worry him, provided that it gave some small hope of getting the wounded crew alive to Shetland.

The two men rowing took one oar each, sharing the midship thwart. The third unwounded man, taking his two hours off from the oars, could not lie down because there was no room, and was occupied with helping the wounded men to shift their positions and to take food and water. Kalve was able to bail with his undamaged hand, and he did so continuously. At four o'clock on the first morning Vika asked for water and aspirins. They had no aspirins, but Larsen gave him the water and he seemed satisfied. When he went to him an hour later he had died. They wanted to bury his body in Norway, but later on their journey they wrapped it in a blanket and lifted it overboard. They remained stubbornly sure that they would reach safety in the end.

At dawn on the first morning, when they had been rowing for six hours, it was still calm and crystal clear. They saw a plane searching the place where the *Bergholm* had been. It flew in increasing circles, and they realised that its crew must have found the wreck, seen that the lifeboat was gone, and started to look for them. Planes remained in sight for the whole of the day, quartering the ocean in which a boat seems dreadfully conspicuous and vulnerable. Whenever the planes approached, the rowers shipped their oars, in case the flash of sunlight on the wet blades should show them up. Often the planes came so close that the men in the boat were certain they had been seen, and nerved themselves to a fresh attack like those of the day before; but each time the plane sheered off, and after a day of suspense at last the darkness fell and covered them. They rowed all night.

On the second day a light breeze came, and as there was no plane in sight they hoisted the sail, and for a time they made good progress. But at dusk it fell calm again, and they rowed for the third night.

The third day was sunny and calm again, and they rowed all day without seeing anything.

During the fourth night they saw a light ahead. They made towards it, and saw it was a fishing boat. They hailed her and drew alongside. Larsen climbed stiffly aboard. He told the fishermen that he and his men had been torpedoed in a merchant ship, and he asked them if they had enough fuel to get to Shetland. The fishermen were friendly and sympathetic, but they said they were only allowed to carry enough fuel to get to the fishing grounds and back, in order to stop them sailing across to the other side. They came from Kristiansund, and were willing to take Larsen and his crew back there with them and to help them to escape; but Larsen was doubtful whether it would be possible to escape from there, so he thanked them but refused the offer. He also refused food, saying they had plenty in the lifeboat. The fishermen gave him his exact position, which was thirty-five miles offshore, and he returned to the boat and started to row again.

At dawn on the next day, their fourth in the boat, they could see land, but it was still a long way off. As they struggled on towards it they saw a lot of fishing boats coming out towards them. This was an unwelcome sight, for it meant that by the evening, when the boats got back to port, the approach of a shipwrecked crew would be common knowledge. But it could not be helped, and when the boats reached them they hailed the first, and Larsen asked again if they had enough fuel to get to Shetland. This time the skipper tried to persuade them against going to Shetland, and after some hedging he came out into the open and said that if they would come back with him he would use his influence to help them; he thought it would only mean a month or two in prison, and then they could join the merchant service for the Germans. Luckily, before the conversation had reached this stage, his crew had given the men in the boat some cooked fish and coffee. It was the first hot food they had had for four days, and they felt much better for it; and they thanked the skipper politely, and went on their way. It turned out later that they had hit on the only local quisling [traitor]. When he got home that evening he reported them to the Germans, and was seen the next day walking in Ålesund with a German officer.

After leaving the fishing boat they rowed at the best speed they could make. They were sure he meant to report them, but they did not think he would lose a day's fishing to do it; so their only hope was to get into hiding on the coast before he could reach home. As they neared the coast a tidal stream against them slowed their progress, and they had a hard struggle to make any headway against it; but about three in the afternoon, very thankfully, they reached the first of the islands, and ran the boat in among some rocks, and waited for darkness.

There were still about ten miles to go, among the islands, to the place where Björnöy lived. They set off at eight, and got there soon after midnight. They were very tired, and some of the wounded men were very ill.

Larsen went ashore and knocked at the door of a man called Nils Sorviknes, who had helped him when he had been there before. It was some time before he could get an answer, and he leaned against the doorpost in the last stages of exhaustion. But at last the door opened, and Sorviknes, astonished to see him again, took him inside. Larsen told him what had happened, and told him he had six men waiting in the lifeboat. He asked what chance there was of getting a boat to go to Shetland. Sorviknes said he would talk to Björnöy, but that it was too late to do anything that night; and when Larsen told him the name of the fishing boat they had spoken to, Sorviknes knew it at once as belonging to a quisling, and was sure that by then the Germans would have been told that they were in the district. So the first essential was to hide them before dawn. He thought for a while, then advised Larsen to go to a man called Lars Torholmen, who lived with his wife and two sisters in the only house on a very small island a couple of miles away. He gave him a letter to Torholmen, and told him to lie low there till he got further instructions.

Back in the lifeboat, Larsen took to the oars for the last time and rowed to the small island. He went ashore again, and woke Torholmen, who took him in without any hesitation. As soon as he gave him the letter from Sorviknes and explained about the wounded men in the boat, Torholmen and his two sisters came down to the shore and between them they carried the wounded men to the house. The mother and the sisters put them to bed and fed them and washed their wounds. It was beginning to get light, and the boat had to be disposed of before daybreak. There was no time to take it out and sink it, so Larsen and Torholmen rowed it round to the other side of the island and hid it in a boathouse. It was a compromising thing to keep on the island, but there was nothing better they could do. As the sun rose they got back to the house, and Larsen was also put to bed. They all slept for the whole of the day.

They stayed with Torholmen for a week, living in two rooms at the top of the house, and being well looked after by the three ladies. With good food and rest their strength began to return, but some of the wounded men were still in great pain from the shell splinters in their bodies.

Björnöy, on whom they were relying to find them a boat to get away, was skipper of a local ferry, and Nils Sorviknes was one of his crew. So they knew that Sorviknes would be able to tell Björnöy about them during the ferry's morning run to Ålesund on the day they arrived. But the story Larsen had been able to tell Sorviknes was incomplete, so one of Torholmen's sisters invented some errands in Ålesund, and went as a passenger on the boat to give him more details. She also asked him whether he knew of a doctor who could be trusted to come to Torholmen to see the wounded men, as she was worried by signs of sepsis and gangrene.

On their second day with Torholmen, which was a Sunday, Björnöy came to see Larsen and to tell him what he was doing. The problem of getting them away had been made much more difficult and dangerous by their meeting with the quisling skipper. As they had expected, he had reported their arrival to the Germans and a tremendous search was going on. Within an hour of their arrival at Torholmen's house the Germans had started an air search of the whole of that part of Norway, and had sent two armed trawlers to the part of the coast the quisling had thought they were making for. They had also dispatched a ferry steamer to land parties of soldiers on each of the string of large islands which ran north from Ålesund; and they had evidently seen or photographed the registration number which was painted on the *Bergholm* at the time, for they sent a detachment of thirty men to the village which the number denoted.

Advertisements offering rewards for their capture were printed in the papers, and everybody in the district was talking about them. The little island where they were hiding was in the very middle of the area which was being searched, and Björnöy thought that until the excitement had died down it would be foolish to risk the slightest move which might draw attention to the place. He did not think it was safe even to bring a doctor out to the island. He offered to take the wounded men to the doctor, in a rowing boat by night, but it would be a dangerous journey, partly over land, where the men would have to be carried and the whole party would be at the mercy of anyone who happened to see them. Larsen and Björnöy agreed that in any case the doctor could not do much unless the men went to a hospital to have the splinters extracted, and they decided to give up the idea unless any of them got much worse.

Björnöy was against using a local boat to escape to Shetland if it could be avoided. The Germans were obviously very anxious to capture the *Bergholm's* crew. If a local boat disappeared they would be sure to guess that the crew had escaped in it, and their punishment of the owners would be severe and might even lead to discovery of the whole organisation to which Björnöy belonged. Although this might be risked as a last resort, he had first got in touch with Karl-Johan, and had a radio message sent to England to ask us to send a boat over to fetch them.

This signal, of course, was the first news we had had in Shetland of what had happened to the *Bergholm*. Knowing that she had been attacked confirmed us all in our opinion that the use of fishing boats was getting too dangerous to be worthwhile. By the time we received it, it was the beginning of April. The nights were already very short, and to send a fishing boat into a district already so thoroughly on the alert would be very risky. A naval M.T.B., on the other hand, would not only have a much better chance of doing the job, but also of fighting its way out if it was spotted. The Navy was very willing to send one; but unluckily the weather by then was very bad, and until it moderated it was impossible for these fast light craft to leave harbour. Every one of the fishing-boat crews which survived at the base was ready and eager to go, and the fishing boats could easily have weathered the gale. But Rogers would not let them. It was natural that everyone's first reaction was to set off at once on a rescue expedition; but when he weighed it up he concluded that it was wrong to take so great a risk of losing a second crew, and that so far as we could tell it was probably safer for the *Bergholm* crew themselves to stay in hiding till an M.T.B. could go, than to embark on a fishing boat which might so very easily be lost on the voyage home. It was hard for him to decide to leave the crew in their dangerous position, but he was certainly right; and the decision was transmitted to Ålesund, and ultimately to the men on the island.

Meanwhile the search continued around and over their hiding place. From the windows of the house they could see aircraft quartering the district, and every day Torholmen brought them news of what the Germans were doing. The search lasted for nearly a week. Then a rumour spread around in Ålesund that a fishing boat had been stolen. Larsen heard it and was pleased, because even though the Germans would not be able to trace it to its source and prove that it was true, they would certainly not be able to prove that it was not, and as time went on they would probably be more inclined to believe it. It would at least offer them a plausible explanation of the disappearance of the boatload of men. He never knew whether it was a spontaneous rumour, or whether it had been started by some friend as a means of bringing the search to an end. At all events it seemed to help.

The intensity of the search gradually died down, and after about ten days the Germans seemed to have given it up as a bad job. Why they missed the little island where the men were hiding remains a mystery. Perhaps it was because it was so small, or because it was so close to the headquarters town of Ålesund; or perhaps they hardly expected that men who had rowed a hundred and fifty miles would row a farther ten among the islands.

As soon as it began to seem that the Germans were convinced the crew had escaped from the district, Björnöy proceeded with his plans for getting them away. He had asked through Karl-Johan that the rescue boat should be sent to the island of Skorpen, a dozen miles farther south, where we had already landed and picked up many agents. Johann Skorpen, the fisherman who lived there, was well used to hiding people and would look after the crew somewhere on his island till the boat could come.

Moving them down there would be the most difficult job. There was a control point on the way at which papers had to be produced, but boats were not usually searched there; and if Björnöy could find a boat with a plausible reason for going through this control, he thought it would be better to risk this than to bring one of our boats too close to Ålesund.

The movement was deputed to Sverre Roald, another member of the organisation, who lived in the island of Vigra, close at hand, and was a neighbour and relation of our foreman shipwright Sevrin Roald. After the men had been a week with Torholmen, Roald came one night to tell them what he had arranged. The next night he came again, and they embarked in his little motorboat. But by then the calm spell which had lasted throughout their journey in the lifeboat had given place to strong southerly winds, and after trying to stem the short seas between the islands they had to give it up and go back to Torholmen.

The next night the wind had dropped a little, and they tried again. This time they reached the island of Vigra in safety, where Roald transferred them to another boat: the small decked fishing boat which was to take them through the control to Skorpen.

There is an important radio station in Vigra, which was guarded by German sentries. The fishing boat was lying within a hundred yards of the station buildings, within sight of the sentries. The trip to Skorpen had to be postponed through bad weather, and the men stayed on board the boat for five days. It was an inconvenient position to be in, because they could not go on deck in daylight but had to stay confined in the little cabin of the boat. But on the other hand it was reasonably safe, because the Germans would not expect the seven men they were looking for to be hiding in a boat under constant watch. Sverre Roald had to be careful in his visits, but he managed to see them every night, bringing them food and the latest news of how things were going. At last they were able to get away. They passed the control quite easily and safely, and reached Skorpen, where Roald handed them over to Johann Skorpen and went back to Vigra. Skorpen installed them in a cowshed on the opposite side of the island to his house, and brought them a primus stove and some food and coffee.

Skorpen was not worried at having them there, because his house and island had been searched only a week before and he did not think the Germans would bother him again for some time. Some M.T.B.s manned by the Norwegian Navy had attacked a convoy in that district, and it seemed that the Germans had not seen the boats leaving the coast and believed they had been sunk and that the crews were hiding. They had been searching for them round Skorpen, just as they had been searching for the *Bergholm* crew round Ålesund, and a party of soldiers had been landed in each island. Luckily Skorpen had seen them coming, and had retreated to the hills, taking with him his radio set, since it was forbidden to possess such a thing, and leaving his wife, who would be less suspect than himself, to deal with the search party. The officer in charge of the party had opened her door and said, 'Where are you hiding them?' It must have alarmed the lady, whose house had harboured so many different agents and refugees; but she pretended not to be able to understand the German officer's Norwegian. This universal means of avoiding difficult questions must have been very annoying for Germans who were perhaps not very sure whether they were really able to make themselves understood or not. It was very effective. The party searched the house and found an old pair of headphones from a disused crystal set, which they took away with apparent satisfaction.

As this search had been made so recently, and as the *Bergholm* crew were now out of the immediate area where the Germans had supposed them to be, they settled down with a feeling of comparative security to wait for the boat from Shetland.

Our headquarters had arranged with Karl-Johan that they should send a code message in the B.B.C. Norwegian news bulletin on the night before the rescue boat was due to arrive at Skorpen. Karl-Johan had warned Skorpen to expect this message, and Skorpen listened every evening on the radio which he had retrieved from the hilltop. When Roald got home and sent a message to Karl-Johan that the men had safely arrived at the rendezvous, a signal was sent to our headquarters and passed on to us in Shetland. The weather was still bad, and although the naval M.T.B.s were ready to sail we had to wait another week before they could leave the harbour. As soon as the wind subsided the code message was broadcast by the B.B.C. and an M.T.B. left Shetland. Skorpen heard the message, and when the boat entered the sound of Skorpen the next evening the seven men were waiting on the shore. Afterwards Larsen said, 'We are glad to be on our way.'

Six

The Wreck of the *Medusa*

Charlotte-Adélaïde Dard

At noon, on the 2nd of July, soundings were taken. M. Maudet, ensign of the watch, was convinced we were upon the edge of the Arguin Bank. The Captain said to him, as well as to everyone, that there was no cause of alarm. In the meanwhile, the wind blowing with great violence, impelled us nearer and nearer to the danger which menaced us. A species of stupor overpowered all our spirits, and everyone preserved a mournful silence, as if they were persuaded we would soon touch the bank.

The colour of the water entirely changed, a circumstance even remarked by the ladies. About three in the afternoon, being in 19° 30' north latitude, and 19° 45' west longitude, a universal cry was heard upon deck. All declared they saw sand rolling among the ripple of the sea. The Captain in an instant ordered to sound. The line gave eighteen fathoms; but on a second sounding it only gave six. He at last saw his error, and hesitated no longer on changing the route, but it was too late. A strong concussion told us the frigate had struck. Terror and consternation were instantly depicted on every face. The crew stood motionless; the passengers in utter despair.

In the midst of this general panic, cries of vengeance were heard against the principal author of our misfortunes, wishing to throw him overboard; but some generous persons interposed, and endeavoured to calm their spirits, by diverting their attention to the means of our safety. The confusion was already so great, that M. Poinsignon, commandant of a troop, struck my sister Caroline a severe blow, doubtless thinking it was one of his soldiers. At this crisis my father was buried in profound sleep, but he quickly awoke, the cries and the tumult upon deck having informed him of our misfortunes.

He poured out a thousand reproaches on those whose ignorance and boasting had been so disastrous to us. However, they set about the means of averting our danger. The officers, with an altered voice, issued their orders, expecting every moment to see the ship go in pieces. They strove to lighten her, but the sea was very rough and the current strong. Much time was lost in doing nothing; they only pursued half measures, and all of them unfortunately failed.

When it was discovered that the danger of the *Medusa* was not so great as was at first supposed, various persons proposed to transport the troops to the island of Arguin, which was conjectured to be not far from the place where we lay aground. Others advised to take us all successively to the coast of the desert of Sahara, by the means of our boats, and with provisions sufficient to form a caravan, to reach the island of Saint Louis, at Senegal. The events which afterwards ensued proved this plan to have been the best, and which would have been crowned with success; unfortunately it was not adopted. M. Schmaltz, the governor, suggested the making of a raft of a sufficient size to carry two hundred men, with provisions: which latter plan was seconded by the two officers of the frigate, and put in execution.

The fatal raft was then begun to be constructed, which would, they said, carry provisions for everyone. Masts, planks, boards, cordage were thrown overboard. Two officers were charged with the framing of these together. Large barrels were emptied and placed at the angles of the machine, and the workmen were taught to say, that the passengers would be in greater security there, and more at their ease, than in the boats. However, as it was forgotten to erect rails, everyone supposed, and with reason, that those who had given the plan of the raft, had had no design of embarking upon it themselves.

When it was completed, the two chief officers of the frigate publicly promised, that all the boats would tow it to the shore of the Desert; and, when there, stores of provisions and firearms would be given us to form a caravan to take us all to Senegal. Why was not this plan executed? Why were these promises, sworn before the French flag, made in vain? But it is necessary to draw a veil over the past. I will only add, that if these promises had been fulfilled, everyone would have been saved, and that, in spite of the detestable egotism of certain personages, humanity would not now have had to deplore the scenes of horror consequent on the wreck of the *Medusa*!

On the 3rd of July, the efforts were renewed to disengage the frigate, but without success. We then prepared to quit her. The sea became very rough, and the wind blew with great violence. Nothing now was heard but the plaintive and confused cries of a multitude, consisting of more than four hundred persons, who, seeing death before their eyes, deplored their hard fate in bitter lamentations.

On the 4th, there was a glimpse of hope. At the hour the tide flowed, the frigate, being considerably lightened by all that had been thrown overboard, was found nearly afloat; and it is very certain, if on that day they had thrown the artillery into the water, the *Medusa* would have been saved; but M. Lachaumareys said, he could not thus sacrifice the King's cannon, as if the frigate did not belong to the King also. However, the sea ebbed, and the ship sinking into the sand deeper than ever, made them relinquish that on which depended our last ray of hope.

On the approach of night, the fury of the winds redoubled, and the sea became very rough. The frigate then received some tremendous concussions, and the water rushed into the hold in the most terrific manner, but the pumps would not work. We had now no alternative but to abandon her for the frail boats, which any single wave would overwhelm. Frightful gulfs environed us; mountains of water raised their liquid summits in the distance. How were we to escape so many dangers? Whither could we go? What hospitable land would receive us on its shores? My thoughts then reverted to our beloved country. I did not regret Paris, but I could have esteemed myself happy to have been yet in the marshes on the road to Rochefort. Then starting suddenly from my reverie, I exclaimed: "O terrible condition! that black and boundless sea resembles the eternal night which will engulf us! All those who surround me seem yet tranquil; but that fatal calm will soon be succeeded by the most frightful torments. Fools, what had we to find in Senegal, to make us trust to the most perfidious of elements! Did France not afford every necessary for our happiness? Happy! yes, thrice happy, they who never set foot on a foreign soil! Great God! succour all these unfortunate beings; save our unhappy family!"

My father perceived my distress, but how could he console me? What words could calm my fears, and place me above the apprehension of those dangers to which we were exposed? How, in a word, could I assume a serene appearance, when friends, parents, and all that was most dear to me were, in all human probability, on the very verge of destruction? Alas! my fears were but too well founded. For I soon perceived that, although we were the only ladies, besides the Misses Schmaltz, who formed a part of the governor's suit, they had the barbarity of intending our family to embark upon the raft, where were only soldiers, sailors, planters of Cape Verde, and some generous officers who had not the honour (if it could be accounted one) of being considered among the ignorant confidants of MM. Schmaltz and Lachaumareys.

My father, indignant at a proceeding so indecorous, swore we would not embark upon the raft, and that, if we were not judged worthy of a place in one of the six boats, he would himself, his wife, and children, remain on board the wrecks of the frigate. The tone in which he spoke these words, was that of a man resolute to avenge any insult that might be offered to him. The governor of Senegal, doubtless fearing the world would one day reproach him for his inhumanity, decided we should have a place in one of the boats. This having in some measure quieted our fears concerning our unfortunate situation, I was desirous of taking some repose, but the uproar among the crew was so great I could not obtain it.

Towards midnight, a passenger came to inquire at my father if we were disposed to depart; he replied, we had been forbid to go yet. However, we were soon convinced that a great part of the crew and various passengers were secretly preparing to set off in the boats. A conduct so perfidious could not fail to alarm us, especially as we perceived among those so eager to embark unknown to us, several who had promised, but a little while before, not to go without us.

M. Schmaltz, to prevent that which was going on upon deck, instantly rose to endeavour to quiet their minds; but the soldiers had already assumed a threatening attitude, and, holding cheap the words of their commander, swore they would fire upon whosoever attempted to depart in a clandestine manner. The firmness of these brave men produced the desired effect, and all was restored to order. The governor returned to his cabin; and those who were desirous of departing furtively were confused and covered with shame. The governor, however, was ill at ease; and as he had heard very distinctly certain energetic words which had been addressed to him, he judged it proper to assemble a council. All the officers and passengers being collected, M. Schmaltz there solemnly swore before them not to abandon the raft, and a second time promised, that all the boats would tow it to the shore of the Desert, where they would all be formed into a caravan. I confess this conduct of the governor greatly satisfied every member of our family; for we never dreamed he would deceive us, nor act in a manner contrary to what he had promised.

About three in the morning, some hours after the meeting of the council, a terrible noise was heard in the powder room; it was the helm which was broken. All who were sleeping were roused by it. On going on deck everyone was more and more convinced that the frigate was lost beyond all recovery. Alas! the wreck was for our family the commencement of a horrible series of misfortunes. The two chief officers then decided with one accord, that all should embark at six in the morning, and abandon the ship to the mercy of the waves. After this decision, followed a scene the most whimsical, and at the same time the most melancholy that can be well conceived. To have a more distinct idea of it, let the reader transport himself in imagination to the midst of the liquid plains of the ocean; then let him picture to himself a multitude of all classes, of every age, tossed about at the mercy of the waves upon a dismasted vessel, foundered, and half submerged; let him not forget these are thinking beings with the certain prospect before them of having reached the goal of their existence.

Separated from the rest of the world by a boundless sea, and having no place of refuge but the wrecks of a grounded vessel, the multitude addressed at first their vows to Heaven, and forgot, for a moment, all earthly concerns. Then, suddenly starting from their lethargy, they began to look after their wealth, the merchandise they had in small ventures, utterly regardless of the elements which threatened them. The miser, thinking of the gold contained in his coffers, hastening to put it in a place of safety, either by sewing it into the lining of his clothes, or by cutting out for it a place in the waistband of his trousers.

The smuggler was tearing his hair at not being able to save a chest of contraband which he had secretly got on board, and with which he had hoped to have gained two or three hundred percent. Another, selfish to excess, was throwing overboard all his hidden money, and amusing himself by burning all his effects. A generous officer was opening his portmanteau, offering caps, stockings, and shirts, to any who would take them. These had scarcely gathered together their various effects, when they learned that they could not take anything with them; those were searching the cabins and storerooms to carry away everything that was valuable.

Shipboys were discovering the delicate wines and fine liqueurs, which a wise foresight had placed in reserve. Soldiers and sailors were penetrating even into the spirit room, broaching casks, staving others, and drinking till they fell exhausted. Soon the tumult of the inebriated made us forget the roaring of the sea which threatened to engulf us. At last the uproar was at its height; the soldiers no longer listened to the voice of their captain. Some knit their brows and muttered oaths; but nothing could be done with those whom wine had rendered furious. Next, piercing cries mixed with doleful groans were heard—this was the signal of departure.

At six o'clock on the morning of the 5th, a great part of the military were embarked upon the raft, which was already covered with a large sheet of foam. The soldiers were expressly prohibited from taking their arms. A young officer of infantry, whose brain seemed to be powerfully affected, put his horse beside the barricadoes of the frigate, and then, armed with two pistols, threatened to fire upon anyone who refused to go upon the raft. Forty men had scarcely descended when it sunk to the depth of about two feet. To facilitate the embarking of a greater number, they were obliged to throw over several barrels of provisions which had been placed upon it the day before. In this manner did this furious officer get about one hundred and fifty heaped upon that floating tomb; but he did not think of adding one more to the number by descending himself, as he ought to have done, but went peaceably away, and placed himself in one of the best boats. There should have been sixty sailors upon the raft, and there were but about ten. A list had been made out on the 4th, assigning each his proper place; but this wise precaution being disregarded, everyone pursued the plan he deemed the best for his own preservation. The precipitation with which they forced one hundred and fifty unfortunate beings upon the raft was such that they forgot to give them one morsel of biscuit. However, they threw towards them twenty-five pounds in a sack, whilst they were not far from the frigate; but it fell into the sea, and was with difficulty recovered.

During this disaster, the governor of Senegal, who was busied in the care of his own dear self, effeminately descended in an armchair into the barge, where were already various large chests, all kinds of provisions, his dearest friends, his daughter and his wife. Afterwards the Captain's boat received twenty-seven persons, amongst whom were twenty-five sailors, good rowers. The shallop, commanded by M. Espiau, ensign of the ship, took forty-five passengers, and put off. The boat, called the *Senegal,* took twenty-five; the pinnace thirty-three; and the yawl, the smallest of all the boats, took only ten.

Almost all the officers, the passengers, the mariners and super-numeraries, were already embarked—all, but our weeping family, who still remained upon the boards of the frigate, till some charitable souls would kindly receive us into a boat. Surprised at this abandonment, I instantly felt myself roused, and, calling with all my might to the officers of the boats, besought them to take our unhappy family along with them. Soon after, the barge, in which were the governor of Senegal and all his family, approached the *Medusa,* as if still to take some passengers, for there were but few in it. I made a motion to descend, hoping that the Misses Schmaltz, who had, till that day, taken a great interest in our family, would allow us a place in their boat; but I was mistaken: those ladies, who had embarked in a mysterious incognito, had already forgotten us; and M. Lachaumareys, who was still on the frigate, positively told me they would not embark along with us.

Nevertheless I ought to tell, what we learned afterwards, that that officer who commanded the pinnace had received orders to take us in, but, as he was already a great way from the frigate, we were certain he had abandoned us. My father however hailed him, but he persisted on his way to gain the open sea. A short while afterwards we perceived a small boat among the waves, which seemed desirous to approach the *Medusa*; it was the yawl.

When it was sufficiently near, my father implored the sailors who were in it to take us on board, and to carry us to the pinnace, where our family ought to be placed. They refused. He then seized a firelock, which lay by chance upon deck, and swore he would kill every one of them if they refused to take us into the yawl, adding that it was the property of the king, and that he would have advantage from it as well as another.

The sailors murmured, but durst not resist, and received all our family, which consisted of nine persons, viz. four children, our stepmother, my cousin, my sister Caroline, my father, and myself. A small box, filled with valuable papers, which we wished to save, some clothes, two bottles of ratafia, which we had endeavoured to preserve amidst our misfortunes, were seized and thrown overboard by the sailors of the yawl, who told us we would find in the pinnace everything which we could wish for our voyage.

We had then only the clothes which covered us, never thinking of dressing ourselves in two suits; but the loss which affected us most was that of several manuscripts at which my father had been labouring for a long while. Our trunks, our linen, and various chests of merchandise of great value, in a word, everything we possessed, was left in the *Medusa*. When we boarded the pinnace, the officer who commanded it began excusing himself for having set off without forewarning us, as he had been ordered, and said a thousand things in his justification. But without believing the half of his fine protestations, we felt very happy in having overtaken him; for it is most certain they had had no intention of encumbering themselves with our unfortunate family. I say encumber, for it is evident that four children, one of whom was yet at the breast, were very indifferent beings to people who were actuated by a selfishness without all parallel.

When we were seated in the longboat, my father dismissed the sailors with the yawl, telling them he would ever gratefully remember their services. They speedily departed, but little satisfied with the good action they had done. My father hearing their murmurs and the abuse they poured out against us, said, loud enough for all in the boat to hear: "We are not surprised sailors are destitute of shame, when their officers blush at being compelled to do a good action." The commandant of the boat feigned not to understand the reproaches conveyed in these words, and, to divert our minds from brooding over our wrongs, endeavoured to counterfeit the man of gallantry.

All the boats were already far from the *Medusa*, when they were brought to, to form a chain in order to tow the raft. The barge, in which was the governor of Senegal, took the first tow, then all the other boats in succession joined themselves to that. M. Lachaumareys embarked, although there yet remained upon the *Medusa* more than sixty persons. Then the brave and generous M. Espiau, commander of the shallop, quitted the line of boats, and returned to the frigate, with the intention of saving all the wretches who had been abandoned. They all sprung into the shallop; but as it was very much overloaded, seventeen unfortunates preferred remaining on board, rather than expose themselves as well as their companions to certain death. But, alas! the greater part afterwards fell victims to their fears or their devotion.

Fifty-two days after they were abandoned, no more than three of them were alive, and these looked more like skeletons than men. They told that their miserable companions had gone afloat upon planks and hen-coops, after having waited in vain forty-two days for the succour which had been promised them, and that all had perished.

The shallop, carrying with difficulty all those she had saved from the *Medusa*, slowly rejoined the line of boats which towed the raft. M. Espiau earnestly besought the officers of the other boats to take some of them along with them; but they refused, alleging to the generous officer that he ought to keep them in his own boat, as he had gone for them himself. M. Espiau, finding it impossible to keep them all without exposing them to the utmost peril, steered right for a boat which I will not name.

Immediately a sailor sprung from the shallop into the sea, and endeavoured to reach it by swimming; and when he was about to enter it, an officer who possessed great influence, pushed him back, and, drawing his sabre, threatened to cut off his hands, if he again made the attempt.

The poor wretch regained the shallop, which was very near the pinnace, where we were. Various friends of my father supplicated M. Lapérère, the officer of our boat, to receive him on board. My father had his arms already out to catch him, when M. Lapérère instantly let go the rope which attached us to the other boats, and tugged off with all his force. At the same instant every boat imitated our execrable example; and wishing to shun the approach of the shallop, which sought for assistance, stood off from the raft, abandoning in the midst of the ocean, and to the fury of the waves, the miserable mortals whom they had sworn to land on the shores of the Desert.

Scarcely had these cowards broken their oath, when we saw the French flag flying upon the raft. The confidence of these unfortunate persons was so great, that when they saw the first boat which had the tow removing from them, they all cried out, "The rope is broken! The rope is broken!" but when no attention was paid to their observation they instantly perceived the treachery of the wretches who had left them so basely. Then the cries of *Vive le Roi* arose from the raft, as if the poor fellows were calling to their father for assistance; or, as if they had been persuaded that, at that rallying word, the officers of the boats would return, and not abandon their countrymen. The officers repeated the cry of *Vive le Roi*, without a doubt, to insult them; but, more particularly, M. Lachaumareys, who, assuming a martial attitude, waved his hat in the air. Alas! what availed these false professions?

Frenchmen, menaced with the greatest peril, were demanding assistance with the cries of *Vive le Roi*; yet none were found sufficiently generous, nor sufficiently French, to go to aid them. After a silence of some minutes, horrible cries were heard; the air resounded with the groans, the lamentations, the imprecations of these wretched beings, and the echo of the sea frequently repeated, "Alas! how cruel you are to abandon us!!!" The raft already appeared to be buried under the waves, and its unfortunate passengers immersed.

The fatal machine was drifted by currents far behind the wreck of the frigate; without cable, anchor, mast, sail, oars; in a word, without the smallest means of enabling them to save themselves. Each wave that struck it, made them stumble in heaps on one another. Their feet getting entangled among the cordage, and between the planks, bereaved them of the faculty of moving. Maddened by these misfortunes, suspended, and adrift upon a merciless ocean, they were soon tortured between the pieces of wood which formed the scaffold on which they floated. The bones of their feet and their legs were bruised and broken, every time the fury of the waves agitated the raft; their flesh covered with contusions and hideous wounds, dissolved, as it were, in the briny waves, whilst the roaring flood around them was coloured with their blood.

As the raft, when it was abandoned, was nearly two leagues from the frigate, it was impossible these unfortunate persons could return to it: they were soon after far out at sea. These victims still appeared above their floating tomb; and, stretching out their supplicating hands towards the boats which fled from them, seemed yet to invoke, for the last time, the names of the wretches who had deceived them. O horrid day! a day of shame and reproach! Alas! that the hearts of those who were so well acquainted with misfortune, should have been so inaccessible to pity!

After witnessing that most inhuman scene, and seeing they were insensible to the cries and lamentations of so many unhappy beings, I felt my heart bursting with sorrow. It seemed to me that the waves would overwhelm all these wretches, and I could not suppress my tears. My father, exasperated to excess, and bursting with rage at seeing so much cowardice and inhumanity among the officers of the boats, began to regret he had not accepted the place which had been assigned for us upon the fatal raft. "At least," said he, "we would have died with the brave, or we would have returned to the wreck of the *Medusa*; and not have had the disgrace of saving ourselves with cowards." Although this produced no effect upon the officers, it proved very fatal to us afterwards; for, on our arrival at Senegal, it was reported to the governor, and very probably was the principal cause of all those evils and vexations which we endured in that colony.

Let us now turn our attention to the several situations of all those who were endeavouring to save themselves in the different boats, as well as to those left upon the wreck of the *Medusa*.

We have already seen, that the frigate was half sunk when it was deserted, presenting nothing but a hulk and wreck. Nevertheless, seventeen still remained upon it, and had food, which, although damaged, enabled them to support themselves for a considerable time; whilst the raft was abandoned to float at the mercy of the waves, upon the vast surface of the ocean. One hundred and fifty wretches were embarked upon it, sunk to the depth of at least three feet on its fore part, and on its poop immersed even to the middle. What victuals they had were soon consumed, or spoiled by the salt water; and perhaps some, as the waves hurried them along, became food for the monsters of the deep.

Two only of all the boats which left the *Medusa,* and these with very few people in them, were provisioned with every necessary; these struck off with security and despatch. But the condition of those who were in the shallop was but little better than those upon the raft; their great number, their scarcity of provisions, their great distance from the shore, gave them the most melancholy anticipations of the future. Their worthy commander, M. Espiau, had no other hope but of reaching the shore as soon as possible.

The other boats were less filled with people, but they were scarcely better provisioned; and, as by a species of fatality, the pinnace, in which were our family, was destitute of everything. Our provisions consisted of a barrel of biscuit, and a tierce of water; and, to add to our misfortunes, the biscuit being soaked in the sea, it was almost impossible to swallow one morsel of it. Each passenger in our boat was obliged to sustain his wretched existence with a glass of water, which he could get only once a day. To tell how this happened, how this boat was so poorly supplied, whilst there were abundance left upon the *Medusa,* is far beyond my power. But it is at least certain, that the greater part of the officers commanding the boats, the shallop, the pinnace, the *Senegal* boat, and the yawl, were persuaded, when they quitted the frigate, that they would not abandon the raft, but that all the expedition would sail together to the coast of Sahara; that when there, the boats would be again sent to the *Medusa* to take provisions, arms, and those who were left there; but it appears the chiefs had decided otherwise.

After abandoning the raft, although scattered, all the boats formed a little fleet, and followed the same route. All who were sincere hoped to arrive the same day at the coast of the Desert, and that everyone would get on shore; but MM. Schmaltz and Lachaumareys gave orders to take the route for Senegal. This sudden change in the resolutions of the chiefs was like a thunderbolt to the officers commanding the boats. Having nothing on board but what was barely necessary to enable us to allay the cravings of hunger for one day, we were all sensibly affected. The other boats, which, like ourselves, hoped to have got on shore at the nearest point, were a little better provisioned than we were; they had at least a little wine, which supplied the place of other necessaries.

We then demanded some from them, explaining our situation, but none would assist us, not even Captain Lachaumareys, who, drinking to a kept mistress, supported by two sailors, swore he had not one drop on board. We were next desirous of addressing the boat of the governor of Senegal, where we were persuaded were plenty of provisions of every kind, such as oranges, biscuits, cakes, comfits, plums, and even the finest liqueurs; but my father opposed it, so well was he assured we would not obtain anything.

We will now turn to the condition of those on the raft, when the boats left them to themselves.

If all the boats had continued dragging the raft forward, favoured as we were by the breeze from the sea, we would have been able to have conducted them to the shore in less than two days. But an inconceivable fatality caused the generous plan to be abandoned which had been formed.

When the raft had lost sight of the boats, a spirit of sedition began to manifest itself in furious cries. They then began to regard one another with ferocious looks, and to thirst for one another's flesh. Someone had already whispered of having recourse to that monstrous extremity, and of commencing with the fattest and youngest. A proposition so atrocious filled the brave Captain Dupont and his worthy lieutenant M. L'Heureux with horror; and that courage which had so often supported them in the field of glory, now forsook them.

Among the first who fell under the hatchets of the assassins, was a young woman who had been seen devouring the body of her husband. When her turn was come, she sought a little wine as a last favour, then rose, and without uttering one word, threw herself into the sea. Captain Dupont being proscribed for having refused to partake of the sacrilegious viands on which the monsters were feeding, was saved as by a miracle from the hands of the butchers. Scarcely had they seized him to lead him to the slaughter, when a large pole, which served in place of a mast, fell upon his body; and believing that his legs were broken, they contented themselves by throwing him into the sea. The unfortunate captain plunged, disappeared, and they thought him already in another world.

Providence, however, revived the strength of the unfortunate warrior. He emerged under the beams of the raft, and clinging with all his might, holding his head above water, he remained between two enormous pieces of wood, whilst the rest of his body was hid in the sea. After more than two hours of suffering, Captain Dupont spoke in a low voice to his lieutenant, who by chance was seated near the place of his concealment. The brave L'Heureux, with eyes glistening with tears, believed he heard the voice, and saw the shade of his captain; and trembling, was about to quit the place of horror; but, O wonderful! he saw a head which seemed to draw its last sigh, he recognised it, he embraced it, alas! it was his dear friend! Dupont was instantly drawn from the water, and M. L'Heureux obtained for his unfortunate comrade again a place upon the raft. Those who had been most inveterate against him, touched at what Providence had done for him in so miraculous a manner, decided with one accord to allow him entire liberty upon the raft.

The sixty unfortunates who had escaped from the first massacre, were soon reduced to fifty, then to forty, and at last to twenty-eight. The least murmur, or the smallest complaint, at the moment of distributing the provisions, was a crime punished with immediate death. In consequence of such a regulation, it may easily be presumed the raft was soon lightened. In the meanwhile the wine diminished sensibly, and the half rations very much displeased a certain chief of the conspiracy. On purpose to avoid being reduced to that extremity, the *executive power* decided it was much wiser to *drown thirteen people*, and to get full rations, than that twenty-eight should have half rations. Merciful Heaven! what shame! After the last catastrophe, the chiefs of the conspiracy, fearing doubtless of being assassinated in their turn, threw all the arms into the sea, and swore an inviolable friendship with the heroes which the hatchet had spared.

On the 17th of July, in the morning, Captain Parnajon, commandant of the *Argus* brig, still found fifteen men on the raft. They were immediately taken on board, and conducted to Senegal. Four of the fifteen are yet alive, viz. Captain Dupont, residing in the neighbourhood of Maintenon, Lieutenant L'Heureux, since Captain, at Senegal, Savigny, at Rochefort, and Corréard, I know not where.

On the 5th of July, at ten in the morning, one hour after abandoning the raft, and three after quitting the *Medusa*, M. Lapérère, the officer of our boat, made the first distribution of provisions. Each passenger had a small glass of water and nearly the fourth of a biscuit. Each drank his allowance of water at one draught, but it was found impossible to swallow one morsel of our biscuit, it being so impregnated with seawater. It happened, however, that some was found not quite so saturated. Of these we ate a small portion, and put back the remainder for a future day. Our voyage would have been sufficiently agreeable, if the beams of the sun had not been so fierce. On the evening we perceived the shores of the Desert; but as the two chiefs (MM. Schmaltz and Lachaumareys) wished to go right for Senegal, notwithstanding we were still one hundred leagues from it, we were not allowed to land.

Several officers remonstrated, both on account of our want of provisions and the crowded condition of the boats, for undertaking so dangerous a voyage. Others urged with equal force, that it would be dishonouring the French name, if we were to neglect the unfortunate people on the raft, and insisted we should be set on shore, and whilst we waited there, three boats should return to look after the raft, and three to the wrecks of the frigate, to take up the seventeen who were left there, as well as a sufficient quantity of provisions to enable us to go to Senegal by the way of Barbary. But MM. Schmaltz and Lachaumareys, whose boats were sufficiently well provisioned, scouted the advice of their subalterns, and ordered them to cast anchor till the following morning.

They were obliged to obey these orders, and to relinquish their designs. During the night, a certain passenger, who was doubtless no doctor, and who believed in ghosts and witches, was suddenly frightened by the appearance of flames, which he thought he saw in the waters of the sea, a little way from where our boat was anchored. My father, and some others, who were aware that the sea is sometimes phosphorated, confirmed the poor credulous man in his belief, and added several circumstances which fairly turned his brain. They persuaded him the Arabic sorcerers had fired the sea to prevent us from travelling along their deserts.

On the morning of the 6th of July, at five o'clock, all the boats were underway on the route to Senegal. The boats of MM. Schmaltz and Lachaumareys took the lead along the coast, and all the expedition followed. About eight, several sailors in our boat, with threats, demanded to be set on shore; but M. Lapérère not acceding to their request, the whole were about to revolt and seize the command; but the firmness of this officer quelled the mutineers.

In a spring which he made to seize a firelock which a sailor persisted in keeping in his possession, he almost tumbled into the sea. My father fortunately was near him, and held him by his clothes, but he had instantly to quit him, for fear of losing his hat, which the waves were floating away. A short while after this slight accident, the shallop, which we had lost sight of since the morning, appeared desirous of rejoining us. We plied all hands to avoid her, for we were afraid of one another, and thought that that boat, encumbered with so many people, wished to board us to oblige us to take some of its passengers, as M. Espiau would not suffer them to be abandoned like those upon the raft.

That officer hailed us at a distance, offering to take our family on board, adding, he was anxious to take about sixty people to the Desert. The officer of our boat, thinking that this was a pretense, replied, we preferred suffering where we were. It even appeared to us that M. Espiau had hid some of his people under the benches of the shallop. But, alas! in the end we deeply deplored being so suspicious, and of having so outraged the devotion of the most generous officer of the *Medusa*.

Our boat began to leak considerably, but we prevented it as well as we could, by stuffing the largest holes with oakum, which an old sailor had had the precaution to take before quitting the frigate. At noon the heat became so strong, so intolerable, that several of us believed we had reached our last moments. The hot winds of the Desert even reached us; and the fine sand with which they were loaded, had completely obscured the clearness of the atmosphere. The sun presented a reddish disk; the whole surface of the ocean became nebulous, and the air which we breathed, depositing a fine sand, an impalpable powder, penetrated to our lungs, already parched with a burning thirst.

In this state of torment we remained till four in the afternoon, when a breeze from the northwest brought us some relief. Notwithstanding the privations we felt, and especially the burning thirst which had become intolerable, the cool air which we now began to breathe, made us in part forget our sufferings. The heavens began again to resume the usual serenity of those latitudes, and we hoped to have passed a good night. A second distribution of provisions was made; each received a small glass of water, and about the eighth part of a biscuit. Notwithstanding our meagre fare, everyone seemed content, in the persuasion we would reach Senegal by the morrow. But how vain were all our hopes, and what sufferings had we yet to endure!

At half past seven, the sky was covered with stormy clouds. The serenity we had admired a little while before, entirely disappeared, and gave place to the most gloomy obscurity. The surface of the ocean presented all the signs of a coming tempest. The horizon on the side of the Desert had the appearance of a long hideous chain of mountains piled on one another, the summits of which seemed to vomit fire and smoke. Bluish clouds, streaked with a dark copper colour, detached themselves from that shapeless heap, and came and joined with those which floated over our heads. In less than half an hour the ocean seemed confounded with the terrible sky which canopied us. The stars were hid. Suddenly a frightful noise was heard from the west, and all the waves of the sea rushed to founder our frail bark.

A fearful silence succeeded to the general consternation. Every tongue was mute; and none durst communicate to his neighbour the horror with which his mind was impressed. At intervals the cries of the children rent our hearts. At that instant a weeping and agonized mother bared her breast to her dying child, but it yielded nothing to appease the thirst of the little innocent who pressed it in vain. O night of horrors! what pen is capable to paint thy terrible picture! How describe the agonizing fears of a father and mother, at the sight of their children tossed about and expiring of hunger in a small boat, which the winds and waves threatened to engulf at every instant! Having full before our eyes the prospect of inevitable death, we gave ourselves up to our unfortunate condition, and addressed our prayers to Heaven. The winds growled with the utmost fury; the tempestuous waves arose exasperated. In their terrific encounter a mountain of water was precipitated into our boat, carrying away one of the sails, and the greater part of the effects which the sailors had saved from the *Medusa*. Our bark was nearly sunk; the females and the children lay rolling in its bottom, drinking the waters of bitterness; and their cries, mixed with the roaring of the waves and the furious north wind, increased the horrors of the scene. My unfortunate father then experienced the most excruciating agony of mind. The idea of the loss which the shipwreck had occasioned to him, and the danger which still menaced all he held dearest in the world, plunged him into a deep swoon. The tenderness of his wife and children recovered him; but alas! his recovery was to still more bitterly deplore the wretched situation of his family. He clasped us to his bosom; he bathed us with his tears, and seemed as if he was regarding us with his last looks of love.

Every soul in the boat were seized with the same perturbation, but it manifested itself in different ways. One part of the sailors remained motionless, in a bewildered state; the other cheered and encouraged one another; the children, locked in the arms of their parents, wept incessantly. Some demanded drink, vomiting the salt water which choked them; others, in short, embraced as for the last time, intertwining their arms, and vowing to die together.

In the meanwhile the sea became rougher and rougher. The whole surface of the ocean seemed a vast plain furrowed with huge blackish waves fringed with white foam. The thunder growled around us, and the lightning discovered to our eyes all that our imagination could conceive most horrible. Our boat, beset on all sides by the winds, and at every instant tossed on the summit of mountains of water, was very nearly sunk in spite of our every effort in bailing it, when we discovered a large hole in its poop. It was instantly stuffed with everything we could find— old clothes, sleeves of shirts, shreds of coats, shawls, useless bonnets, everything was employed, and secured us as far as it was possible. During the space of six hours, we rowed suspended alternately between hope and fear, between life and death. At last towards the middle of the night, Heaven, which had seen our resignation, commanded the floods to be still. Instantly the sea became less rough, the veil which covered the sky became less obscure, the stars again shone out, and the tempest seemed to withdraw. A general exclamation of joy and thankfulness issued at one instant from every mouth. The winds calmed, and each of us sought a little sleep, whilst our good and generous pilot steered our boat on a still very stormy sea.

The day at last, the day so desired, entirely restored the calm; but it brought no other consolation. During the night, the currents, the waves, and the winds had taken us so far out to sea, that, on the dawning of the 7th of July, we saw nothing but sky and water, without knowing whither to direct our course; for our compass had been broken during the tempest. In this hopeless condition, we continued to steer sometimes to the right and sometimes to the left, until the sun arose, and at last showed us the east.

On the morning of the 7th of July, we again saw the shores of the Desert, notwithstanding we were yet a great distance from it. The sailors renewed their murmurings, wishing to get on shore, with the hope of being able to get some wholesome plants, and some more palatable water than that of the sea; but as we were afraid of the Moors, their request was opposed. However, M. Lapérère proposed to take them as near as he could to the first breakers on the coast; and when there, those who wished to go on shore should throw themselves into the sea, and swim to land. Eleven accepted the proposal; but when we had reached the first waves, none had the courage to brave the mountains of water which rolled between them and the beach.

Our sailors then betook themselves to their benches and oars, and promised to be more quiet for the future. A short while after, a third distribution was made since our departure from the *Medusa*; and nothing more remained than four pints of water, and one half dozen biscuits. What steps were we to take in this cruel situation? We were desirous of going on shore, but we had such dangers to encounter. However, we soon came to a decision, when we saw a caravan of Moors on the coast. We then stood a little out to sea. According to the calculation of our commanding officer, we would arrive at Senegal on the morrow.

Deceived by that false account, we preferred suffering one day more, rather than to be taken by the Moors of the Desert, or perish among the breakers. We had now no more than a small half glass of water, and the seventh of a biscuit. Exposed as we were to the heat of the sun, which darted its rays perpendicularly on our heads, that ration, though small, would have been a great relief to us; but the distribution was delayed to the morrow. We were then obliged to drink the bitter seawater, ill as it was calculated to quench our thirst.

Must I tell it! thirst had so withered the lungs of our sailors, that they drank water salter than that of the sea! Our numbers diminished daily, and nothing but the hope of arriving at the colony on the following day sustained our frail existence. My young brothers and sisters wept incessantly for water. The little Laura, aged six years, lay dying at the feet of her mother. Her mournful cries so moved the soul of my unfortunate father, that he was on the eve of opening a vein to quench the thirst which consumed his child; but a wise person opposed his design, observing that all the blood in his body would not prolong the life of his infant one moment.

The freshness of the night-wind procured us some respite. We anchored pretty near to the shore, and, though dying of famine, each got a tranquil sleep. On the morning of the 8th of July at break of day, we took the route for Senegal. A short while after the wind fell, and we had a dead calm. We endeavoured to row, but our strength was exhausted. A fourth and last distribution was made, and, in the twinkling of an eye, our last resources were consumed. We were forty-two people who had to feed upon *six biscuits* and about *four pints* of water, with no hope of a further supply.

Then came the moment for deciding whether we were to perish among the breakers, which defended the approach to the shores of the Desert, or to die of famine in continuing our route. The majority preferred the last species of misery. We continued our progress along the shore, painfully pulling our oars. Upon the beach were distinguished several downs of white sand, and some small trees. We were thus creeping along the coast, observing a mournful silence, when a sailor suddenly exclaimed, "Behold the Moors!" We did, in fact, see various individuals upon the rising ground, walking at a quick pace, whom we took to be the Arabs of the Desert. As we were very near the shore, we stood farther out to sea, fearing that these pretended Moors, or Arabs, would throw themselves into the sea, swim out, and take us. Some hours after, we observed several people upon an eminence, who seemed to make signals to us. We examined them attentively, and soon recognised them to be our companions in misfortune. We replied to them by attaching a white handkerchief to the top of our mast.

Then we resolved to land, at the risk of perishing among the breakers, which were very strong towards the shore, although the sea was calm. On approaching the beach, we went towards the right, where the waves seemed less agitated, and endeavoured to reach it, with the hope of being able more easily to land. Scarcely had we directed our course to that point, when we perceived a great number of people standing near to a little wood surrounding the sand-hills. We recognised them to be the passengers of that boat, which, like ourselves, were deprived of provisions.

Meanwhile we approached the shore, and already the foaming surge filled us with terror. Each wave that came from the open sea, each billow that swept beneath our boat, made us bound into the air; so we were sometimes thrown from the poop to the prow, and from the prow to the poop. Then, if our pilot had missed the sea, we would have been sunk; the waves would have thrown us aground, and we would have been buried among the breakers. The helm of the boat was again given to the old pilot, who had already so happily steered us through the dangers of the storm. He instantly threw into the sea the mast, the sails, and everything that could impede our proceedings. When we came to the first landing point, several of our shipwrecked companions, who had reached the shore, ran and hid themselves behind the hills, not to see us perish; others made signs not to approach at that place; some covered their eyes with their hands; others, at last despising the danger, precipitated themselves into the waves to receive us in their arms.

We then saw a spectacle that made us shudder. We had already doubled two ranges of breakers; but those which we had still to cross raised their foaming waves to a prodigious height, then sunk with a hollow and monstrous sound, sweeping along a long line of the coast. Our boat sometimes greatly elevated, and sometimes engulfed between the waves, seemed, at the moment, of utter ruin. Bruised, battered, tossed about on all hands, it turned of itself, and refused to obey the kind hand which directed it. At that instant a huge wave rushed from the open sea, and dashed against the poop; the boat plunged, disappeared, and we were all among the waves. Our sailors, whose strength had returned at the presence of danger, redoubled their efforts, uttering mournful sounds.

Our bark groaned, the oars were broken; it was thought aground, but it was stranded; it was upon its side. The last sea rushed upon us with the impetuosity of a torrent. We were up to the neck in water; the bitter sea-froth choked us. The grapnel was thrown out. The sailors threw themselves into the sea; they took the children in their arms, returned, and took us upon their shoulders; and I found myself seated upon the sand on the shore, by the side of my stepmother, my brothers and sisters, almost dead. Everyone was upon the beach except my father and some sailors; but that good man arrived at last, to mingle his tears with those of his family and friends.

Instantly our hearts joined in addressing our prayers and praises to God. I raised my hands to Heaven, and remained some time immoveable upon the beach. Everyone also hastened to testify his gratitude to our old pilot, who, next to God, justly merited the title of our preserver. M. Dumège, a naval surgeon, gave him an elegant gold watch, the only thing he had saved from the *Medusa*.

Let the reader now recollect all the perils to which we had been exposed in escaping from the wreck of the frigate to the shores of the Desert—all that we had suffered during our four days' voyage—and he will perhaps have a just notion of the various sensations we felt on getting on shore on that strange and savage land. Doubtless the joy we experienced at having escaped, as by a miracle, the fury of the floods, was very great; but how much was it lessened by the feelings of our horrible situation!

Without water, without provisions, and the majority of us nearly naked, was it to be wondered at that we should be seized with terror on thinking of the obstacles which we had to surmount, the fatigues, the privations, the pains and the sufferings we had to endure, with the dangers we had to encounter in the immense and frightful Desert we had to traverse before we could arrive at our destination? Almighty Providence! it was in Thee alone I put my trust.

SEVEN

The Last Cruise of the *Saginaw*

George H. Read

WITH THE HOMEWARD-BOUND PENNANT FLYING FROM THE MAINMAST head and with the contractor's working party on board, we sailed from the Midway Islands on Friday, October 29, 1870, at 4 p.m. for San Francisco. We had dragged high up on the beach the scow from which the divers had worked, secured the house doors, and taken a last look at the blinding sand with thankful hearts for leaving it.

As Doctor Frank, our surgeon, and myself were walking down the beach to the last boat off to the ship, there occurred an incident which I will relate here for psychological students.

He remarked, as we loitered around the landing, that he felt greatly depressed without being able to define any cause for it and that he could not rid himself of the impression that some misfortune was impending. I tried to cheer him up; told him that the "blues" were on him, when he ought to be rejoicing instead; that we had a fair wind and a smooth sea to start us on a speedy return to the old friends in San Francisco. It was in vain, however; he expressed a firm belief that we should meet with some disaster on our voyage and I dropped the subject with a "pooh pooh."

As soon as we reached the open sea, the captain ordered the ship headed to the westward and the pressure of steam to be reduced, as with topsails set we sailed along to a light easterly breeze. It was his intention, he stated, to come within sight of Ocean Island about daylight and to verify its location by steaming around it before heading away for San Francisco.

The evening following the departure passed quietly in our wardroom quarters and in fact all over the ship. Officers and men were more than usually fatigued after the preparations for sea both on shore and on board. There was none of the general hilarity accompanying a homeward cruise. There was also a prevailing dread of a long and tedious journey of over three thousand miles, mostly to be made under sail, and we all knew the tendency of the old *Saginaw* in a headwind to make "eight points to leeward," or, as a landlubber would say, to go sideways. We occupied ourselves in stowing and securing our movables, and after the bugle sounded "Out lights" at 9 p.m. the steady tramp of the lookouts and their half-hour hail of "All's well" were all that disturbed the quiet of the night.

The night was dark, but a few stars were occasionally visible between the passing clouds. The sea continued smooth and the ship on an even keel. When I turned in at ten o'clock I had the comforting thought that by the same time tomorrow night we should be heading for San Francisco. We were making about three knots an hour, which would bring Ocean Island in sight about early dawn, so that there would be plenty of time to circumnavigate the reef and get a good offing on our course before dark.

How sadly, alas! our intentions were frustrated and how fully our surgeon's premonitions were fulfilled! My pen falters at the attempt to describe the events of the next few hours. I was suddenly awakened about three o'clock in the morning by an unusual commotion on deck; the hurried tramping of feet and confusion of sounds. In the midst of it I distinguished the captain's voice sounding in sharp contrast to his usual moderate tone, ordering the taking in of the topsails and immediately after the cutting away of the topsail halliards. Until the latter order was given I imagined the approach of a rain squall, a frequent occurrence formerly, but I knew now that some greater emergency existed, and so I hastily and partly dressed myself sufficiently to go on deck.

Just before I reached the top of the wardroom ladder I felt the ship strike something and supposed we were in collision with another vessel. The shock was an easy one at first, but was followed immediately by others of increasing force, and, as my feet touched the deck, by two severe shocks that caused the ship to tremble in every timber. The long easy swell that had been lifting us gently along in the open sea was now transformed into heavy breakers as it reached and swept over the coral reef, each wave lifting and dropping with a frightful thud the quaking ship. It seemed at each fall as though her masts and smokestack would jump from their holdings and go by the board.

To a landsman or even a professional seaman who has never experienced the sensation it would be impossible to convey a realizing sense of the feelings aroused by our sudden misfortune. There is a something even in the air akin to the terror of an earthquake shock—a condition unnatural and uncanny. The good ship that for years has safely sailed the seas or anchored in ports with a free keel, fulfilling in all respects the destiny marked out for her at her birth, suddenly and without warning enters upon her death-struggle with the rocks and appeals for help. There is no wonder that brave men—men having withstood the shock of battle and endured the hardships of the fiercest storms—should feel their nerves shaken from their first glance at the situation.

The captain had immediately followed his orders, to take in the sails that were forging us on towards the reef, by an order to back engines. Alas! the steam was too low to give more than a few turns to the wheels, and they could not overcome the momentum of the ship. In less than an hour of the fierce pounding the jagged rock broke through the hull and tore up the engine and fireroom floor; the water rushed in and reached the fires; the doom of our good ship was now apparent and sealed.

I hastily returned to my stateroom, secured more clothing, together with some of the ship's papers, then ascended to the hurricane deck to await developments or to stand by to do rescue work as ordered. I had participated in the past in drills that are called in Navy Regulations "abandoned ship." In these drills everyone on board is supposed to leave the vessel and take station as assigned in one of the ship's boats. I had only taken part in these drills during calm weather at sea, and thought it a pretty sight to see all the boats completely equipped and lying off in view of the deserted vessel. Here, however, no programme could help us. Our captain's judgment and quickness of decision must control events as they developed.

The night was clear and starlit, but we could see nothing of any land. Perhaps we had struck on some uncharted reef, and while strenuously employed in getting the boats over the side opposite the sea we waited anxiously for daylight. The scene was one for a lifelong remembrance and is beyond my power adequately and calmly to describe.

There was at first some confusion, but the stern and composed attitude of the captain and his sharp, clear orders soon brought everyone to his senses, and order was restored.

A few of the more frightened ones had at first, either through a misunderstanding or otherwise, rushed to our largest boat—the launch—hanging at the starboard quarter and partly lowered it before the act was noticed. A large combing sea came along and tore it from their hold, smashing it against the side of the ship and then carrying its remnants away with its tackles and all its fittings. This was a great loss, we felt, if we should have to take to the boats, for we did not know at that time where we were.

The same wave also carried off one of the crew, a member of the Marine Guard, who had been on the bulwarks; and whisking him seaward, returned him miraculously around the stern of the ship to the reef, where his struggles and cries attracted the notice of others. He was hauled over the lee side, somewhat bruised and water-soaked, but, judging from his remarks, apparently not realizing his wonderful escape from death.

As the night wore on, the wind increased and also the size of the breakers. The ship, which had first struck the reef "bows on," was gradually swung around until she was at first broadside to the reef, and then further until the after part, to which we were clinging, was lifted over the jagged edge of the perpendicular wall of rock. She was finally twisted around until the bow hung directly to seaward, with the middle of the hull at the edge. Thus the ship "seesawed" from stem to stern with each coming wave for an hour or more and until the forward part broke away with a loud crash and disappeared in the deep water outside. Our anchors, which had been "let go," apparently never touched bottom until the bow went with them.

All that was left of our good ship now heeled over towards the inner side of the reef; the smokestack soon went by the board and the mainmast was made to follow it by simply cutting away the starboard or seaward shrouds. Over this mast we could pass to the reef, however, and there was comparative quiet in the waters under our lee. This helped us in passing across whatever we could save from the wreck, and in this manner went three of our boats, the captain's gig, one of the cutters, and the dinghy, without much damage to them. We also secured in this way an iron lifeboat belonging to the contractor.

As the first gray streaks of dawn showed us a small strip of terra firma in the smooth water of the lagoon and not far from the reef, many a sigh of relief was heard, and our efforts were redoubled to provide some means of prolonging existence there. At any rate, we knew now where we were and could at least imagine a possible relief and plan measures to secure it.

Although the sea had robbed us of the larger part of our provisions, in the forward hold there were still some of the most important stowed within the fragment we were clinging to, which contained the bread and clothing storerooms. With daylight our task was made easier.

A line was formed across the reef and everything rescued was passed over the side and from hand to hand to the boats in the lagoon, for transfer to the island. Thus we stood waist-deep in the water, feet and ankles lacerated and bleeding, stumbling about the sharp and uneven coral rock, until five in the afternoon, and yet our spirits, which had been low in the dark, were so encouraged by a sight of a small portion of dry land and at least a temporary escape from a watery grave that now and then a jest or a laugh would pass along the line with some article that suggested a future meal.

At five o'clock in the afternoon the order was given to abandon the wreck (which was done while hoping that it would hold together until tomorrow), and as the sun went down on the "lone barren isle," all hands were "piped" by the boatswain's whistle to supper.

A half-teacup of water, half a cake of hardtack, and a small piece of boiled pork constituted our evening meal, to which was added a piece of boiled mutton that had been intended for the wardroom table.

After this frugal meal all hands were mustered upon the beach to listen to a prayer of thankfulness for our deliverance and then to a few sensible and well-timed remarks from the captain enjoining discipline, good nature, and economy of food under our trying circumstances. He told us that by the Navy Regulations he was instructed, as our commanding officer, to keep up, in such sad conditions as we were thrown into, the organization and discipline of the Service so far as applicable; that he would in the event of our rescue be held responsible for the proper administration of law and order; that officers and crew should fare alike on our scanty store of food, and that with care we should probably make out, with the help of seal meat and birds, a reduced ration for some little time. He would detail our several duties tomorrow. Then we were dismissed to seek "tired nature's sweet restorer" as best we could.

With fourteen hours of severe labor, tired, wet, and hungry, we were yet glad enough to sink to rest amid the bushes with but the sky for a canopy and a hummock of sand for a pillow. In my own case sleep was hard to win. For a long time I lay watching the stars and speculating upon the prospects of release from our island prison. Life seemed to reach dimly uncertain into the future, with shadow pictures intervening of famished men and bereaved families.

I could hear the waves within a few rods of our resting-places—there was no music in them now—lapping the beach in their restlessness, and now and then an angry roar from the outside reef, as though the sea was in rage over its failure to reach us. I realized that for more than a thousand miles the sea stretched away in every direction before meeting inhabited shores and for treble that distance to our native land; that our island was but a small dot in the vast Pacific—a dot so small that few maps give it recognition. Truly it was a dismal outlook that "tired nature" finally dispelled and that sleep transformed into oblivion; for I went to sleep finally while recalling old stories of family gatherings where was always placed a vacant chair for the loved absent one should he ever return.

On the Island

Sunday, October 30. No pretensions to the official observance of the Sabbath were made today. We always had religious services on board the ship when the weather permitted on Sunday, but today every effort has been made to further the safety of our condition.

The captain, executive officer, and many of the crew went off early to the wreck in order to make further search for supplies and equipment.

The wreck appears from the island to be about as we left it, for the wind has been light and the sea calm during the night.

I remained on shore with a few men to assist in sorting out and making a list of the articles rescued yesterday and to assemble them in the best place suitable for their preservation. We spread out in the sun the bread, bags of flour, and other dry foodstuffs, even to the smallest fragments, and it was early apparent that unless much more food was secured we shall be compelled to live upon a greatly reduced ration and that our main source of food would be the seal and brown albatross (or "goonies," as they are commonly called). Both of these seemed plentiful and are easily captured.

The seal succumb quickly to a blow upon the head, a fact we discovered early in our first visit to the Midway Islands. One of the boat's crew, when pushing off from the beach, carelessly and without intent to kill, struck a nearby seal on the head with an oar, and the next morning it was found dead, apparently not having moved from the spot. Its mate had found it and was nosing it about, while moaning in a most humanlike voice.

These seal are quite different from the Alaska fur seal, of such great value for their fur. These have a short lustreless hair, and their principal value is in the oil that is extracted by the few seal hunters who seek them. They frequently exceed two hundred pounds in weight, and are savage fighters if one can judge by the many scars found upon them. We never thought, when, a few months ago, we amused ourselves on the verandas of the Cliff House at San Francisco in watching their disporting about Seal Rock, that we should make such a close acquaintance with them.

The "goonies" also are easy to capture, although they are large and strong and a blow from the wing would break a man's limb. I measured one of them from tip to tip of wing, and it was over seven feet. They are, however, very awkward on their feet, and, having a double-jointed wing (that is, a joint in it like an elbow) can only rise from the ground when the wind is in their faces. Owing to this fact one only needs to get to the windward of them with a club and look out for the wings. We should like to add some of their eggs to our bill of fare, but dare not for fear of driving the birds away. I imagine it would take but a few of the eggs, if eatable, to go around, for I saw one at the Midways that was as large as those of the ostrich.

Fresh water will, however, apparently be our greatest cause for anxiety; for we have secured but a small supply, considering our number—ninety-three. A few breakers or kegs only, which were stowed in the boats, were secured. Rain, of course, we count upon; but to conserve our scanty supply until it comes is most necessary. Today several wells have been dug in various parts of the island, but the water found in them is near the surface and is too brackish for any use.

The old timbers of a former wreck, probably of the *Gledstanes*—the "bones" as sailors call them—lie near on the beach and look as though they would yield us fuel for a long time. Our fire, which was started last evening by a match that Mr. Bailey, the chief diver, had fortunately kept dry, has been constantly going for lack of more lighting material.

Evening. The reef party returned at sundown, reporting a strenuous day on the wreck. We all had a supper of "scouse" (a dish of pork, potato, and hardtack), and before sleeping the campsite was laid out, the sails and awnings which had come on shore temporarily set up, to our greater comfort. Besides the sails and awnings, more food supplies were captured from the after storeroom and a particularly fortunate prize secured in a small portable boiler that had been lashed to the after deck. This had been used by the contractor's party in hoisting to the scow the blasted coral from the reef, at Midway Islands.

There were also in one of the wheelhouses of the wreck some distilling coils, which the engineer's force with our chief engineer successfully rescued after hard labor, for the sea was washing through the wheelhouse with terrible force. The boiler, suspended between two boats, was successfully landed on the beach, and we are greatly encouraged at the promise of fresh water tomorrow. We secured a barrel, also, partly filled with sperm oil, and a lantern in good condition. These two articles ensure us a supply of lighting material for the cooking-fire, which can now be put out at night and much fuel saved. Considerable clothing was secured from the officers' staterooms, and I was fortunate enough to find some of mine rolled up in one of the large wet bundles; and a few soaked mattresses and blankets were also brought in. The carpenter's chest, too, came ashore intact, and altogether we feel our situation greatly improved.

Mr. Talbot tells me that they are literally "stripping" the wreck, and nothing movable will be left on it if the weather will but hold good long enough. No one stops to question the utility of an article found adrift; it is seized hastily and thrown out on the reef to be transported later to the island. Pieces of rigging, boxes of tinned coffee, canned goods, tools, crockery, sails, awnings, etc., all come to the beach in a promiscuous mass to be sorted out later.

—◦—

Tuesday, November 1. The crew was formed into several messes today, and also into watches. Each mess was provided with a tent, that for our mess (the wardroom) being made from the *Saginaw's* quarter-deck awning. Such of our dry goods and bedding as had been rescued were removed to them, and our little camp begins to take on the appearance of comfort.

The duties of every member of the ship's company have been so arranged that it is hoped and expected that no one will have much time to brood over our situation or the future.

Wednesday, November 2. The bad weather we have feared has arrived. It came on suddenly this morning from the southeast with a high wind and a heavy rainfall, and before we had been able firmly to secure the tents. After strenuous exertion, however, we saved them from being blown over, but were wet to the skin when they were finally safe in place.

Fortunately the wreck on the reef has been thoroughly explored and there is very little material there now that could be of use to us, unless it may be the timbers themselves, to help us in building a seaworthy boat should it be necessary to do so in a final effort to get away. The idea of sending a boat to the Sandwich Islands for relief has been already revolving in our minds, and today was revealed by an order from the captain to the senior officers. After a consultation singly with us, he has directed each one to file with him an opinion on the feasibility and necessity of doing so—each written opinion to be without knowledge of the others.

It is probable that the hulk will be considerably broken up before the wind and sea go down, for one can see it rise and fall with the breakers, and occasionally a piece is detached and floated across the reef into the lagoon. As soon as it is safe to launch the boats, the work of securing these pieces will be started.

The boats are now resting at the highest part of the island in the centre of the camp, for even with the protecting reef the sea in the lagoon has been so rough that combers have reached within a few feet of our tents. As I write my journal we are a wet and sad party of unfortunates.

Our captain and his boat's crew must be having an experience worse than ours, however. They left this morning in the cutter for the sandspit near and to the west of us, to collect driftwood, and are "marooned" there in the storm. They can be seen, with the glasses, huddled together beneath the upturned boat. They do not, however, seem to be in imminent danger, and have made no signals of distress; so we expect them to return as soon as the sea abates.

Thursday, November 3. It has been still too rough today to launch the boats for work in the lagoon. We have, however, busied ourselves in erecting a storehouse for the better preservation of our food supplies, and tonight have them safely under cover. Last night the rats robbed us of a box of macaroni, and, therefore, we have put our storehouse on posts and two feet above the ground with inverted pans upon the posts.

We made the acquaintance of the rats last night in our tent when a noisy fight over a piece of candle disturbed our sleep. We had seen a few of them before, but did not suppose them to be so very numerous—as on first thought there seemed to be so very little for them to eat. We now found them to have good lungs and appetites, however, and a good deal of thrashing around with boots, etc., was necessary to expel them. We discussed them before we went to sleep again in the light of a future food supply—an addition to our one-quarter ration—and the opinion was general that should the seal and goonies desert us the rats would become more valuable. At any rate, they would thrive on the refuse of the food we had now.

The captain returned this morning from his expedition and gives a sad story of their luck. They had to literally bury themselves to the neck in the sand and lie under the boat to prevent being drenched by the rain. During the height of the storm they had one streak of good luck. They found some companions that the rough sea had induced to seek the shelter of the lagoon and beach. They were large sea turtles, and he and his crew turned them on their backs to prevent their escape. Today we have them added to our food supply and they are very welcome, notwithstanding the sad plight of their captors when they returned.

We have also added to our fresh water a supply of about fifty gallons caught in the rainstorm of yesterday, and doled out an extra cupful to each person.

Sunday, November 6. We were mustered for divine service today, and it being the first Sunday of the month the roll was called and each man answered "Here" as his name was called. After that prayers were read by the captain and an extra cup of water served out from the quantity caught during the recent gale. Work was suspended so far as possible, but the lagoon being so quiet it was thought necessary to launch two of the boats and tow in some of the floating timbers. We were overjoyed thus to receive and haul up free of the water a large fragment of the old hurricane deck. We can imagine some value in almost any piece of timber, but in this particular we are confident of securing much material for the building of our future boat, it being of three-inch-thick narrow planking. We believe we can make one-and-a-half-inch stuff from it by rigging up a staging and converting our one bucksaw into a jigsaw with a man above and one below. The blacksmith believes that he can extract a good supply of nails, and in many ways it is evident that we are not going to wait supinely for the relief we hope for from our brave comrades' voyage.

Today we killed our first goonies and had some for supper. They were very tough and "fishy," and Solomon Graves, once the *Saginaw*'s cabin cook, but now "King of the Galley" on Ocean Island, says that he cooked them all day. Only a portion of the bird could be masticated. However, it was voted superior to seal, the latter being so tough that Graves has to parboil it overnight and fry it in the morning. The hardtack is exhausted, but so much of the flour has been found good that we are to have a tablespoonful every other day and the same quantity of beans on the alternate days as substitutes for the hardtack. A cup of coffee or tea every day for the morning meal. Supper we have at five.

We had a luxury after supper. There are nine of us in the wardroom mess who smoke, and each of us was generously supplied with a cigar by Passed Assistant Engineer Blye, whose chest was rescued the second day; it contained a box of five hundred Manila cigars.

Monday, November 7. The mainmast is ready to raise tomorrow. An excavation has been made at the highest point of the island, near the captain's tent, and the mast rolled up to it with the rope guys ready to hold it upright. The carpenter's gang have been busy all day in sorting out material for the gig's deck and for raising her sides eight inches.

While the weather is fine, there seems to be a considerable swell at sea from the late storm, and the wreck is gradually, as it were, melting away. Today a piece of the hull floated towards us and a boat was sent after it. When it reached the beach I recognized the remains of my stateroom, with twisted bolts protruding from the edge where it had been wrenched away from the rest of the hull. I viewed mournfully the remnant of my longtime home and reflected how it had once been my protection and that now fate had turned me out of its shelter.

Many of the hopes that were bred within its wooden walls have been shattered by its destruction, and I thought it would be appropriate to bury it on the beach with an epitaph above it showing the simple words "Lights out" which I had so often heard at its door when the ship's corporal made his nightly rounds at the "turning-in" hour. However, it was valuable even in its ruin for building and burning material. Besides, we are not ready yet to think of anything like a funeral.

Sunday, November 13. Ship breaking up rapidly and boats out to pick up driftwood. Had prayers (read by Captain S.) at 3 p.m., and he addressed us with remarks as to necessity in our situation of working on Sabbath. Thousands of rats about. Put extra night watch on storehouse, for fear of further depredations.

Thursday, November 17. Blowing hard from north. Tea at 7 a.m. The gig anchored off shore. Mr. Bailey and I fixed up the well where fresh water was found when mast fell; goodbye to the old condenser. "The little cherub that sits up aloft" doing good work for us all.

The Sailing of the Gig

Friday, November 18. The weather has been fine since the breaking up of the storm of the second.

As to work, everyone has had his duties portioned out to him, and there is no doubt of the captain's wisdom in providing thus an antidote to homesickness or brooding. Faces are—some of them—getting "peaked," and quite a number of the party have been ill from lack of power to digest the seal meat; but there are no complaints, we all fare alike. Medicines are not to hand, but a day or two of abstinence and quiet generally brings one around again. In the evenings, when we gather around the smoking lamp after supper, there are frequent discussions over our situation and prospects.

They are, however, mostly sanguine in tone, and it is not uncommon to hear the expression "when we get home." No one *seems* to have given up his hope of eventual relief. It has been very noticeable, too, at such times that no matter where the conversation begins it invariably swings around, before the word is passed to "douse the glim," to those things of which we are so completely deprived—to narratives of pleasant gatherings—stories of banquets and festival occasions where toothsome delicacies were provided. It would seem as though these reminiscences were given us as a foil to melancholy, and they travel along with us into our dreams.

Upon one point we are all agreed, that we are very fortunate in being wrecked in so agreeable a climate, where heavy clothing is unnecessary. The temperature has been, aside from the storm we had soon after the landing, between seventy and seventy-five degrees during the day and around fifty degrees at night. We are very sensible of the discomforts that would be ours if tumbled upon some of the islands of the northern ocean in winter.

The moonlit nights have been grand, and calculated to foster romance in a sailor's thoughts were the surroundings appropriate. As it is, the little cheer we extract from them is in the fact that we see the same shining face that is illuminating the home of our loved ones.

Often in my corner of the tent, Mr. Foss and I pass what would be a weary hour otherwise, over a game of chess, the pieces for which he has fashioned from gooney bones and blocks of wood.

Mr. Main has made a wonderful nautical instrument—a sextant— from the face of the *Saginaw's* steam gauge, together with some broken bits of a stateroom mirror and scraps of zinc. Its minute and finely drawn scale was made upon the zinc with a cambric needle, and the completed instrument is the result of great skill and patience. Mr. Talbot has tested it and pronounces it sufficiently accurate for navigating purposes.

Another officer has made a duplicate of the official chart of this part of the Pacific, and still another has copied all the Nautical Almanac tables necessary for navigation.

I have been directed by the captain to make a selection from the best-preserved supplies in the storehouse most suitable for boat service, and calculate that Talbot will have the equivalent of thirty-five days' provender at one-half rations, although many of the articles are not in the regular ration tables.

This morning the boat was surrounded by many men and carried bodily into water that was deep enough to float her. There she was anchored and the stores carried out to her. Mr. Butterworth, standing waist deep in the water, put on the last finishing touches while she was afloat by screwing to the gunwales the rowlocks for use in calm weather.

There was expended from store-book the following articles: ten breakers (a small keg) of water, five days' rations of hardtack sealed in tin, ten days of the same in canvas bags, two dozen small tins of preserved meat, five tins (five pounds each) of desiccated potato, two tins of cooked beans, three tins of boiled wheaten grits, one ham, six tins of preserved oysters, ten pounds of dried beef, twelve tins of lima beans, about five pounds of butter, one gallon of molasses, twelve pounds of white sugar, four pounds of tea and five pounds of coffee. A small tin cooking apparatus for burning oil was also improvised and furnished.

I had intended putting on board twenty-five pounds of boiled rice in sealed tins, but discovered one of the tins to be swollen just before the provisions were started off. Hastily the tins were opened and the rice found unfit for use. The desiccated potatoes were at once served out in place of the rice, the cans scalded and again sealed.

With the navigating instruments and the clothing of the voyagers on board, the boat was pronounced ready and we went to dinner. There was little conversation during the meal. The impending departure of our shipmates hung like a pall of gloom over us at the last and was too thought-absorbing for speech. Talbot seemed to be the most unconcerned of all, but as I watched him I felt that the brave fellow was assuming it to encourage the rest of us. I had a long friendly talk with him, last evening, during which he seemed thoroughly to estimate the risk he was to take, and entrusted to me his will to be forwarded to his parents in Kentucky in case he should not survive the journey.

The hour set for the boat's departure (four o'clock) arrived and we were all mustered upon the beach. Prayers were read by the captain, after which final farewells were said and the brave men who were to peril their lives for us waded off to the gig and climbed on board. They quickly stepped the little masts, spread the miniature sails, raised their anchor, and slowly gaining headway stood off for the western channel through the reef. With full hearts and with many in tears, we gave them three rousing cheers and a tiger, which were responded to with spirit, and we watched them until the boat faded from sight on the horizon to the northward.

As I write this by the dim light of a candle the mental excitement due from the parting with our shipmates seems still to pervade the tent and no one is thinking of turning in.

Mr. Bailey, the foreman of the contractor's party, came into the tent soon after we had gathered for the evening. He had in his hand a small book and on his face a smile as he passed it around, showing each one an open page of the book; when he reached me I saw it was a pocket Bible opened at the fifty-first chapter of Isaiah, where Mr. B.'s finger rested under the words, "The isles shall wait upon me and on my arm shall they trust." He did not speak until I had read, and then said he had opened the Bible by chance, as was his habit every evening. Poor Bailey! We all feel very sorry for him. He is a fine character, well advanced in years; and having by economy accumulated considerable money, had bought himself a home, before coming out, to which he was intending to retire when this contract was completed.

By invitation from the captain I accompanied him in walking around the entire island, avoiding, however, the extreme point to the westward, where albatross were nesting. He talked but little, and I saw that his eyes often turned to the spot where the gig had disappeared from view. As we separated in front of his little tent he said with a voice full of pathos to me, "Goodnight, Paymaster; God grant that we see them again."

I find that I have so far omitted to give the personnel of Talbot's crew. As stated before there were many volunteers, but the surgeon was ordered to select from a list given him four of the most vigorous and sturdy of the applicants and report their names to the captain. There was considerable rivalry among them. In fact I was accidentally a witness to a hard-fought wrestling match between two of the crew who sought the honor of going and risking their lives. The defeated one, I was told, was to waive his claim in favor of the victor.

WAITING

Thursday, November 24. Thanksgiving Day—at home; the noble bird, roast turkey, has not graced our tarpaulin-covered table. He has been replaced by a tough section of albatross. Nor was there any expression of thanks at the mess table until one of the officers, having finished the extra cup of coffee served in honor of the day, said, "Say, fellows, let's be thankful that we are alive, well and still with hope."

Last evening about nine o'clock we were given another flurry of excitement over expected relief. The storehouse sentry reported a light to the eastward and in a "jiffy" our tent was empty. Sure enough, there was a bright light close to the horizon which, as we watched, appeared to grow larger and nearer. The captain was called, and I joined him with Mr. Cogswell (our new executive officer since Talbot left) in front of his tent. After watching the light for a few minutes, the captain turned to us and said, "Gentlemen, it is only a star rising and the atmosphere is very clear. Better turn in again"; and he entered the tent.

Sunday, November 27. Last Sunday and today we have had divine service led by the captain reading the prayers of the Episcopal ritual.

Work has been steadily pushed on the schooner. The keel has been hewed out of the *Saginaw's* late topmast and is blocked up on the beach. We are ripping the old deck planks in two with our old bucksaw and one handsaw, and while it is slow work we can see our boat planking ahead of us when the frame is ready. The schooner is to be forty feet long, of centre-board, flat-bottomed type, and the captain has settled upon her shape and dimensions after experimenting with a small model in company with the contractor's carpenter, who has had experience in boat-building.

This morning about sunrise the camp was roused to excitement by the loud cry of "Sail ho!" I found on joining the crowd at the landing that the captain had ordered a boat launched and her crew were already pulling away in a northerly direction.

I could see nothing from the crow's nest at the masthead, but the statement of one of the crew that he had seen a sail was positive; and the camp was full of a nervous expectancy until nine o'clock, when the boat returned with the disappointing news that the alleged sail was only a large white rock on the north end of the reef that had reflected the sun's rays. As the sun rose to a greater angle the reflection disappeared. An order was at once given out that no one should again alarm the camp before permission from the captain was obtained.

Sunday, December 25. Christmas Day!! Merry Christmas at home, but dreary enough here! Still the salutation was passed around in a halfhearted manner. It is the first day since the wreck that depression of spirit has been so contagious and camp-wide. The religious services, as we stood in the sand bareheaded (some barefooted also), hardly seemed to fit our situation, and the voice of the captain was subdued and occasionally tremulous. I had donned my best uniform coat, which had come ashore when the wreck was stripped, and tried also to put on a cheerful face. No use; I could not keep up the deceit, and I slipped out of line before the service was ended, to change back to the blue sailor shirt and working clothes. I felt that I had been "putting on airs." It has been my first really blue day, for the pictures in my mind of the Christmas festivities at home but emphasized the desolation of the life here.

Strangely enough, Doctor Frank has seemed to a certain extent to be more cheerful than usual. It seems queer that he, pessimist as he appeared to me when he predicted disaster before we sailed from the Midway Islands, should now be the optimist and attempt to dispel our gloom. Some expert in psychical research may be able to discern, as I cannot, why the doctor's belief in Talbot's success should now have influence enough to change my melancholy into a firmer hope than ever.

We borrowed the chart from the captain and followed in pure imagination the course of the gig; and when we folded it, the doctor said that he believed Talbot had arrived at the end of his journey and we should be relieved. Talbot has now been away thirty-seven days, and our several estimates of the time he would consume have been between thirty and forty.

Every afternoon, when work is suspended for the day and we have repaired to the tent, the expression of Talbot's whereabouts is the first note of discussion; as though it had not been in our minds all the long weary day of work.

As the possible failure of Talbot's brave effort begins to enter our calculations, the greater is the exertion to provide in the near future another avenue of escape. So, with gradually weakened strength, owing to lack of sustaining food, the labor we find arduous and exhausting; I, being included in the carpenter's gang on the schooner, realize that fact thoroughly. Yesterday the captain and myself made another circuit of the island, and both were glad to rest on the return to the camp.

The captain has ordered the cutter to be also fitted for a voyage to the Midway Islands. There he intends to have a sign erected stating, briefly, our situation; to serve in case the Navy Department should send (as we expect it will) a searching vessel for us. Twice every day I have climbed the rope ladder on the mast and searched with anxious eyes through my rescued opera glasses the shipless horizon; sometimes with such a strain of nerves and hope that phantom vessels plague my vision. The loneliness and solitude of the vast expanse of water surrounding us is beyond expression. Truly, it is the desert of the Pacific Ocean, and more dangerous than that upon the land, for there are no trails or guideposts for the weary traveler when the sky is obscured. One might easily fancy that beyond the line of the horizon there exists only infinite space. As the Prince of the Happy Valley observes in "Rasselas," after an ocean voyage, "There is no variety but the difference between rest and motion."

I do not remember the cry of "Sail ho!" during all of our cruising between the Hawaiian and Midway Islands save in the vicinity of the former.

The rats are more in evidence of late. At first small and timid, they are now growing larger and bolder; running about and over us in the tents during the night. We are getting quite accustomed to their visits, however, and, rolling ourselves in blankets or whatever covering we have, pay small attention to them. If we stay here, though, our attention will become more acute; for they begin to loom up in importance as a food supply.

The seal, on the contrary, are growing less in numbers, although great care has been taken not to frighten them away. Also, we have not lately attempted fishing on the reef, for fear of reducing their food. We have been prevented from trying the eggs of the albatross, that their nesting may continue without interruption. They will probably leave, too, when the hatching season is over and the young have been taught to fly.

So far as our present ration is concerned, with the exception of beans, flour, and coffee from which our small daily issue is made, we are situated as though no provisions had been rescued from the wreck; for the captain has wisely ordered that all the rest must be held intact to provision the schooner. So, with all the nerve we can muster, the work on the schooner is being pushed. Today the frame stands ready for the planking, and the captain thinks that in another week her mast can be ready for stepping.

Sunday, January 1, 1871. New Year's Day—"Happy New Year"! I think no one but the marine sentry at the storehouse saw the birth of the new year or cared to see the new year come in. For myself I hope there will be no more holidays to chronicle here except it may be the one that liberates us from these surroundings. They have—the three we have had here—aroused too many sombre reflections in contrasting those of the past with the present.

Talbot has now been away forty-three days and it seems almost beyond probability that he should have reached the Sandwich Islands before the food was exhausted. There is a lingering hope, however, that some delay in starting relief for us may have occurred or that he may have reached some island other than Oahu, where Honolulu is situated, and that communication with Oahu may be limited. We are "threshing out" the whole situation tonight in earnest discussion between the sanguine and non-sanguine members of the mess.

Rescued

Tuesday, January 3. At midnight. It is near an impossibility sanely and calmly to write up my journal tonight—my nerves are shaken and my pencil falters. I have climbed into the storehouse to get away from the commotion in the tent and all over the camp. No one can possibly sleep, for I can see through a rent in the canvas men dancing around a huge fire on the highest point of the island, and hear them cheering and singing while feeding the fire with timbers that we have been regarding as worth their weight in coin. To a looker-on the entire camp would seem to have gone crazy. I will tell what I can now and the rest some other time.

At half-past three this afternoon I was working on the schooner near Mr. Mitchell, one of the carpenters of the contractor's party. I was handing him a nail when I noticed his eyes steadily fixed on some point seaward. He paid no attention to me, and his continued gaze induced me to turn my eyes in the same direction to find what was so attractive as to cause his ignoring me. I saw then, too, something that held my gaze. Far off to the northeast and close to the horizon there was something like a shadow that had not been there when I had last visited the lookout. It appeared as a faintly outlined cloud, and as we both watched with idle tools in our hands it seemed to grow in size and density. Very soon he spoke in a low voice, as though not wishing to give a false alarm: "Paymaster, I believe that is the smoke of a steamer," and after another look, "I am sure of it"; and then arose a shout that all could hear: "Sail ho!"

The order concerning alarms was forgotten in his excitement, but as the captain stood near and his face beamed with his own joy, no notice was taken of the violation. He directed me at once to visit the lookout, and I did so, rapidly securing my glasses. By the time I reached the top of the mast I could see that the shadow we had watched was developing into a long and well-marked line of smoke and that a steamer was headed to the westward in front of it. I notified the eager, inquiring crowd at the foot of the mast and still kept my glasses trained on the steamer until her smokestack came into view. She was not heading directly for us, and I cannot describe the anxiety with which I watched to see if she was going to pass by—my heart was thumping so that one could hear it. I could not believe she would fail to see our signal of distress that waved above me, and pass on to leave us stricken with despair.

When she arrived at a point nearly to the north of us, I saw her change her course until her masts were in line, and then I shouted the fact to those below, for it was evident she was bound for Ocean Island.

The long dreary suspense was over; our relief was near, and I slid down the Jacob's ladder, pale and speechless. The few moments of tense watchfulness had seemed to me like hours of suspense, and it is slight wonder that it took some time to recover my speech. When I did so I acquainted the captain with all I had seen. By the time I had completed my statement the steamer was in view from the ground, and then I witnessed such a scene as will never be forgotten.

Rough-looking men—many of them having faced the shocks of storm and battle—all of them having passed through our recent misfortunes without a murmur of complaint—were embracing each other with tears of joy running down their cheeks, while laughing, singing, and dancing.

By the time we had finished supper she was very near and was recognized as the *Kilauea*, a vessel belonging to the King of the Sandwich Islands. She came within half a mile of the reef where the *Saginaw* was wrecked and dipped her flag and then slowly steamed away in a southerly direction. This manoeuvre we understood, for, as it was getting late in the day, our rescuers were evidently intending to return tomorrow.

Thursday, January 5. The *Kilauea* appeared at daybreak and anchored near the west entrance of the lagoon, and very soon after her captain came to our landing-place in a whaleboat. I recognized in him an old Honolulu friend—Captain Thomas Long, a retired whaling captain—and as he stepped from his boat, we gave him three rousing cheers while we stood at attention near the fringe of bushes around the camp. Captain Sicard went down the beach alone to receive him, and after a cordial greeting, they conferred together for a few minutes. Together they came towards us apparently in sober thought, and Captain Sicard held up his hand as a signal for silence. He uncovered his head and said, in a tremulous voice, "Men, I have the great sorrow to announce to you that we have been saved at a great sacrifice. Lieutenant Talbot and three of the gig's crew are dead. The particulars you will learn later; at present, Captain Long is anxious for us to remove to the *Kilauea* as quickly as possible."

He bowed his head and a low murmur of grief passed along our line. From a cheering, happy crowd we were as in an instant changed to one of mourning. All the dreary waiting days we had passed seemed to fade into insignificance in the face of this great sorrow.

—◆—

Our captain has made the following report to the Secretary of the Navy, which adds to and confirms the story of the lone survivor of the gig:

Honolulu, Hawaiian Islands,
January 18, 1871.
Sir: I forward herewith the brief report called for by regulation of the death of Lieutenant J.G. Talbot (and also three of the crew of the United States Steamer Saginaw*) at the island of Kauai (Hawaiian Group).*

I feel that something more is due to these devoted and gallant friends, who so nobly risked their lives to save those of their shipmates, and I beg leave to report the following facts regarding their voyage from Ocean Island and its melancholy conclusion.

The boat (which had been the Saginaw*'s gig and was a whaleboat of very fine model) was prepared for the voyage with the greatest care. She was raised on the gunwale eight inches, decked over, and had new sails, etc.*

The boat left Ocean Island November 18, 1870. The route indicated by me to Lieutenant Talbot was to steer to the northward "by the wind" until he got to the latitude of about 32 degrees north, and then to make his way to the eastward until he could "lay" the Hawaiian Islands with the northeast trade winds. He seems to have followed about that route. The boat lost her sea anchor and oars in a gale of wind and a good deal of her provision was spoiled by salt water. The navigation instruments, too, were of but little use, on account of the lively motions of the boat. When she was supposed to be in the longitude of Kauai she was really about one and one half degrees to the westward; thus, instead of the island of Kauai she finally sighted the rock Kauhulaua (the southwestern point of land in the group) and beat up from thence to the island of Kauai. She was hove off the entrance of Hanalei Bay during part of the night of Monday, December 19, and in attempting to run into the bay about 2:30 a.m. she got suddenly into the breakers (which here made a considerable distance from the shore) and capsized.

I enclose herewith a copy of the deposition of William Halford, coxswain, the only survivor of this gallant crew; his narrative being the one from which all accounts are taken. I have not seen him, personally, as he left here before my arrival.

Peter Francis, quartermaster, and John Andrews, coxswain, were washed overboard at once and disappeared. Lieutenant Talbot was washed off the boat, and when she capsized he clung to the bottom and tried to climb up on it, going to the stern for that purpose; the boat gave a plunge and Halford thinks that the boat's gunwale or stern must have struck Mr. Talbot in the forehead as he let go his hold and went down.

James Muir was below when the boat struck the breakers, and does not appear to have come out of her until she had rolled over once. He must have suffered some injury in the boat, as he appears to have been out of his mind and his face turned black immediately after his death. As will be seen by Halford's statement, Muir reached shore, but died of exhaustion on the way to the native huts.

The body of John Andrews did not come on shore until about December 20. All clothes had been stripped from it. The body of Peter Francis has never been recovered.

The bodies are buried side by side at Hanalei (Kauai). The service was read over them in a proper manner. Suitable gravestones will be erected over them by subscription of the officers and crew of the Saginaw.

As soon as we had gotten on Ocean Island after the Saginaw's *wreck, Lieutenant Talbot volunteered to take this boat to Honolulu, and the rest volunteered as soon as it was known that men might perhaps be wanted for such service.*

Mr. Talbot was a very zealous and spirited officer. I had observed his excellent qualities from the time of his joining the Saginaw *(September 23, 1870) in Honolulu. During the wreck and afterwards he rendered me the greatest assistance and service by his fine bearing, his cheerfulness, and devotion to duty. His boat was evidently commanded with the greatest intelligence, fortitude, and gallantry and with the most admirable devotion. May the Service always be able to find such men in the time of need.*

The men were fine specimens of seamen—cool and brave, with great endurance and excellent physical strength. They were, undoubtedly, those best qualified in the whole party on Ocean Island to perform such a service. Both Lieutenant Talbot and his men had very firm confidence in their boat and looked forward with cheerfulness to the voyage. Such men should be the pride of the Navy, and the news of their death cast a deep gloom over the otherwise cheerful feelings with which the Kilauea *was welcomed at Ocean Island.*

I do not know that I sufficiently express my deep sense of their devotion and gallantry; words seem to fail me in that respect.

Previous to the sailing of the boat from Ocean Island I had enlisted John Andrews and James Muir as seamen for one month. Since I have ascertained their fate I have ordered them to be rated as petty officers (in ratings allowed to most of the "fourth rates"), as I have thought that all the crew of that boat should have stood on equal footing as regards the amount they might be entitled to in case of disaster, as they all incurred the same risk.

Andrews and Muir belonged to the party of Mr. G.W. Townsend (the contractor at Midway Islands), and it was made a condition, by them, of their enlistment that it should not interfere with their contract with Mr. Townsend. It was intended as the security of their families against the risk incurred while performing the great service for the shipwrecked party. I have forwarded their enlistment papers to the Bureau of Equipment and Recruiting.

I am very respectfully,
Your obedient Servant,
Montgomery Sicard,
Lieut. Comdr. U.S.N. Comd'g.
Hon. George M. Robeson,
Secretary of the Navy.

EIGHT

Treacherous Passage

Douglas A. Campbell

THE SEA WAS IN A FURIOUS MOOD. PILED ON ITS SURFACE WERE GREAT, gray waves, living monsters who could humble even the greatest warships. Yet, the USS *Flier* was but a submarine, at about 300 feet, one of the smaller vessels in the navy. Even when submerged, it pitched and rolled like a slender twig. But inside *Flier* were no ordinary sailors. They were submariners: men—most of them quite young—selected from the ranks for their virtues of fearlessness and its companion trait, optimism. Their mood was bright. Despite the beastly roar and hiss of the sea above them, none believed that on this day his death was at hand.

The Reaper might come later, when their boat reached the actual battle lines in this, the third year of World War II. And probably not then, either, they thought. The momentum of the conflict had turned in their favor. There was a sense, pervasive on board, that destiny was with the Allies. Everyone expected to be around for the final victory. These were young men—many of them green—led by a handful of sailors creased by the experience of having survived at sea. Death was for someone else, the enemy, even on January 16, 1944, even on the Pacific Ocean, the greatest naval battleground in history, a place where tens of thousands of Americans had already died.

But the men aboard the *Flier* could not ignore the thrashing as she bucked and twisted. For the one young cowboy in the crew, it had to make him think rodeo bull. He and his mates joked uneasily about the sobriety of the welders who had built the submarine back in Groton, Connecticut.

In these angry seas they approached the atoll known as Midway, one of the navy's refueling depots. Once beyond Midway, their first wartime patrol aboard *Flier* would begin, and their record—distinguished or dreadful—would be tallied in tons of enemy shipping sunk. With young hearts and a sense of invincibility, they knew that the slamming of their submarine by the sea was only a tune-up for the coming combat. And they had no fear.

On August 12, the now-battle-tested *Flier* approached Sibutu Passage like a slugger stepping into the batter's box. On the far side of this strait was the Sulu Sea, nearly 90,000 square miles of unbroken blue water shaped roughly like a baseball diamond. Sibutu Passage was home plate. The opposing team—the Japanese soldiers and sailors—had taken all the land around that diamond two years earlier. They were scattered along the first-base line, a string of islands called the Sulu Archipelago that ended in Mindanao, more than 200 miles to the northeast. More Japanese troops were strung along the islands from first base to second—Mindoro, at the top of the diamond, 500 miles due north. The enemy also held third base—the small island of Balabac to the northwest. And the huge island nation of Borneo, due west of Sibutu Passage, was thick with supporting troops, like the bench-dwellers in the dugout. Throughout the more than 7,000 Philippine Islands and their Indonesian and Malaysian neighbors, the Japanese navy and army were arrayed in what until now had been an almost impenetrable defense. Americans entered the Sulu Sea only by submarine, and when they did, they knew it was kill or be killed in this deadly World Series.

Flier's general orders, drafted back in Fremantle, became specific on the evening of August 13 as the submarine approached Balabac Strait. The word came around dinnertime, the normal hour for submarine headquarters in Australia to broadcast the war news along with any special instructions for the submarines on patrol. On this, the third consecutive day, there was a message for the submarine *Robalo*, which was scheduled to return from its most recent patrol. The message asked for the boat's location and estimated time of arrival in Fremantle. There was no urgency in the transmission. A returning submarine could easily be a few days late.

There was a message for *Flier*, as well. When the radioman's message was typed into the machine, the officer informed the captain, Commander John Crowley, of the new orders. The submarine *Puffer*, which had been patrolling in the northern Philippines, had encountered a Japanese convoy heading south. *Puffer* had sent torpedoes into several of the ships in the convoy and was now trailing "cripples," the message said. The rest of the convoy, thwarted by *Puffer* from entering Mindoro Strait on the northern end of Palawan, was now traveling southwest, along the western shore of Palawan in the South China Sea. Until now, *Flier*'s assignment had been to patrol the South China Sea, looking particularly for four Japanese submarines making supply runs from Vietnam. The new orders directed *Flier* to go after *Puffer*'s convoy. There was no need for Crowley to change course. *Flier* was already headed for Balabac Strait, and that would take the submarine right into the path of the approaching convoy.

Crowley was energized. The patrol had just begun and already there were targets. The word was passed along by intercom, and the crew knew they were back in the war.

On this evening, Baumgart had lookout duty after dinner, so he donned a pair of red glasses after seven o'clock and wore them for a half hour before he went to the control room. At eight o'clock, he climbed the ladders up through the conning tower. The glasses, filtering the harsh incandescent submarine lighting, prepared his eyes for scanning the darkened ocean. He was wearing his navy denims and boots. The warmth of a night in the tropics required nothing else. And despite his continuing anger over the way he had been assigned this duty, he was beginning to enjoy the hours he spent standing on the A-frame above the deck, cooled by the breeze as *Flier* made eighteen knots across the surface.

The conning tower was crowded with its usual complement of officers and crew. Jim Liddell, the executive and navigation officer, stood at the foot of the ladder leading to the bridge so that he could talk with Crowley, whose stool was on deck beside the hatch. Jim Russo stood beside Liddell, helping him with the charts. Arthur Gibson Howell was at the rear of the compartment, operating the radar. Beside him, Charles Pope, the hero who nearly drowned on the trip between Midway and Hawaii, ran the sonar.

Howell's radar presented him with an image of the nearest shoreline, many miles away. They had traveled on the surface throughout the day and had seen neither Japanese ships nor aircraft, and the radar screen still showed no enemy threats. The night was going as easily as had the day.

Admiral Ralph W. Christie's orders directing *Flier* through Balabac Strait remained unchanged by the message the radioman had transcribed earlier. Crowley was to take the deepest water route through the strait that he could. In deep water, it was assumed, mines could not be anchored. Specifically, the orders directed Crowley to use the Nasubata Channel, one of eight channels between the Sulu and South China seas allowing east and westbound ships to pass through the reef-strewn Balabac Strait. Nasubata Channel was the deepest—more than 500 feet deep in spots— and the broadest, with about five miles' leeway between Roughton Island's reefs to the north and Comiran Island to the south.

As he approached the channel, Crowley had several concerns, as would any skipper. While the ability to navigate safely around natural obstructions such as reefs was always a consideration, in wartime a captain had two more problems to solve. He had to give himself enough room to maneuver if an enemy ship attacked, and he also had to be wary of shallow water where mines could be anchored. Roughton Island's extensive reefs to the north took away maneuvering room and presented a navigation problem. Crowley, talking the matter over with Liddell through the conning-tower hatch, decided he would try a more southerly route through the channel. If he stayed in fifty fathoms—300 feet or more of water—Crowley believed *Flier* would pass through the channel untroubled.

Mines were the only military threat Crowley felt he faced that night. He trusted his radar and its operator, Chief Howell, and felt the device could find a target the size of a surfaced submarine—with the possible exception of a midget submarine—at a range of more than three miles. Unless the Japanese had developed a superior night periscope, he believed that on a night as dark as this one, a submarine could not make a submerged attack. And as Howell reported from below what he was seeing on the radar, Crowley was convinced the only things out there in the dark were islands and mountains, a few of which he knew harbored enemy soldiers. *Flier* could make it through.

Chief Howell relayed a constant stream of radar readings to Liddell, who passed them along to the skipper. And Chief Pope, watching the sonar, gave depth readings. With the radar showing the nearest land about 5,000 yards away, *Flier* was traveling in sixty-five to ninety fathoms of ocean when Pope reported a reading of forty-one fathoms. *Flier* wasn't about to scrape bottom, but the depth was shallow enough to raise Crowley's concern about mines. He asked Liddell, a veteran of a Philippine tour before the war, what he thought.

Crowley was standing in the forward end of the bridge, leaning over the open hatch in the bridge floor to talk with Liddell about taking a new course, when the explosion came. The blast caused the entire submarine to whip to one side and then snap back like an angry stallion trying to throw its rider. Crowley felt the violent motion, but the concussion was without sound, like the thunder from the electrical storms that played their lightning fingers across those distant mountains.

Jim Russo's job had been simply to help handle the conning-tower charts. He was at Liddell's side when the explosion rocked the boat as if it had rammed a wall. Instinctively, he looked down at the hatch to the control room. Something slammed into his cheek below his eye, ripping his flesh like a bullet. A shaft of air was venting straight up from below, blasting out through the hatch to the bridge. Blood was draining down his cheek when Russo felt himself lifted by the column of air, along with Liddell, the 200-pound ex-football-player, straight up to the bridge. Once above deck, Russo—by instinct and without hesitation—followed Liddell, whose shirt had been ripped off by the blast, to the rear of the bridge where, at the railing, they dove into the ocean. When Russo turned around in the water, *Flier* was gone.

Wesley Miller, standing on the A-frame above the bridge, was nearly thrown from his watch but managed to hook his legs over a railing to avoid falling. He was confused. Somehow, he had lost his binoculars, and he was concerned about the discipline that would result. Then there was screaming coming from below and air was blasting out of the hatch in the bridge floor under him. He stood frozen on the A-frame for an instant, although it seemed longer, until he heard someone yell, "Abandon ship!" and saw the bow of the submarine go under. Then the ocean was swelling around him, dragging him down into its darkness. The radio antenna had snagged him. Miller struggled to free himself and then swam and swam, reaching for the surface. Then he was alone in the water, and the submarine was gone.

Al Jacobson, lost in his reverie, watching the lightning and the mountains silhouetted in the darkness, felt the blast of air and, curiously, found Lieutenant Reynolds standing on the deck beside him, complaining that his side hurt. Jacobson told Reynolds to lie down, and then he crouched over the lieutenant, hoping to help him. He assumed that an air bank, used to store compressed air for use in diving and surfacing, had blown, and he told Reynolds to lie still. But as he talked with Reynolds, he saw Ensign Mayer and Ed Casey diving over *Flier*'s side. Just then, water rose around Jacobson and Reynolds, and the submarine sank below them, sucking them down with it. The image in Jacobson's mind was of the two huge propellers at the rear of the boat, still spinning as they passed him, slicing him to bits. He struggled to swim up and away from his death. It took a few seconds before he surfaced in a slick of diesel fuel that floated on warm, calm seas. Baseball-size chunks of cork from inside *Flier* floated around him. He could feel them. But there was no light to see what, or who, else was there.

Crowley, who had been standing to port at the front of the bridge, saw a geyser shoot toward the sky from the forward starboard side of the submarine. The next thing he knew, he was standing against the aft railing of the bridge, near Jacobson. He ran forward to trigger the collision alarm that was mounted on the bulwark just above the conning-tower hatch. When he got there, he smelled diesel fuel. He looked down into the conning tower but it was dark. There was no time!

"Abandon ship!"

The skipper's yell carried across the deck and perhaps a short way down into the submarine, where many in the crew already were being thrown about by the air blast and the flooding that made Crowley's command superfluous. On the bridge, the skipper felt the shaft of air rising from within the submarine, carrying with it the sounds of rushing water and the screams of seventy-one men trapped inside. Some men were climbing the ladder from the conning tower, just in time because the deck was heading under, *Flier's* engines still driving it like a train entering a tunnel. Crowley found himself in a raging stream of water as the sea poured around the bulwark and into the bridge, and then he was washed out the rear of the bridge, into the sea. In a matter of just twenty seconds after the blast, *Flier* was gone, and after its passing, the ocean was calm. The dead sailors of the Japanese minelayer *Tsugaru* had once again struck from their graves.

A mine had touched the side of *Flier*—just a glancing blow, but enough to trigger its explosives. The geyser had appeared near the rear of the forward torpedo room. The explosion, quiet as it was on the surface, would have been enough to punch a hole through the submarine's superstructure and one or more of its watertight welded-steel compartments.

On this night, Crowley had ordered battle stations for the conning tower, but the rest of the crew was not on alert. If the watertight doors were not dogged in place with their big handles, the blast from the mine—having opened a huge hole in *Flier's* side—flooded the forward torpedo room and the officers' quarters immediately. At the same time, a rupturing of the tanks full of compressed air sent a shockwave through the submarine's ductwork ahead of the flooding water. The seawater raced to the rear, in seconds reaching the control room where Ensign Behr would have been among the first in its path, followed by the bow and stern planesmen and the other sailors handling the various controls.

The flooding would stop the engines as *Flier* sank deeper, and the darkness that Crowley had seen when he looked down the hatch from the bridge would spread throughout the submarine. For the men in the rear, there was but one hope to temper their panic—an escape hatch in the aft torpedo room. If they could get the hatch open, then for the first time since their submarine training in Connecticut, they would strap on their air tanks and take their chances floating to the surface.

But what then?

The darkness was nearly absolute. Al Jacobson could see nothing, but he could taste diesel fuel on his lips. His body felt the warm, wet embrace of the sea as his uniform clung to his arms and legs. All was quiet except for the lapping of small waves. And then there were shouts, the sounds of a human voice, the first indication to the ensign that he was not alone. He began swimming toward the voice, floating easily in the salt water but slowed by the weight of his shirt, trousers, and boots. The strap of his binoculars was still around his neck, and the glasses floated harmlessly by his chest as he did the sidestroke. *Flier*'s sinking had disoriented him, snatching him from the tranquility of a warm ocean night, plunging him into a struggle for survival.

Several of the men had responded to the same yell that had drawn Jacobson. Once they were all together, they shared what they knew and tried to decide what had happened to *Flier*. It could have been an explosion in the batteries, but Crowley discarded that notion. The diesel engines had been running and the batteries were idle, not a situation in which they were likely to explode. The other topic concerned who else from the crew had escaped the boat. With almost no light, they could not expect to see other survivors, so their only choice was to call for them. Soon they had gathered more men into their group. A headcount was taken.

A total of fifteen men responded to the roll call. All fifteen men were already getting a lift. Not only had they escaped the terrifying death of their seventy-one trapped shipmates, but they had also surfaced on a sea that was unusually docile for this time of year. Summer is monsoon season, and storms can whip the Sulu Sea into a froth. Swimming in those waves would have been exhausting, and the chances of all these men finding and communicating with each other would have been slim. With lightning flashing on distant islands, there remained the possibility that a storm could still come, funneling winds between the mountains. But for now, here on the open ocean, the wind was light and the waves were gentle. As long as each man could stay afloat, he could remain with the group. For the next two hours, as they assessed their situation and developed a plan, that is what the men did.

There was a sense shared by most of the men that they were still part of a military unit. Perhaps this was because of their training, to always follow the lead of Crowley and Liddell. It took time for them to realize that there was no longer a formal chain of command, and that neither Crowley nor Liddell was in charge. They needed a plan.

The first thing to consider was their location. The skipper and his executive officer knew where they were. Liddell began explaining the options, most of which everyone already understood. There was land on three sides, Liddell said. To the west was Balabac, the largest chunk of land in the vicinity, roughly ten miles away. Each man was aware that the Japanese occupied that mountainous island. They could swim in that direction and with some certainty, due to the island's long shoreline, land on Balabac's beaches. To the south was Comiran Island, less than two miles away. Every survivor could probably swim that far, despite injuries. But there was a problem with this option: Comiran was tiny—only a few hundred feet across. If, swimming in this opaque darkness, they missed Comiran, they would have another forty miles of ocean before they reached land on one of northern Borneo's islands.

The lightning occasionally lit a mountainside to the northwest, but judging from what they could see, that land was about thirty miles away.

And if they headed toward any eastern quadrant, the Sulu Sea threatened them, with hundreds of miles of ocean, uninterrupted by land of any kind.

These were the options Liddell presented, each one unpromising. And none was worth even attempting right now. There were no stars to guide the men, and no moon, only clouds overhead. And the occasional lightning flash on the horizon, while it gave them something of a beacon, left their eyes blinded for several minutes.

But even the strongest among the survivors could not expect to stay afloat forever, and so they adopted two rules. First, they would turn so that the waves were lapping their left cheeks, and then they would swim in the direction they were facing. The course was randomly chosen, as far as young Jacobson knew. Perhaps Crowley and Liddell had a reason. But the skipper and his second in command did not share their thinking.

The second rule was Crowley's idea—a death sentence for several of the men, and everyone knew it: It would be each man for himself. The cruel reality was that wherever they were going, it was a long way off. Some of the injured men could not swim the distance without help, and if the whole group waited for the injured, the chances were overwhelming that no one would survive.

Crowley was uninjured, but he was the oldest, at thirty-five, and his physique after several years of sedentary submarine service was not particularly athletic. Crowley could be among the first victims of his edict. But like their skipper, all of the men agreed to the pact, and all fifteen began swimming across the waves, which lifted them a few inches and then gently lowered them in a mesmerizing rhythm.

Chief Pope called out in the night for Jim Liddell, asking the distance that lay ahead of them before they reached shore. After two hours in the water, the men still felt little wind. Liddell, pondering Pope's question, knew the entire swim could be fifteen miles or more, but he wanted to be encouraging.

"About nine miles, Chief," Liddell replied.

"Oh, fuck it!" Pope said in disgust. With that, the chief stopped swimming and said no more, his faint image dissolving forever behind the swimmers in the night.

It was not much later that Jacobson, keeping pace with Ed Casey, saw him veer. Instead of calling him back to the course as he had done before, the ensign swam over to his mentor.

"Ed, rest a minute, and then just float on your back and put your feet on my shoulders and I'll push you back," Jacobson offered.

"Remember, we agreed every man for himself?" Casey said, refusing his young friend's gesture. But the two of them swam back toward the group, talking as they went. They were joking about a blowout party they had planned to throw in Perth when the patrol was over, and as they talked, they reached the wake of the others.

Ten minutes later, Casey disappeared in the darkness. When Jacobson and the others called to him, there was no response. The lieutenant had chosen not to burden his shipmates any longer.

Paul Knapp had been struggling like Casey, but was keeping in line with the others. Jacobson saw him swim off to the side without a word. The ensign thought little of it until Knapp did not return. Then he realized the courage it had taken for Knapp to separate himself.

As the night wore on, one after another of the men, when they felt they could swim no more, silently turned to the side and disappeared, each man choosing for himself when his time had come.

If anyone among the survivors were thinking about the beasts that swam below them, none gave voice to the image. But the reefs of the Sulu Sea were habitat for a vast assortment of large animals. Sharks of every description shared the water with barracudas and rays. Some were harmless, like the white and blacktip sharks, and the guitar sharks. But others were legendary, like the hammerheads and bull sharks, predators that would eat another shark as quickly as they would consume a human being.

If the swimmers were ignoring the carnivores beneath them, it may have been because their minds were filled with the death they had just dodged, and, not that far below the sea, their shipmates already dead inside *Flier*. The thing that now would keep these men alive was their determination to keep swimming.

The overcast sky that had kept the stars hidden was overcome at about three o'clock that morning by the moon, rising grudgingly in the east to give the swimmers a navigational beacon. By now, only nine of the original fifteen survivors remained in the group. Wesley Miller straggled far behind the main pack but could hear their voices in the dark, and shouted to them to maintain contact.

At about five o'clock, when the first hint of daybreak was tingeing the sky from black to gray, helmsman Gerald Madeo began to panic. He fell below the surface, and after seven hours in the water, no one had the strength to help him. They simply continued swimming, led away from Madeo by the moon toward an unknown destination.

The trio of Howell, Baumgart, and Jacobson kept pace with each other throughout the morning, cooled under the blazing tropical sun by the same glass-clear sea that had warmed them during the night. Slowly, they drew toward their island, probably helped by a change in the tide or the currents.

It was one o'clock in the afternoon when Jacobson checked his wristwatch. The approaching drone of an airplane came from a distance, and when the men stopped swimming to look, they saw a low-flying Japanese craft, coming directly toward them. A half-dozen heads on the surface of the Sulu Sea were too tiny for the pilot to notice, however, and the plane kept going. The swimmers resumed their strokes, their luck apparently intact.

Choosing Freedom

The jungle island floated in the distance like a thin, green wafer. Little about its shore could be determined, but it was closer than anything else, and distance was important for the men, who by now had been in the water for nearly seventeen hours. Jacobson, Howell, and Baumgart had managed to stay close to each other since they had first spotted land. If there was anyone else afloat, they were no longer in sight. There were only the three and the island.

And then ahead, almost on a line toward the island, the men noticed something else in the water. It was long, and above it rose some perpendicular objects. Perhaps it was a native fishing boat, they thought, and the objects were the fishermen. They waved, but there was no response, so they decided to avoid the unfriendly thing. Swimming the straight route toward the island, they nevertheless drew closer to it and discovered it was a bamboo tree, its buoyant trunk riding lightly on the surface, its limbs rising toward the afternoon sun. Eager for some rest, they swam to the tree and Jacobson climbed up to have a look at the surrounding area. Howell and Baumgart struggled up beside where he balanced as the ensign scanned the sea. A short way off he saw more swimmers. He began shouting, joined by his mates, their voices carrying across the now-choppy water, their arms waving in excited arcs.

At daylight, when the island was first spotted, Crowley had given the order to anyone within shouting distance: Swim toward land at your own pace. He soon fell behind the rest, alternately swimming and resting when exhaustion overcame him. That he continued to swim is indisputable. What kept him moving is less certain.

Early in the afternoon, Crowley had seen Liddell ahead of him, clinging to another floating tree. The skipper and his executive officer stayed together then until they heard the shouts from Jacobson's group. It took a few minutes for Crowley and Liddell to reach the larger tree and cling to it. For the skipper, the plant had become a lifesaver. Exhausted, he had felt—even with the island in sight—that he could no longer swim. But the shouts from Jacobson and the others gave him new energy.

Breaking branches from the tree for paddles, the five men now straddled its trunk, urging the tree toward the shore. Off to one side, they saw Don Tremaine, swimming alone. He waved back when they shouted and gestured, but he avoided them. Tremaine had seen them but he could not hear them, and had assumed they were natives. If they were too unfriendly to pick him up, he reasoned, he would not chance swimming toward them.

The water changed from dark blue to a pale aqua a few hundred yards from the shore where the coral reef began, and then it was shallow enough for the men to walk. Their feet were wrinkled and white from seventeen hours in the water, and the entire seabed on which they stepped was coral. It was like walking on crushed glass rather than gravel, and the sharp coral edges sliced into the soft soles of their feet. Abandoning their bamboo tree, they stumbled, trying to keep their balance as the hot afternoon sun dried the salt water from their backs. The pain in their feet was numbed by their eagerness to feel dry land. And up on the beach stood Jim Russo, urging them on.

Staggering ashore, the men could, for the first time since *Flier* sank, see each other from head to toe. The sight was shocking. In the ten hours since daylight, the unrelenting rays of the sun had bombarded their water-softened white flesh. Now, where their skin was exposed, they were scalded red. Baumgart alone had long trousers on, saving his legs from the scorching. But like the others, he waded from the ocean with his face and arms as red as if the seawater had been boiling, and his blood drained into the sand from the coral slashes in his feet.

Byan Island, roughly triangular in shape, is just east of Mantangule Island. In 1944, the island was uninhabited by humans. A few hours after the men reached Byan Island, the sun settled beyond sprawling Mantangule and the air grew cool. Crowley and Liddell believed they were on Mantangule Island and that the big land to the west was Balabac, which they knew was occupied by the Japanese. To build a fire, if they could manage it, might attract attention, so they faced a night of cold. Even before sunset had cooled the air, they were swept alternately by fever chills and sweats. In the dusk, they huddled together for warmth, lying directly on the sand and, having successfully outlasted death for a day, sought the peace of sleep.

Neither sleep nor peace was to be theirs, however. Roused by their fevers, they would seek a more comfortable position, only to have the grains of the beach rasp across their sunburned flesh like sandpaper. At times, they were awakened by rats nibbling on their feet. Young Jacobson lay awake, his body shaking, the watch on his wrist slowly ticking off the seconds and minutes. He wanted nothing more than for the hours to pass and the day to come, bringing with it warmth.

~⁓

They had learned, in their first stumbling hours ashore before nightfall, that the area near the beach offered neither food nor water. So when the sun rose on August 15, 1944, the *Flier* survivors knew they had to begin a search. Crowley directed Tremaine, Russo, and Howell, who had injured his knee when he had jumped off the submarine, to stay on the beach and improve the lean-to shelter. Jacobson and Baumgart were to head east and scout out the island, while Crowley and Liddell would head the other way.

Howell, Russo, and Tremaine started gathering scraps of wood and palm leaves in the hope of creating some real shelter for the coming night. At the same time, Ensign Jacobson and Baumgart hobbled along the shore, Baumgart in trousers and an undershirt, the ensign in his underwear with binoculars dangling from his neck. There were coconuts everywhere along the water's edge. They picked up the ones that looked whole and opened them with their bare hands by smashing them on coral. But each one that broke open left them disappointed, its meat rotten, its milk spoiled.

They trudged for hours without success. And then they rounded a point and ahead they saw a string of islands. Still ankle-deep in the sea and standing on coral beds, they splashed forward until they found a sandy beach where driftwood had gathered. Then they decided it was time to head back. Realizing that if they crossed the island, it should take less time than circling the beach, they tried to climb ashore up the coral cliffs. But the thorns and vines repelled them, and they waded once more into the shallows across the coral, retracing their painful steps toward their shipmates.

They had another reason for leaving together: They wanted to talk about the prospects for the group's ultimate survival. Crowley was familiar with the territory only from having studied nautical charts. Liddell had served on a submarine in the Philippines before the war and had a deeper understanding of the locale. What they had found so far was that they could not stay on this island. It was little more than a coral reef with no food or shelter. The jungle that began at the shore was a tangle of thorns and vines.

Rounding the western tip of the island, they saw their two options: To the northeast, beyond two more small islands, lay a large island. Liddell identified it as Bugsuk Island. And behind them, to the southwest, beyond long, flat Mantangule Island, was the mountainous mass they knew had to be Balabac. Intelligence reports that they had reviewed back in Australia said the Japanese were on Balabac. But from what they remembered, there was less chance of finding the enemy on Bugsuk, which was about five or six miles away. The trip could be made manageable by hopping only to the next island, Gabung, and resting before going on. There were tremendous currents that funneled between islands like these, Crowley and Liddell knew, and in their weakened state, the survivors could easily be swept out to sea if they tried to swim across. They needed another plan, and more information. So Liddell decided to leave Crowley behind and explore a bit further on the northern side of the island. The lieutenant had walked some distance when, coming around a curve in the shore, he saw a man ahead on the beach—a white man, clothed only in underwear.

⌁

At daybreak the day before, Wesley Miller had lost contact with the other swimmers. But he saw several islands on the horizon, and, since it was in the direction he had been swimming, he kept going for the closest one. As the afternoon wore on, however, he found that the current was sweeping him to his left, past the nearest island. He would never be able to reach it, he knew, so he began to swim for the next island. But when he was perhaps two miles from his target, the current increased, carrying him fast along the beach. Still he swam toward the shore, cutting the distance in half when, to his left, he saw the end of the island approaching. After that, there was nothing, and Miller believed that his long trek from the Oregon ranch to the middle of the Pacific Ocean was at an end.

It was startling when, letting his feet fall below him, Miller felt his toes touch the bottom. He began walking now, and soon the water was only waist-deep, and to his left the coral actually rose above the surface. Then the sun set over Balabac and Mantangule and the water grew deeper. He no longer could wade, but although he must swim again to survive, his arms and legs were unwilling to move. So he willed himself toward the beach, and when he could touch bottom again, he was too tired to stand. Sand and coral rose beneath him, and he leaned forward in the water so that his knees, not his feet, propelled him ashore while his body and arms floated listlessly. Crawling as an infant might, he worked his way out of the sea and partway up the sand, where his thoughts and his will ceased and he fell asleep. Awakened in the middle of the night by rising water, he dragged himself to higher ground, up against the coral cliff, and slept once more.

In the morning, Miller began to walk along the shore, looking for a way to scale the cliffs. As he stumbled on, he searched for clams in the sand. In a mile of hiking, he had found only solid rock cliffs along the bank, with jungle growth snarling out of their cracks.

Then Liddell found Miller and led him back to Crowley. The skipper, perhaps noticing the sailor for the first time, realized that this crewman was little more than a boy, a child who was pathetically grateful to find that he was not a sole survivor.

Later that afternoon, everyone assembled at the beach and reported on their work. Jacobson and Baumgart had found neither food nor water, but they told of locating a pile of driftwood on the northern beach. Howell, Russo, and Tremaine, when they were not working on the lean-to, had set out seashells to collect water should it rain. And they had found water seeping out of the coral cliffs. They had set some shells below the cliffs and collected some water, one drip at a time—three shells full, in all. Everyone shared it, each person drinking a couple of teaspoons. It was merely seawater that had splashed onto the coral at high tide, but their thirst convinced the men they were getting fresh water.

If they continued to wet their lips with this water for long, they were going to be doomed. The human body, in order to rid itself of excess salt, passes the salt through the kidneys where it is washed away in urine. That means that the body is losing water as well as salt. The more salt in the system, the more water must be expelled. In a short time, the consumption of salt water will actually dehydrate the body, increasing the level of salt in the bloodstream and damaging bodily tissues. Soon, the drinker will die. But first, normal body functions will be damaged. Saliva will dry up, leaving the mouth and tongue without lubrication, exposing them to infection. Drying of the tongue may cause it to swell and split. Death might be preferable.

With the other reports submitted, Crowley told the men of their options. They could head west, eventually reaching Balabac where there was food and shelter—and Japanese soldiers. They would probably be captured and become prisoners of war. (Earlier in the afternoon, another Japanese patrol plane had flown low over the island, the red rising sun insignia on its wings easily seen by the survivors.) Or, they could use the driftwood that Jacobson and Baumgart had found, build a raft, try to reach Bugsuk, and, accepting the uncertainty of finding food and water there, remain free men.

To a man, they chose freedom. They would begin work in the morning.

Sunrise brought all the men back onto their feet. The agony of standing on those festering cuts was not enough to keep them on the beach, and soon the eight were hobbling in the shallow water, where vegetation coated some of the coral, making it less sharp. Splashing up Byan Island's eastern shore, they could see Gabung Island in the distance. When they reached the place where the two islands were closest together—just under a mile separated them—they began building their raft. Liddell and Russo, both strong men, reached into the jungle from the edge of the beach and tore out vines. As some of the men used the vines to lash the bamboo driftwood logs together, Chief Howell sat on the beach, improvising two paddles by splitting slender bamboo poles partway, inserting small pieces in the split crossway, and then tying them in place with thin vines. Occasionally, he would lick moisture that he found on leaves.

Crowley saw how his men slowed in their work as the day wore on, their movements becoming uncoordinated, their attention wandering. Thirst was on everyone's mind. But even though they scoured the coast looking for edible coconuts, they found none all day.

It was about two-thirty that afternoon, just before slack tide, when the eight men surrounded their little raft and pushed it out toward Gabung. Ahead of them was a crossing of slightly less than one mile. The water was the pale blue of reef water out for several hundred yards off the beach, and the reef resumed on the far side of the channel, where dark blue water indicated a depth that no one would be able to wade. They had brought two long poles with them, and for the first quarter of the voyage, the younger men took turns poling the raft, on which Crowley was the only permanent passenger. The rest of the men leaned on the raft for support as they walked in the shallows across another long bed of razor-sharp coral. Crowley paddled.

Before they had made it halfway across the channel, they saw the daily patrol plane coming in low. Crowley and the man poling slipped into the water, and everyone tried to hide under the raft. The plane kept going, and the men, clinging to the sides, kicked in the deeper water, slowly moving the raft across the channel.

Now on the open water, they found themselves directly in the path of an oncoming squall. Abruptly, they were pelted with large, pure droplets, delicious on their lips, and everyone tipped his head back and opened his mouth. But while the raindrops splattered off their foreheads and cheeks, none of it seemed to find their tongues before the squall passed on into the ocean, leaving the scorching sun in its wake.

They had not yet reached the reef on the far side of the channel when the tide seemed to shift and a new current swept between the islands. With only a quarter of a mile to go, they suddenly seemed unable to make any progress, and the raft appeared to be drifting away from Gabung Island.

The men on the sides kicked with all their feeble power and Crowley, feeling like a very elderly thirty-five, paddled, and the raft circled the end of the island and settled in its lee, the current having deposited the men close enough to shore that they could swim the final leg.

It was seven o'clock, more than four hours since they had left Byan Island a mile to the south, and the sun had already set. They found a sandy beach and were content to collapse where they could find room. The little slivers of coconut they had eaten earlier had done little to curb their appetite, and their thirst was only growing. But no one had the energy to forage. More than food and water, right now they wanted sleep.

Sunrise the following morning—August 17—brought with it relief from the tremors of the night and hope that this would be the day the men would eat. Before launching their raft, they gathered to discuss their next steps. It would be another nine or ten hours until the tides allowed them to leave this island for the next one in the chain. Crowley and Liddell took suggestions, and the group decided that their time could be best used by traveling around the island the long way. There would be more chance of finding food if they were covering a longer shoreline. It meant more walking, but now empty stomachs and parched mouths were overpowering the screaming pains from their feet and the swollen and blistered burns on their backs and arms. They pushed the raft into the shallow water and began circling the island to the west. Once more, the coral in the shallow water was softened by plants that grew on it, so wading was less painful than it might have been. But there was a trade-off, because when they were not swimming, their burns were always exposed to the sun as it rose high above the island.

On the eastern side of Byan the day before, the men had walked along the beach with open ocean to their right. Now, walking along Gabung's western coast, they felt surrounded by islands. Mantangule's long, low bulk stretched out to the southwest, and Bugsuk's broad sweep consumed the view to the northeast, only three or so miles across the reef-strewn water. To the north, another large island—Pandanan—was indistinguishable from Bugsuk. And to the northwest, more, smaller islands rose above the reefs to hide the horizon. With their goal of Bugsuk in sight, the men could think of food and water and let those images draw them ahead. But there were distractions. Swarms of stinging insects flew around them, and their thoughts drifted uncontrollably, clouded by the lack of food and water.

Apo Island was on the far side of a strait nearly two miles across, with the dark blue of deep water again in the middle, between the two shores. The men had about two hours to wait for slack tide and the passing of the next enemy patrol plane, and they gathered more coconuts from the beach, but as so often before, none was edible. Surrounded by a sea full of fish and water, they were dying of thirst and starvation.

The airplane arrived on schedule and continued south over the island. Certain the danger had passed, the men pushed their raft back to sea. The water was shallow enough for them to wade and to keep the weight off their feet as they leaned on the raft. Pushing and splashing, they moved their craft into the dark blue of the deeper water.

They were midway between the two islands, with no retreat possible, when someone noticed the fins. Two sharks cruised just beneath the surface, looking for food. The men kept paddling, splashing and kicking, and the sharks, perhaps sensing the hunger that drove these eight beings, stayed clear.

Aided by the shallow water, the raft crossed between Gabung and Apo islands in only three hours, and the men found a sandy beach just before dark. By now, they knew what to expect. They posted their rat guards and waited in troubled dreams and fitful sleep for the morning.

Sunrise was again their alarm clock, but they lingered until about eight o'clock before gathering around their sole possession, the raft, and heading to the west. Apo is a small, round island, but in all other ways it seemed no different from Byan and Gabung. Again, the men had chosen to take the long way, and each grudging step along the curved shoreline revealed some new aspect of the land ahead. Before noon, they had found the first indication of humans—a dugout canoe abandoned on the beach. The boat was riddled with holes and useless, so they left it and went on. Then they saw a trail leading up over the coral cliff, and Jacobson and Baumgart decided to explore. A trail like this meant human activity. But after a few hundred yards of walking on the coral pavement of the path, the men turned back, leaving the place to the monkeys that chattered and scampered in the trees around them. Joining the other men, they continued north along the shore.

Ancient trees, their trunks varicose and black, their roots writhing like serpents, the weave of their arched branches creating darkened tunnels, grew out from the coral cliffs along the northwestern shore of Apo Island. The men walked under the trees, hidden from observation, until, in the distance, they saw the green shoreline of their destination, Bugsuk Island.

They stood transfixed, for there, under coconut trees that swayed like tall, slender dancers lining the edge of a broad, sandy beach, were houses. There were no Japanese launches on the shore and no sign of activity around the buildings. That did not mean there were no risks. So they would wait and watch.

But not for long.

SPIRITS OF THE LAND

There were eyes behind the towering coconut trees that swayed in the sea breeze along Bugsuk Island's sparkling beach in a gentle hula. The eyes were watching the *Flier* survivors.

All that Crowley and his men saw when they looked toward the island were the apparently tranquil settlement of houses and, in their imaginations, food and water. But they were cautious. With their raft in tow, they worked their way around the northern edge of Apo Island to a point on the beach where they could no longer see the houses. Their plan was to arrive on Bugsuk just before sunset and to use the half-light of dusk to sneak toward the settlement. By now, their starvation and thirst had robbed the men of whatever athletic ability they had once possessed, so when they swam across the narrow channel between the islands, they would lack the strength to swim against the flow. But if they judged the current correctly, they would land about a mile and a half from the houses. Then they would have enough cover to sneak closer, undetected. There was no more than a half-mile between Apo and the far shore, and all of it was the pale blue of reef water. They expected no problems.

Late that afternoon, they pushed the raft off the sandy beach. Most of the men waded at its side, and when they reached the far shore, they climbed out of the water, not on coral but with another long stretch of white-sand beach under their tender feet. Stowing the raft, they walked west toward the setting sun. They were on a narrow peninsula, on the far side of which was the tidal mouth of a saltwater stream. Crossing the peninsula with a wary eye toward the far shore, they waded into the stream. When they climbed the far bank, they were on the same beach that, to the west, passed in front of the Bugsuk houses. Here a grove of baring trees, a species that, like mangroves, sinks its roots in salt water, blocked their view of the settlement. The men worked their way through the shallow water under the trees, with the low rays of the sun slanting between the tree trunks, and then moved ashore, peering through the grove at what appeared to be a once-thriving but now-abandoned village. The houses that they had seen from Apo Island were surrounded by a coconut grove, and between the survivors and those houses were the remnants of bamboo and palm-leaf native huts.

Jacobson and Baumgart were the last to arrive, their arms filled with coconuts. For the first time in five days, the *Flier* survivors would have unspoiled food to eat, and apparently a place to sleep. The main building in this settlement—well built of bamboo and lumber, with a thatched roof—looked like the home of a person of wealth. But the home had been ransacked, the furniture carted out of its now-barren rooms, and any remnant of the former owners' presence stripped from the now-naked walls.

The house had a good wooden floor for sleeping, probably free from rats and certainly protected from sand crabs. But weary as they were, the men were also excited by their discoveries and were not yet ready for rest. They wanted to explore. Standing in front of the main house and looking south, they could imagine that they were in an exotic resort. A lawn fifty yards deep or more and shaded by the high canopy of coconut trees led to the beach of pure, white, soft sand, framed in this view by drooping coconut palm fronds. Beyond the beach was an island paradise. Stretching out to the left was the chain of islands the men had spent the last four days hopping, and between the last—Byan—and Mantangule, on the right, rose the distant blue mountains of Balabac. A good-size wooden boat— Al Jacobson guessed it was thirty-eight feet long—was beached in front of the house and looked like it had been intentionally destroyed. Nearby was another launch of about the same size that appeared to have been under construction. On either side of the house and inland from it were several clearings, which suggested that the owners had raised vegetables. And farther inland, some of the men reported, there was a stream. In its clear water swam schools of fish, meals for days to come.

Exploring by himself, Earl Baumgart found a curious concrete structure just behind the main house. It stood about five feet high and was another six feet long, and when he climbed atop it he was elated. Someone had built a cistern to collect rainwater, probably from the roof of the house. There was all the water the men would ever need, and more! He called out his discovery to the others, who came running.

Once more, the skipper lived up to his reputation for cautiousness outside of the realm of battle. He told his gathered crew that they should drink sparingly from the cistern. They wanted to guzzle to their thirst's content, he knew. But having gone without water for five days, and with almost no food in the same period, their bodies could not handle much. When he had explained this, each man took a small sip from Baumgart's pool and then went away. Only Chief Howell ignored Crowley's caution. He drank until his belly was full, and then he drank some more.

Now Jacobson and some others set about opening the good coconuts. They found a sharp rock in the ground and smashed each nut against it until they had removed the soft green outer shell. Then they punched out the eye of the inner, hard brown shell, drained the milk, and crushed the nut into pieces that could be chewed.

With these small pleasures, the men began to settle in for the night. Jacobson found a bamboo door that he laid on the floor as his mattress, and he stretched out on it, content. Images filled his head as the palm leaves rustled above him. There were fish and coconuts to eat, a roof over his head, water to drink, and, it appeared, no enemies within miles. There was no more need to walk, so his feet could heal. There was shade from the sun, so his blisters would dry and disappear. This was a place where a man could wait out the war, if he had to.

Not long after Chief Howell drank his fill from the cistern, he began to feel ill. His condition worsened during the night, but there was no help for him. If some of the others showed little sympathy, it may have been because they knew his sickness, self-inflicted as it was, was not lethal. In time, his body would acclimate. The little bit of coconut in their stomachs had satisfied their appetites, and they knew there would be more meals to come. With a home around them to keep away the chilling breezes, they succumbed to their exhaustion, dreaming untroubled dreams.

Once more, they arose with the sun and began planning their day. There was work to be done, and Crowley and Liddell started organizing teams. One group would catch some fish, while another would build a fire for cooking. They had no matches, but Jacobson still had his binoculars, and their lenses would make perfect magnifying glasses for focusing the sun's rays in an incendiary beam on dry tinder. Someone needed to scout the area, and the group would need more coconuts.

Jacobson was the first one up, and he was standing looking out a window toward the rear of the house and the jungle beyond when he saw two small boys—they might have been thirteen or fourteen—emerge from the trees. Jacobson told his shipmates what he saw, and they all were quickly on their feet. It was obvious to them that the boys knew the sailors were there, so they filed out of the house and approached the visitors. The boys were wearing ragged shorts and tattered shirts, and their feet were bare, like the sailors'. Crowley stepped forward.

"Americans or Japanese?" he asked.

"Americanos!" one of the boys, Oros Bogata, said, smiling. "Japanese!" he said, drawing a finger across his throat as if slitting it.

The men felt a collective wave of relief. Then the boy pointed to the cistern by the house.

"Don't drink water," he said.

Perhaps they misunderstood his puzzling words, they thought. But with their *Que sera, sera* attitude, they disregarded that comment and asked whether the boys had any food. Oros patted his small stomach.

"Rice," he said, and he motioned for the men to follow him and his silent friend back into the jungle. Stepping in line behind the boys, they found themselves on a narrow path. The boys, seeing that they were being followed, scampered ahead to a spot where they had left poles with small packs tied at the ends. Each balanced his pole on his shoulder, and then Oros led the file of hobbling, nearly naked men while his friend followed, sweeping the trail behind them to camouflage evidence of the group's passing.

In a short distance, they reached an abandoned sugarcane field. Oros motioned for the men to sit down, and he and his companion cut sections of cane a yard long and offered each man his own piece. The heart of the cane was a sweet and juicy bundle of fibers, and for the next half-hour, Crowley and his men chewed in bliss, until they simply had no more strength left in their jaws.

Back on the path, the boys led the men a short way to a clearing about the size of a football field. In one corner of the field was a raised wooden platform with a thatched roof supported on bamboo poles, but with no walls. Again the boys motioned for the men to sit and rest. Then they dropped their poles and opened their packs. One took a stick, sharpened at one end, and placed the tip in a notched piece of wood that he drew from his pack. He spun the stick between his palms, and in less time than it would have taken to remove a match from a box and strike it, he had some tinder smoldering. Jacobson, the Eagle Scout who had been taught to start fires with a bow and a stick, was impressed.

Then the boys produced a small pot, and one left and got water from a nearby stream. They poured rice from their pack into the pot, and while the fire brought the water to a boil, they cut leaves from a banana tree and made plates for their guests. Now the same boy who had cautioned them against drinking from the cistern gave them a cup of muddy water and, by sign language, told them they should drink it. The men hesitated, so the boy drank some himself. *Que sera, sera!* The men drank, as well.

When the rice was cooked, the boys spread it on the banana leaves. Then they produced three dried fish from the bounty of their packs and divided them among the men. There was enough for everyone.

Four days earlier, Crowley and his men had chosen survival with freedom over survival with food when they had elected to head away from Balabac. Theirs was a decision that prolonged the pain of hunger and thirst, which might easily have been cut short had they allowed themselves instead to come under Japanese control. Now, without hesitation, they had turned themselves over to the authority of two small boys whose friendship they accepted as a stray dog does that of a man with a scrap of food. Led by their stomachs, the sailors had followed the boys into the jungle with only the promise of rice, and now, with the smell of steaming hot rice and fish rising to their nostrils, they attacked their meal.

Their focus changed abruptly when, looking up from his food, one of them saw nine men, bristling with weapons—rifles, blowguns, and bolos—stepping into the clearing from every point of the compass.

They were surrounded!

The *Flier* survivors had traded their safety for scraps of sustenance. The price of their meal now stared across the clearing at them.

Wesley Miller was ready to bolt like a startled fawn, but these fierce-looking warriors were everywhere. No one budged. The shredded soles of their feet precluded it.

"Hello!" one of the armed men called. His voice was cheerful and a smile lit his face. He dashed across the grass to the platform where the sailors still sat. Crowley struggled to his feet, as did his men at the approach of this stranger. When the man reached them, he grasped the hands of the *Flier* crew, shaking them vigorously.

"Welcome to Bugsuk Island," the man said. "I am Pedro Sarmiento."

Sarmiento said he was the leader of the local bolo battalion, indicating the men who were with him. Sarmiento had instructions from the guerrilla headquarters that if he found any Allied survivors, he was to ship them to a guerrilla outpost on Palawan's southern tip.

Crowley and Liddell were becoming comfortable with Sarmiento, and they were prepared to follow his instructions. At this point someone recalled the earlier direction from the two boys, to not drink the water in the cistern, and asked Sarmiento to explain.

Oh, he replied, earlier in the war, when the Japanese had driven the owner of the home from his property, Sarmiento had poisoned the water with arsenic in hopes that Japanese soldiers would drink it!

Everyone looked at Chief Howell. The man had a cast-iron gut!

A Japanese patrol would reach Bugsuk later in the morning, Sarmiento told the sailors, so they could not remain at the schoolhouse. The Japanese soldiers would inspect the area and then would spend the night in the house where Crowley and his men had slept so peacefully the night before. So the sailors would have to hike at least a mile inland to be safe. The Japanese were afraid to penetrate the center of the island, Sarmiento said.

Sarmiento reported that his instructions from the guerrilla leader, Captain Mayor, were to take any survivors all the way north across the center of Bugsuk and then to bring them by boat to the guerrilla outpost at Cape Buliluyan, the southernmost tip of Palawan. He told Crowley and Liddell that it was important to begin the hike soon. When they said they were ready, he told them to finish their breakfast. Then he sent the two boys back to the beach to make sure the Americans had not left any evidence behind.

A few minutes later, the boys returned with the lens that the sailors had removed from Jacobson's binoculars, with which they had planned to start their fires. Someone offered the lens to Sarmiento, who produced a pipe and tobacco that he lit with the lens. He smiled with gratitude. Then, seeing that they had finished their rice and fish, he invited the men from *Flier* to begin their cross-island trek.

NINE

Seventy Days in an Open Boat

Guy Pearce Jones

ON THE NIGHT OF WEDNESDAY, AUGUST 21, 1940, THEY HAD LUNCHEON sausage and meatballs for tea on the *Anglo-Saxon*. The ship was making way steadily in a southwesterly direction and had left the Azores five hundred miles behind.

Widdicombe thought very little of the menu. It would be his wheel at eight o'clock, Paddy's lookout and Tapscott's standby. So he passed up his tea and slept instead.

Shortly before going forward, he rolled a half dozen cigarettes to take with him to the wheelhouse. It was against orders, but the *Anglo* steered like a yacht in heavy weather and like an automaton in calm. Two long hours of virtually no movement, with the binnacle paralyzing the optic nerves like a hypnotist's mirror, made it very hard for a man to keep his eyes open. Cigarettes helped.

Four explosions, so close together that they seemed one, shook the ship from stern to stem. The men stared at one another, the dreaded question in their eyes: mine or torpedo?

As he reached deck, a blinding glare struck Tapscott like a blow in the eyes. It lighted up the fireman's back against the curtain of blackness in front of them. The fireman plunged forward. Tapscott had only one idea: he must not lose sight of that back. He sprang after the fireman, struggled for balance, and the whole world seemed to blow up behind him in one terrific roar and shocking blast. He felt himself fly through the air and crash into something hard; then he knew nothing.

Tapscott came to on the starboard side of the deck twenty feet from the companionway. He was flat on his face, his nose jammed against the deckhouse bulkhead. He tried to move, but his muscles refused. He felt no pain—nothing at all. He wondered if he were dead. He lay there for what seemed a long time. Actually, it was only a few seconds.

It was 8:20 when the first salvo from the raider plowed into the *Anglo-Saxon*'s poop, demolishing the gun and killing everyone in the starboard fo'castle. Widdicombe knew the time to the tick, for he had just glanced at the wheelhouse clock and noted with satisfaction that twenty minutes of his trick was behind him.

A tearing crash and explosions shook the ship. Widdicombe ran out of the wheelhouse to the port end of the bridge. He could see nothing—only blackness and the water alongside. He ran back across the bridge to the starboard end and peered over the weather cloth. About a quarter of a mile away a dark shape was racing obliquely toward them, gun flashes stabbing from her as she came.

A raider!

Widdicombe tore back to the wheel and put it hard aport.

The hail of lead and steel that was pouring into the ship aft moved forward. It cut through the *Anglo*'s upper works with machine-like precision. It dropped to deck level and raked her fore and aft.

A breastwork of concrete building blocks protected the wheelhouse. Bullets were hammering into it. Shell fragments and shrapnel tore the ship all along the starboard side. Incendiary bullets crisscrossed into her in burning lines.

The Third Mate, whom Widdicombe had been unable to find, ran in from the bridge.

"Put her hard aport," he yelled.

"She's hard aport now," Widdicombe yelled back.

The raider was within a hundred yards now. Widdicombe could see her clearly. She was firing with everything she had. A red glow lighted up the *Anglo*'s poop. The starboard lifeboat was burning; the jolly boat on that side was smashed.

Widdicombe looked directly below. A body was slumped against the bulwark, just outside the Captain's quarters. It was Captain Flynn's. A machine-gun burst had caught him full in the chest as he was dumping the ship's papers overboard.

The storm of fire was moving forward again. Widdicombe ran back to the wheel. The First Mate was coming up the port ladder two steps at a time, followed by the Chief, Sparks.

"Antennas are all shot away and sets smashed, sir," Chief Sparks said. "No hope of an S.O.S. now."

"Right," said the Mate. "Hold her where she is," he ordered Widdicombe. "I'll be back in a minute."

The Mate returned to the bridge. "The Captain's gone," he said. "Bear a hand. I'm going to get the port boat away."

Widdicombe left the wheel and followed the Mate. They ran to the port jolly boat, the Mate fumbling for his knife as he ran. He got the knife opened and sawed at the ropes of the gripes. It seemed incredible to Widdicombe that they could be so tough and resistant.

Widdicombe stood by the after-fall. As the Mate's knife bit into the last strands of the gripe the boat went down with a run. The after-fall fouled round Widdicombe's body, pulling his hand into the block and jamming it there. The whipping rope stripped his trousers from his hips and seared his arm as it went. The boat hung by the stern.

Working frantically and in great pain from his jammed hand, Widdicombe managed to clear the block. The Mate leveled the boat and they lowered away. As it passed the deck below, two men leaped into it.

In a boat drill it was Tapscott's routine job to fend off. Automatically, after falling into the dropping jolly boat, he found the boat hook and held it off the *Anglo*'s side. The boat settled smoothly into the sea, rising and falling with the brisk swell. It was also his job to unhook the forward fall. He did this and then realized that there was no one to free the after-fall. He clambered over the hapless Penny, cast off, and went forward again to stand by the boat rope.

The Chief Mate was first down the lifeline. He slid so rapidly that the skin of his fingers and palms was badly burned. Widdicombe was next. As he swung off the ship, the Second, Sparks, came running up. He had on a hat and carried a sweater and an attaché case. "Wait for me," he begged.

A moment later Sparks came down the lifeline, just in time. Tapscott took only one turn of the boat rope—which is fastened fore and aft from ship to boat. Having reckoned without the fact that the ship was going full speed ahead, the rope ripped through his hands, burning and lacerating them when he tried to hold fast. The jolly boat went rapidly astern.

It was Widdicombe's job, too, to fend off. He and Tapscott attacked it with the energy of fear. The *Anglo*'s propeller, churning powerfully, was drawing them into the stern. The easterly swell made it difficult to keep away from the ship. One touch of the whirling blades and all would be over.

As they swept by amidships, the men in the jolly boat saw the smashed lifeboat over them and faces peering down. Two of the men overhead dropped into the boat. Tapscott and Widdicombe, frantically plying boat hook and oar, did not even see them. They gave two last mighty shoves against the ship's side and the boat swept around the stern, clearing the propeller by inches.

The *Anglo*'s poop was ablaze now and the raider was closing in to finish her. The men in the jolly boat crouched like hunted animals and scarcely breathed. The swell was carrying them right across the raider's bows. They waited for a burst from her guns.

It seemed impossible that they would not be discovered. But the raider was so intent on the kill, she hung on the *Anglo*'s blazing trail. Hunter and hunted rushed ahead. The jolly boat drifted away on the swell. The boat was taking water badly but the men in her dared not move. When they were a good half mile astern they put out their oars, headed the boat into the sea and pulled.

They settled into their swing and made the boat leap. They were congratulating themselves on making good progress in their escape when, dead ahead, the moon rose, flooding the sea with brightness and throwing them into sharp relief. The men froze on their oars and swore.

Water had been coming over the side. After heading the boat to the swell there should not have been as much of it as there was. It was now slopping about their calves.

"That drainage plug must be loose," Tapscott said. No one paid any attention.

Widdicombe and Tapscott seized bailers and attacked the rising water. Pilcher and Morgan relieved them at the oars. But bail as fast as they could, the water did not lower as it should. The Mate plunged his arm into it and groped along the bottom of the boat. He found the drainage plug. Tapscott had been right; the plug was half out of the hole and water coming in around it. He drove it in with his axe and they were able to get the water down to the level of their ankles.

Between the boat and the *Anglo*, lights suddenly appeared bobbing up and down on the crests of the waves. "The life rafts!" exclaimed the men in the boat. The Mate tried to signal them with his torch; but, fearing the raider would see them, he stopped. They put the boat about and rowed toward the rafts. As they neared them, the raider swung its guns, and streams of incendiary bullets poured into them. On the rise of the next swell, the men in the boat saw, the bobbing lights were gone. The life rafts and the men clinging to them had been obliterated.

At nine o'clock by the Mate's wristwatch an explosion rent the *Anglo*'s poop, followed, five minutes later, by another. "The magazines," said the men in the boat. Their ship's bow was rising now. When almost perpendicular, it snapped back with a jerk and she went down by the stern. There was a great hissing as the water reached her fires, and a cloud of steam shot up from her. It took less than a minute. The waves closed over her. Only a pall of black steam overhead remained to mark where she had been. The men in the boat watched silently. Even Morgan, the garrulous, had nothing to say. It's a terrible thing, Tapscott thought, to see your ship go down.

The raider, her work of destruction over, headed off into the east.

Tapscott and Widdicombe rigged the drogue and paid out the line. It brought the bows of the jolly boat into the sea but was not large enough to enable them to dispense with the oars altogether.

"Right," said the Mate, when he saw how matters stood. "We'll have to stand watches. Tapscott and Widdicombe will take the first. Keep her head into it or we're liable to swamp."

Changing places, Pilcher groaned.

"What's the matter?" the Mate asked.

"My foot. I think it's blown off."

"It can't be as bad as that. How could you have rowed? I'll take a look at it."

The Mate flashed his torch. The bottom of the boat was awash with bloody water and was full of the smell of blood. Tapscott's seat was smeared with it, from the shrapnel wounds in his back.

"You've been hit, right enough," said the Mate, straightening up, "but you still have a foot. I'll dress it for you in the morning. . . . Everybody try to get some sleep now."

No one could sleep; they were too cold, wet and miserable. The swell pounded the boat and the spray rained down in clouds. At midnight the Mate and Hawkes relieved the two A.B.'s. Tapscott and Widdicombe lay down where Hawkes and Denny had been, but could sleep no better than the rest. In the end they all gave it up and talked in lowered voices.

The sun rose at six o'clock on seven cold, sad, wet and thoroughly miserable men. As the long, level rays lighted up the surface of the sea and a golden light flooded the sky, with one accord all who could stood up and scanned the sea. In all that tossing circular plane they could see nothing, nothing save empty miles of water, nothing on the surface of the ocean and nothing in the sky. They were completely and singularly alone.

"Well," said the Mate, briskly, when he had satisfied himself that there was nothing human to be seen in the whole circle of the sea, "the sooner we start, the sooner we'll be there."

"Be where?" the men asked.

"The Leeward Islands," the Mate said. "There's no use going east. Wind and current are against us. Finding the Azores would be like looking for a needle in a haystack."

"Yes," said Widdicombe, "but supposing we miss the Leeward Islands?"

"Even if we sail right through them," the Mate said, "there is the Caribbean and the whole coast of North and South America."

Pilcher's wounded leg had stiffened so that it stood out straight before him. In daylight they saw that he was much more badly wounded than he had led them to believe. Shrapnel or a dum-dum bullet had torn through the length of his left foot, reducing it to a pulp of tissue and shattered bone. The men marveled that he could have rowed as he did in the first hours of their flight from the ship. "I didn't feel it," he said deprecatingly. They moved him forward into the bow-sheets, fashioning a sling from his scarf to keep his stiff leg from moving with the motion of the boat.

The gunner, Penny, had a badly torn hip, where shrapnel had caught him as he ran across the *Anglo-Saxon's* deck. The bullet that had gone through his right forearm as he lay with Tapscott in the shelter of the bridge had left a hole, comparatively clean. Both wounds being on his right side, they arranged the gunner forward on his left, bolstering him as best they could against the roll.

Morgan, the second cook, had a jagged tear just above his right ankle, where shrapnel or flying metal of some variety had caught him as he scrambled to the boat. His whole foot was bruised and swollen. He had a badly contused hand as well.

Tapscott had the Mate check him up for wounds. One of his front teeth, which had been broken off, exposing the nerve, when he was hurled through the air by the explosion of a shell, was now paining him considerably, but blood had stopped seeping down his back. The Mate found that a small piece of shrapnel had buried itself in Tapscott's left buttock, another in the muscles of his back and another in the palm of his left hand. A long splinter, evidently spent, had gone through his shorts into his right groin. It had burned him painfully but had not penetrated his flesh.

The wounded men disposed of, the able men got in the sea anchor, stepped the stubby mast they found in the boat and set sail. They headed the boat due west to make west–southwest, a note on the compass advising them that it was out several points. A good breeze was blowing from the east. They were on their way to shelter and safety, they felt, doing all of four knots.

They took stock of the boat and supplies. The boat, eighteen feet long and six wide, was stoutly built and in sound condition. Seats ran fore and aft on either side inboard, converging at the bow. These were rounded off at the stern to join a roomy seat across it, underneath which was a locker. Two stout thwarts completed the seating arrangements.

The boat was propelled by a dipping lug, a powerful sail in the hands of experts. It was large enough to carry the boat along at decent speed but not so large as to be dangerous in squally weather. It is the favorite rig of fishermen and trawlers on the English coast. It has the disadvantage, however, of having to be lowered every time the boat is tacked, no maneuver for amateurs. This is the only way the spar from which it is suspended can be passed to the other side of the mast. Hence the name.

For equipment there was a sea anchor, a boat hook, six pairs of oars, a steering oar, an axe, the Mate's knife, two bailers, a rope painter, the boat's canvas cover, badly worn and torn, and a few ends of rope. In the locker under the stern seat was a boat's compass, a colza oil lamp with a bucket large enough to hold it—this for signaling in Morse—a dozen red flares in watertight canisters, a dozen matches in a watertight container and a medical kit.

Further to equip it as a lifeboat, three airtight tanks had been built into it—one in the bow, and two on either side in the middle—and a lifeline within easy reach from the surface of the sea fixed along both of the boat's sides.

Food supplies consisted of three tins of boiled mutton, weighing six pounds each; eleven tins of condensed milk and thirty-two pounds of ship's biscuit in an airtight metal tank fixed forward under the first thwart. Behind this was the water breaker, a keg in a cradle, with a wide bung in the top, and two long-handled, narrow-mouthed dippers for scooping up its contents.

Tapscott had, in addition to his underwear, khaki shorts, a singlet, heavy knitted Air Force socks and heavy shoes. Widdicombe had underwear, a pair of tattered trousers and a cotton shirt. Penny wore the khaki shirt and trousers of the Marine undress uniform. Morgan had denim cook's trousers and a singlet.

The sun was now high enough to shine down hotly. The men took off their soaked clothing and spread it dry.

Routine having been established, the Mate opened the medical kit. It consisted of a bottle of iodine, two rolls of bandage, a packet of medical lint and a pair of scissors. "Just the thing for taking to a picnic in the New Forest!" he said, on seeing the size of it. There were several rubber finger cots in the kit. He put these on his fingers that had been burned sliding down the lifeline from the ship; they were now raw and painful.

Sparks was treated first. With the aid of the Third Mate and Tapscott, the Mate bathed Sparks' mangled foot in seawater and cleaned it as best he could. On close examination it seemed crushed beyond any hope of saving; the shattered bone protruded through a bloody pulp.

"Man," said the Mate, shaking his head, "how could you have pulled a boat with a foot like that?"

"It wasn't anything," Sparks said. "I tell you I didn't feel it."

"If we were in port I am afraid the doctor would have it off," the Mate said.

Sparks was silent. Fever was already coursing through his depleted veins; he had lost a great deal of blood. "I know we must be careful with the water," he said, "but do you think that I might have a drop? Just enough to wet my throat."

They gave him a drink. It was then that the Mate discovered that the water breaker had lost some of its contents; it was little over half full—about four gallons.

After sterilizing and binding up the wounds of the injured men and settling them as comfortably as they could, the able men bailed the boat, made ready the lifeboat lamp and set up as orderly a routine as possible in quarters so cramped.

The Mate returned to his log and wrote:

Thursday, August 22nd, 1940. Wind N.E. 3, slight sea, slightly confused easterly swell. Course by compass W. All's well. Medical treatment given.

The men had their first rations that evening at six: a ship's biscuit apiece. No one asked for water. As night fell the wounded and the men off watch made themselves as comfortable as they could under the tattered boat cover. It kept off some of the spray.

When they came to light the small colza oil binnacle lamp—the compass was housed in a hoodlike affair of metal with the lamp fixed inside—they could not get it to ignite. They tried to light the large lamp with no better success.

"Too bad," said the Mate. "We'll have to steer by the stars."

They changed watches regularly during the night. The wind held and the boat ran before it, taking water now and then, which was promptly bailed out by the man on standby.

Everyone got some sleep. Those who could not sleep lay quietly. Now and again, one of the wounded men groaned in spite of himself. Underneath the canvas, someone snored.

Tapscott shifted about on his hard plank bed, trying to settle his hip bone so as to give him some ease. The boat was sailing handily. Seas struck it sharply and ran hissing by. Occasionally it rose on the crest of a wave and dropped with a booming shock that vibrated its timbers and sent a cloud of spray raining down.

⚫︎⚫︎

The day passed uneventfully. Everyone's spirits were good, but conversation lagged. They had worn out their slim stock of conundrums. The sun was warm but not in the least oppressive. The wounded and the men off watch slept a good deal. It was not unlike their routine aboard ship, where sleep occupied most of their time off duty.

Physical functions practically ceased; their bodies had no waste to eliminate.

At six in the evening they had their biscuit and half dipper of water, changed the watch, and settled down for the night. They knew by this time every bolt head, rib, knot and protuberance of the boat's planking. They had learned, too, how to dodge spray so as to get the minimum wetting. Under the tattered boat cover they were out of the wind and most of the wet; the night was appreciably warmer; they enjoyed good hours of sleep.

Tapscott and Widdicombe had finished their watch at ten o'clock and had turned in when they were awakened by a stir within the boat. It was eleven o'clock by Widdicombe's wristwatch, which was still functioning.

"What is it?" they asked, sleepily.

"Ship," said the Mate, fumbling hastily in the locker under the stern seat.

"Where?" they demanded, wide awake now and straining their eyes into the surrounding darkness.

The whole boat awoke and sat up eagerly trying to see.

"Aft," said Hawkes, who had the standby.

The Mate was unscrewing the top of the container that held the flares. As their eyes adjusted themselves to the light they saw a ship in outline heading north–northeast. She was blacked out; but they could see her clearly.

The Mate extracted a flare, struck it on the milled top of the container and held it, spluttering and hissing, over his head. The boat and the sea for yards around were lighted up with a dazzling red glare. They sat silent while the flare burnt itself out. When the last bead of the chemical composing it had melted, flamed, charred and gone out, the night closed in, blacker than before. The Mate flung the smoking stick into the sea. They brought the boat into the wind and waited.

When they could again see, the ship had turned and was coming back to them in a wide circle, as if afraid of a trap. They started to cheer. The Mate silenced them curtly. As she swung around they could see what he feared. Her build was German, or, at least, very like a German.

"I don't like the looks of her," said the Mate.

The stranger was now almost opposite them.

"Lower the sail," the Mate ordered. They dropped the dipping lug and lay to.

"If she's British she will put a searchlight on us," Widdicombe said.

"Stow it," the Mate said, "and lie low."

They crouched down in the boat and waited while the stranger hung off to the starboard.

"A Jerry, or I'm a Chinaman," said the Mate. "Look at the way she acts."

They waited there, their hearts stepping up to a higher beat. After some minutes of cruising at slow speed the stranger turned, gathered speed and made off to the north–northeast.

The next morning, after dealing out the early ration, the Mate cut another notch of his toll of days in the gunwale and wrote up his log for the previous one.

August 23rd. Friday. Wind E.N.E. 3, slight sea, slightly confused easterly swell, partly cloudy. Half a dipper of water per man 6 a.m. Also half a biscuit with a little condensed milk. Sighted a vessel showing no lights at 11 p.m. showed sea flare, she cruised around but was of the opinion she was raider as she was heading N.N.E. We were about a hundred miles from our original position. Kept quiet let her go off.

Saturday passed without incident. While everyone was cheerful enough, there were long periods of silence. The wind had hauled around to the northwest; the sky was cloudy. The Mate peered anxiously into the bung of the water breaker and noted the lowering level.

Sunday dawned cloudy with a slight swell on the sea. The wind had dropped during the night until the boat had lost all way. A light wind sprang up from the north–northwest. The watch trimmed sail hopefully and the boat moved forward once more. Everyone was cheerful over his half biscuit and pittance of water. Their bodies were so dehydrated it was impossible to swallow the hard biscuit without wetting it first. The Mate's eyes narrowed every time he looked inside the breaker. He scanned the sky anxiously for rain clouds, but nowhere in the idly moving mass was one remotely resembling the cloud he sought.

Pilcher and Morgan were suffering increasing pain in their wounds. Their lacerated feet had swollen during the night and were swelling more. It was necessary to loosen their bandages. When this had been done, an odor permeated the boat, an odor no man ever forgets once he has smelled it—the horrible stench of gangrene. The Mate examined the wounds intently, but said nothing. He returned to the stern sheets with another weight on his already heavily burdened sense of responsibility.

The men dozed as they drifted, or, sitting up, scanned the empty reaches of the sea. In all that space there was nothing but sky and water to be seen; not a bird, not a patch of seaweed, not even a drifting log.

The sun was sinking in red glory, betokening fair weather to come. The men made ready for the night. The Mate wrote up his log for the day. Had it not been for the disquieting smell of gangrene, which, once in the boat, infected the air, they might have been on a pleasure cruise, so well were they feeling after their hearty meal.

In the morning, Monday, August 26th, their fifth day in the open boat, a bos'n bird appeared to the men of the *Anglo-Saxon*. It planed over them in a leisurely way, wheeled, came back and flew low over them again.

"Mean-looking blighter, he was," Widdicombe said. "Had that look in his eye: 'Just wait. I'll get you yet.'" He stared back at the bird malevolently. "Not me you won't get," he said.

The wind, which had been falling, now dropped away to an occasional fitful gust and the boat drifted or lay becalmed under the burning sun. To men without hats the direct rays were torture. Those who took shelter under the canvas boat cover found themselves in an oven.

They were very thirsty now. Their pores, denied any liquid to evaporate, closed up; their skin scorched and crisped; salivation ceased. The morning half dipper of water, gulped with such eagerness, was like a drop on a blotter.

They prayed for squalls and a decent wind.

"We should sight a vessel any time now," the Mate said; and they accepted this as inspired knowledge.

After breakfast, the Mate and the Third dressed the injured men's wounds. Pilcher's mangled foot had swollen to twice its natural size. Without the bandage it was a green and black gangrenous horror. The boat was almost untenable. They gave him the best treatment they could devise with the scant knowledge and means at their disposal. They got his leg over the gunwale. Tapscott bailed salt water over the wound for an hour. The Mate then bound it up with the last linen bandage. Pilcher never flinched, although in exquisite pain. He apologized for giving them so much trouble. "He has guts that one," Widdicombe said to Tapscott. "A proper man if I ever saw one."

Morgan's smashed ankle was swelling badly, too. They gave him the same treatment.

The bullet hole in the gunlayer's right forearm was still clean. They bathed it with a little of their precious fresh water, saturated it with iodine and bound it up again. The wound in his thigh, however, was not doing at all well. And they were at the end of their medical supplies.

As the sun reached meridian they writhed and twisted on the hot planking of the boat like fish on a griddle. Their mouths and throats were so parched that talking was painful. The able men bailed seawater over the wounded, and when they had them thoroughly doused, went over the side themselves, being careful to keep their faces out of water. Naked, they noted with surprise how much weight they had lost.

"At any rate," the Third said to Tapscott, "you're much better-looking without that fat belly."

They made good progress during the day. Whenever they spoke, which was seldom, they heard the changed notes of their voices distorted by thirst. Cracked and swollen lips, tightened skin and salient cheek bones gave them new expressions. They noticed that they were not so sure of their footing as before.

During the night the boat did a steady four knots on the port tack heading S.W. true. The sun, the Mate noted, had set at 6:42.

The trade wind held all the next day. In the morning a bos'n bird and a common gull flew over them. "There's that bloody bird again," Widdicombe said, shaking his fist at it. "What's he want hanging about like this?" The men laughed. But Widdicombe was serious. "He had mean eyes," he said. "It made me fair narked."

The sun beat down tropically. The Mate, the Third, Tapscott and Widdicombe dipped their bodies overside again, holding on to the lifelines that festooned the side of the boat. Their bodies took up the water through their pores, leaving their skin white with salt. Saliva returned to their mouths. They all felt better.

The reek of gangrene was terrible now. Penny's torn hip was going the way of Pilcher's foot. No matter how brisk the breeze, it seemed impossible to get that devastating stench out of their nostrils. Sparks was apologetic. It was the only sign of suffering he allowed himself. Morgan's wound was gangrening, too. Everyone assured Sparks that it was nothing that could be helped, but on awakening to it, after the unconsciousness of sleep, their stomachs turned over.

In the morning Sparks' foot "went dead." He no longer felt pain in it. He no longer felt anything there. It was surcease of a sort but bought at the expense of his whole body. He was failing and they caught in his eyes the expression of a man who is looking beyond life.

The wind was strong and the sea boisterous. They bowled along handily, making fine time and shipping buckets of water. No one cared about the water. They were soaking wet, yet all they talked of were liquids. They talked of peaches, pears, oranges, the juice of pineapples. In the end, they talked of beer: light beer, dark beer, beer in glasses, mugs and tankards; English, Danish, French and German beer; beer foaming from inexhaustible taps.

They made ready for a wet night cheerfully. This, they told themselves, in voices croaking with thirst, was the last lap.

In the morning the wind dropped and the swell lessened. After the first bite no one cared to go on with his quarter of a ship's biscuit. It was impossible to swallow. The half dipper of water gave them a few moments' release from the grip at their throats; then it was gone, a splatter of rain in the desert of their desiccated tissues.

Pilcher lay very quietly now under the shelter of the boat cover. As the sun climbed the sky and the temperature mounted and the men bailed water over one another. Morgan, the cook, seemed better; he could move his stiffened leg. Penny seemed better, too; so much so he took a short trick at the tiller.

Everyone remarked that they had stopped sweating, even at noon. The dryness of their throats crawled up their tongues, which, thick and discolored, filled their mouths like a gag of hot felt. They grinned at each other now and then as if sharing a painful, sardonic joke.

In the evening, the wind fell away completely. The boat pitched, tossed and drifted on the swell. It was hard to rest, much less to sleep, thrown about on a narrow seat. They were awake until late at night.

Just as, fatigued to the point of sleep, some of them achieved an uneasy doze, Pilcher's voice rose from the bow in a long and plangent wail.

An inhuman quality in it, a severance from all direction of the intellect, brought them awake with a start.

"What is it, Sparks?" the Mate asked.

There was no answer.

The Mate went forward to him. He was lying face upward, staring unseeingly into the sky.

"What's the matter?" the Mate repeated.

The glazed eyes showed no flicker of recognition. A voice, a detached caricature of Pilcher's, apostrophized an unseen, abstract personage in bitter, obscene invective. The voice, matter and manner were utterly unlike the normal, gentle Sparks! Then he laughed—hysterical bursts of unmotivated laughter, which stopped as abruptly and unreasonably as they had started.

"Off his head," the Mate said, "and that's a fact."

Sparks was singing now, a street ballad of the most scabrous nature, a song they would not have thought him capable of. He sang it to the end, then started again. He sang it over and over.

"For God's sake, stop him!" Morgan, who lay next him, begged the Mate.

The Mate tried again to quiet the delirious operator, but to no use. Sparks, insulated by hysteria, gave no sign of hearing anything. All they could do was wait uneasily for the seizure to wear itself out.

After a bit Sparks subsided into low moans and a running mutter of talk. The men settled themselves again. They could not sleep, no matter how they twisted and turned; expectancy of what they did not want to hear kept them tense. It came very soon, heralded by that long-drawn, rising, animal cry—singing, invective, bursts of maniacal laughter.

Toward the morning Sparks drifted off into sleep or semi-coma.

At sunup the next morning the Mate called the able men to him.

"We've got to do something about Sparks's foot," he said.

All of the previous day Sparks had alternated between delirium and comatose sleep. He had been off his head most of the night and was now exhausted but lucid.

"What can we do?" they asked.

"Amputate it."

"With what?" Tapscott asked.

"The axe. If we don't, he's going to die."

Tapscott was shocked. The axe was rusty, dirty and dull. They had no antiseptic. He was certain, too—but he did not mention this to the others—that Sparks was going to die anyway. Why torture him with a clumsy operation that would in all likelihood end in him bleeding to death?

The men looked uncertainly at one another.

"I know it's taking a long chance," the Mate said, "but that foot is poisoning him. It will have to come off."

Hawkes and Widdicombe agreed that the Mate was right, but Tapscott still demurred.

"Very well," said the Mate, "we'll put it up to Sparks himself."

They went forward to Pilcher, who lay in the bow-sheets, weak but uncomplaining.

"Sparks, old chap," the Mate said, "your foot is in bad shape."

"I know it," Sparks said, feebly.

"We think it will have to come off. The sooner the better. Do you want us to do it?"

"Yes. Please. Anything," Pilcher said, his face contorted with pain.

The Mate fetched the axe. They removed the boat cover from Pilcher. Widdicombe and Hawkes stood by to hold him. But when it came to the actual business of lopping off Sparks' foot with the axe, even the resolute Mate quailed. "I can't do it," he said. "He'll just have to take the chance."

Everyone breathed a sigh of relief.

The Mate rearranged the boat cover over Pilcher so as to keep the sun off his face. "Carry on, old boy," he said. "We're not going to do it now. We're certain to be picked up soon and a proper doctor will make it right for you."

Pilcher smiled weakly and closed his eyes.

Saturday night was grim and miserable. They were so thirsty they could not sleep. In the morning the Mate wrote in his log:

During Saturday night crew felt very thirsty; boiled mutton could not be digested and some felt sick. Doubled water ration that night.

This was a triumph of understatement. When the Mate used the word "sick" he did not mean ill, as Americans do, but, literally, nauseated. Nor did he say that of the "some" who were sick he was the sickest. Nausea and cramps seized him early in the night, causing him to retch agonizedly. Had the others not been so tormented themselves, they would have been more concerned.

When the morning dawned, they saw to their consternation that he, the symbol of discipline and fountainhead of knowledge, had suffered some sort of internal collapse. His face was livid and lined with pain. All of his strength seemed to have gone from him. His abraded fingers were suppurating badly, and his flesh, even where burned by the sun, had a lifeless, claylike appearance.

Pilcher, too, was very low. He was so weak he could hardly speak. He was lucid, though. When they took him his morning ration of water he turned his head from the dipper and told them to give it to someone who needed it more than he.

They went about the business of the boat in a vague and silent fashion. The sun was already hot enough to be uncomfortable. It reflected back from the sea, giving them a taste of the burning misery to come.

At eight o'clock, Morgan, from his place next to Pilcher in the bow-sheets said, suddenly: "I say, I think Sparks has gone."

The Mate, the Third, Tapscott and Widdicombe went forward. Morgan had spoken the truth. Sparks had, indeed, gone, as silently and unobtrusively as he had done everything in life. They looked at one another incredulously. So soon! It couldn't be possible. But when the looked at Sparks' fallen jaw and saw the subtle changes that had already taken place in the contours of his face, they knew that it could not be otherwise. They stood impotently by, overwhelmed by the awful finality of death.

In curt, low orders the Mate arranged all that was left to do. Tapscott and the Third lifted the body over the gunwale and lowered it gently into the sea. They had nothing to wrap it in and nothing with which to weigh it.

The wind was south–southwest; the boat was making several knots. The body drifted away on the swell, off into the immensity of the Atlantic. They watched it until they could see it no more.

Very little was said in the boat the rest of that day.

When the sun came up the next morning, their twelfth in the open boat, there was no expectant stir, no sense of a new day. Pilcher's death was heavy upon them and the Mate's condition gave them new cause for alarm. He could scarcely crawl to the breaker to issue the morning half dipper of water. His face was ghastly, his will and vitality almost gone.

Several of them refused the ration of dry ship's biscuit. Those who took it gave up trying to eat; they were unable to chew.

Penny, the gunner, lay quiet in the bow. He was visibly much weaker. Morgan, who had lain beside him, almost as quietly, since the ordeal by thirst began, now chattered and sang.

Widdicombe, too, seemed bordering on hysteria, alternately violently optimistic, confident that they would come through all right in the end, or sunk in apathetic pessimism. He suffered more than the others from the heat. He attributed this to a sunstroke he had experienced on a voyage through the Arabian Sea. Frequently he would be overcome while taking his turn at the tiller and would have to get Tapscott to relieve him until the faintness had passed.

Tapscott, engrossed in his own misery, brooded over this. He doubted Widdicombe's peculiar susceptibility as he doubted many of Widdicombe's stories. He had never liked Widdicombe and he felt that his watchmate was exploiting him now, trading on his good nature to get out of onerous duty. This growing resentment blazed forth in open quarrel that morning, which might have ended tragically had the Third not intervened. Discipline, obviously weakening, was restored for the time.

Discipline now was sustained only by a symbol, the Mate. So long as he lived and retained his reason he held command. But as the sun rose higher and the heat increased, violent nausea and spasms of pain racked him. He lay in the bottom of the boat, retching horribly. After one of these spells he would lie exhausted, in a state of semi-coma. His arms were a mass of blisters and scales. In spite of all this, he took a turn at the tiller whenever he could.

To Morgan, also, they gave a trick at the rudder. It seemed to allay his growing dementia, and weak as they now were, everyone had to help. But Morgan gave them more trouble than aid. He seemed incapable of grasping the first principles of sailing a boat. He yawed and blundered, shipping water and nearly capsizing them several times.

They made little progress that day. No one had the energy to dip himself overside. They simply lay and suffered, protecting themselves from the worst of the sun with the boat cover.

That evening the Mate made the last entry he was able to write in the log. He reported their condition with his habitual understatement. As ill and despairing as he was, he remained the officer. He included a suggestion for bettering lifeboat equipment based upon his all-too-actual experience. In a hand that could just trace the letters he wrote:

Sept. 2nd. Monday. 6:15 a.m. issued half a dipper of water per man and same in evening with a little condensed milk diluted with it. Crew now feeling rather low, unable to masticate hard biscuit owing to low ration of water.

Suggestion for lifeboat stocks. At the very least two breakers of water for each boat, tins of fruit such as peaches, apricots, pears, fruit juices and lime juices, baked beans, etc. Our stores consisted of—

One tank filled with dry biscuit.
11 tins condensed milk
3 tins each 6 pounds boiled mutton.
One breaker of water, half filled.

These were the last words of any kind the Mate ever wrote. He was ill all during the night and so weak in the morning he could not get to his feet. They made a bed for him in the thwarts, using boards and life belts. He was too ill now to command.

Whatever was in store for them, they must keep going west. It was their only hope. They trimmed sail and kept the boat on her course.

When the Third went to the water breaker Widdicombe proposed issuing a whole dipperful instead of the usual ration. Tapscott objected; he was as thirsty as anyone but he felt they should maintain the ration the Mate had decided upon up to the very end. And that would be all too soon, they knew; the water was very near the bottom of the breaker now.

The Third hesitated. The Mate was too ill to intervene. Penny and Morgan were nullities so far as making decisions was concerned; Penny was nearly as weak as the Mate and Morgan had to be handled like a feebleminded child.

"The water won't last much longer anyway," Widdicombe insisted, "so why not have a decent drink now?"

In the end Hawkes and Tapscott gave in. There was that in Widdicombe's voice and manner which caused them to fear that he would attempt to take the water by force. They did not want a fight to complete their distress. A fight was the last thing in the world they wanted at that moment.

That day they made better time than on the day before. They took their turns at the tiller, bailed the boat and sought shelter from the sun under the boat cover, trying not to think of the thirst that was consuming them.

They were dull with apprehension, but, whatever their thoughts were, they did not express them. Each man was wholly preoccupied with his chief concern, his own life. That is, all but Morgan, who kept up a babble of senseless talk and singing until one of them, driven into a passion of irritation, would silence him temporarily with a curse.

Tapscott thought of nothing in particular; he was sunk into a heat-drenched stupor, a sort of anesthesia. He was not despondent, though. Things were pretty bad, he realized, but they need not inevitably end in disaster. He was nineteen years old, and life, even in such circumstances as these, was essentially a hopeful affair.

Widdicombe, mercurial in his calmest moments, alternated between energetic optimism and angry despair. This he relieved at times by cursing, long and fervently, an abstract fate that could not be reached with his fists and feet.

The older men, one poisoned with gangrenous wounds, the other, ravaged by some internal disorder in addition to the thirst and starvation they were all suffering, said nothing. Neither could have had much hope, unless that of a miraculous landfall or rescue ship, but neither of them would admit it. Both must have known that rescue for them would be too late now.

The night was chill and wet. Their teeth chattered as they huddled together for warmth. The Mate kept them awake with the violence of his vomiting, the cook with hysterical ramblings and complaint. Toward morning the cook became quieter.

The sun rose on a calmer sea. The wind fell off and the boat made slow progress under a sky that promised no escape from another day of unbearable heat and thirst. They had the morning ration of water. It was plain that after the next drink there would be no more. They were at the very end of their tether.

The noon sun reduced them to such an agony of thirst they voted to drink the last of the water then and there. It was measured out, the three able men jealously watching that an exact division was made.

Tapscott sat on the starboard seat. Widdicombe and the Third were at the breaker. Morgan was lying in the bow-sheets and the Mate on his bed of boards amidships. Penny had just taken the tiller. He said nothing, but there was nothing unusual in that. Normally taciturn, Penny had practically quit speech in the last few days.

The boat yawed suddenly. Tapscott turned to see what the helmsman was up to. But there was no helmsman to be seen. Where Penny had sat there was an empty seat and the rudder handle swinging purposelessly. Tapscott sprang to his feet and searched the sea. Then he saw Penny. He was floating away rapidly, face downward, his arms outstretched before him. "Like doing the dead man's float," Tapscott said. He was making no attempt to swim. He had not gone over for that.

Even if they had been able to bring the boat about in time—which was impossible—it is doubtful anyone would have moved to go after the gunner. He was doing what he deemed best. Unwritten law gave a man in these circumstances, provided he was or appeared to be in his right mind, the inalienable right to choose his own way out of his suffering. The gunner had "gone over the side."

It was hard to take in, but, they had to admit, this very likely *was* the end. It confronted them suddenly with a horrible actuality. There was nothing more for them, saving a miracle, than prolonged torture, madness and inevitable death. They had known that it was a possibility but had kept it so buried in their minds, resolutely determined not to admit it, it seemed a new and unfair hardship, considering what they had already endured.

Better end it now and spare themselves further suffering. That would be the sensible course, they agreed. But a physical lassitude weighed down their bodies and paralyzed their wills. No one wanted the initiative in so final a move. In the end they did nothing but mechanically sail the boat, and there was no more talk of going over the side.

Night brought escape from the heat, at least. They sprawled or lay in misery, all power gone from their limbs. When they moved to relieve one another at the tiller the physical action lagged appreciably behind the act of will. It seemed too great an effort to get themselves from the bow to the stern of the boat.

The wind was slight and fitful. The boat drifted or sailed listlessly. At times it seemed to float stationary, its only motion a slight heaving with the swell.

The Mate was scarcely breathing. Morgan had quieted down. There was no sound just before dawn, save the sighs of the sleeping men and the murmur of the sea.

Morgan sat up suddenly, pushed away the canvas that was muffling him, stared into the void and said peremptorily: "I want my mother."

＊ ＊

Day dawned to the five men of the *Anglo-Saxon*—their thirteenth in the open boat—as the morning of execution to a condemned man.

The sun came up from the sea; the breeze freshened; the boat picked up speed. But the unkempt, hollow-eyed, thirst-tortured creatures in it hardly stirred.

From habit they edged toward the water breaker. Then, remembering, they sat down again. They were heavy with apprehension. Each regarded the other warily, awaiting the gesture or word they all knew would come.

As if to put the seal of finality on disaster, the rudder, which lacked a lower pintle when they left the ship, was carried away by a heavy swell. The Mate was steering at the time. He watched it disappear as if it were his last hope for life, dropped the useless tiller, went to his bed of life belts and boards, and lay down with closed eyes.

Tapscott and Widdicombe got out the steering oar and shipped it in place of the lost rudder. The Third, who had been watching the Mate narrowly, stretched himself out beside him. The two lay this way for a long time, while the sun, mounting higher, burned into their eyelids and whipped up the demon inside, which was relentlessly squeezing the juice of life from them.

They sailed for long hours this way, hearing nothing, seeing nothing. Then the Mate opened his eyes, raised himself on his elbow and said from swollen and discolored lips, "I'm going over. Who's coming with me?"

"No, no! Don't! You can't! Don't leave me! You won't, will you?" Morgan cried from the bow-sheets.

"Shut up!" Widdicombe ordered him, menacing him with a gesture.

Morgan was still.

Tapscott, Widdicombe and the Third stared at one another, each waiting for the other to speak.

"I'll go," the Third said, finally; "only you'll have to help me, you know."

The Mate nodded assent. He turned his eyes to Morgan.

"No, no, no!" Morgan cried. "I can't. I can't. I don't want to die."

The Mate turned next to Tapscott. Tapscott thought a minute before answering. "No," he said. He felt that he must explain. "I mean to say," he added, "it isn't like I was dying; and you can't tell; we may be picked up yet."

The Mate turned to Widdicombe. Widdicombe shook his head violently. "No fear," he said, showing the whites of his eyes like a nervous horse.

The Mate lay back with eyes closed.

"That settles that," said the Third. "I might as well have some sleep myself before we go." He lay down beside the Mate again.

The dread of what they must see overwhelmed the other three. Morgan lay back in the bow-sheets staring at the self-condemned men. It was the formal end; those in command were laying down their arms.

Maybe, Tapscott thought, they'll change their minds. He could not imagine anyone making such a dreadful decision and then going calmly to sleep.

Neither Tapscott nor Widdicombe would have dreamed of remonstrating or trying to interfere. Not only were the two officers senior to them and entitled to make decisions without question, but they had decided the most private question in life. Interference would have been presumptuousness of the most outrageous character. Moreover, they were too dazed and miserable themselves to formulate more than their own desire to hold on until the last. Tapscott did not even think that far; blind instinct had spoken for him, an instinct he had never thought to question.

There was something awesome in this vigil. They sailed for an hour or more in this fashion.

Somewhere near ten o'clock Hawkes sat up and said: "Ready?"

The Mate opened his eyes and then got to his feet with surprising speed and sureness, considering how weak he had been. He picked up the axe and placed it on a thwart near the port gunwale.

"Just a minute," Hawkes said, almost gaily. "I'm going to have something to eat and drink."

He dipped a can of water from the sea and gulped it down greedily. He filled the can again and drank that off. Then he softened a biscuit in seawater and ate it.

The Mate drew off his signet ring and handed it to Widdicombe. "Give it—my mother—if you get through," he gasped.

They shook hands all around.

It was then that Hawkes had a moment of bitterness. "To think," he said, "that I put in four years of training—to come to this."

The Mate took off his coat. Hawkes removed his, too.

"Give it to me," Widdicombe said.

"No," the Third said, "I can't. I promised it to Bob if anything happened to me."

"Then give me your trousers," Widdicombe said. "You won't need them."

"Can't do that either," the Third said, grinning through cracked and blistered lips; "I might meet a mermaid where I'm going."

Tapscott's eyes were blinded with unexpected tears when the Mate took his hand.

"Keep going west," the Mate said, scarcely able to force the words through his stiffened lips. His voice fell off into a throaty croak; he gestured loosely with his left hand and struggled to achieve what he wanted to say. "No more south."

The Mate and the Third then stood up in the thwarts near the port gunwale. They shook hands. Tapscott turned his head away and held his breath. He heard a crunching thud, a great splash, and, when he dared look again, the Mate and the Third were floating yards away, clasped, apparently, in each other's arms.

The Third's hair, the lightest of yellows normally, had bleached to white in the boat. Long and untrimmed, it floated out on the sea like a patch of bright sea-growth, a brilliant note in the monotone of blue water. The men in the boat could see it for a long time. Getting smaller and smaller, they found and lost it in the swell until it, too, became a part of the heaving whole.

The passing of the Mate and the Third Engineer had a curious effect upon Widdicombe. It vitalized him into hope and action. He took to himself command.

Morgan and Tapscott were sunk in despair. Widdicombe, on the contrary, was full of energy. He trimmed sail, set the course and rallied the others to new effort. They had nothing to maintain life—neither food nor water—but Widdicombe was sure that somehow, perhaps miraculously, they would come through.

They moved now like figures in a slow-motion film. They had to rest continuously to husband what little strength they had left. They divided the day into hour watches, which they kept more or less accurately, although they had to shorten or lengthen them often according to their physical state.

The mere thought of food gave Tapscott a painful contraction of the stomach, which seized him like a cramp. He would have to lie down while suffering it and wait until it had passed before he could do a thing.

Widdicombe suffered more and more from the sun. It gave him fits of vertigo that rendered him useless for whatever he was doing at the time. They tried Morgan on the steering oar and it seemed to steady him for a time. But, always, in the end, they had to snatch it away from him to avoid disaster. He could not stay on the wind or learn the rudiments of handling the boat in the swell. They took bucketfuls of water which had to be laboriously bailed out. And they could scarcely stand on their legs.

The second day after the Mate and the Third went over was very like the first, save that the breeze lessened and the heat increased. They bailed seawater over each other and dipped their heads over the side when the sun was at its worst. Tapscott noticed impersonally, as if it was not his body he was considering, that his skin was cracking and scaling, and that he was covered with boil-like eruptions. The piece of shrapnel in his left palm was working to the surface. It made a painful lump there which prevented him from grasping anything firmly. As consumed as he was by his thirst, he drank no more seawater. The Third's last actions before going over made him somehow chary of that.

Morgan, on the other hand, drank seawater in greater quantities. It did no good to warn him not to or to stop him in the act. At night he could dip it up when he chose.

That night they lay hove to again, but got very little sleep. Morgan kept them awake with his noise and lamentations. The next day he was worse. They put him in the bow-sheet under the boat cover, wedged in well with life belts, and ordered him to lie still. Tapscott had no sooner made his way aft again than Morgan was out of his shelter and working his way aft. Or, worse, he would pull himself up on the gunwale and try to walk, at imminent peril of falling overboard.

The breeze was lighter and the humidity intense. Widdicombe sat a great deal of the time with his head in his hands. His burst of optimism and energy had departed as suddenly as it had arrived. He would shut out Morgan's ravings with the palms of his hands, or bear them until his frayed nerves recoiled. Then he would stagger up and rave and curse like a madman himself.

In the heat of the day, while staring at nothing, Widdicombe got up suddenly, went to the water breaker, took the keg from its cradle and hurled it into the sea.

"That's a damn silly thing to do," Tapscott said to him. "What did you want to do that for?"

"Why is it sitting there with nothing in it?" Widdicombe demanded furiously.

"Now what will we put the water in when it rains?" Tapscott asked.

"We aren't going to get any water. It's never going to rain. What do I care, anyway?" Widdicombe shrieked.

Tapscott mentally shrugged his shoulders. He wondered if Widdicombe, too, were going completely off his head.

They lay to that night and tried to get some sleep. The second cook was in and out of the bow-sheets all the time. When not raving he sank into coma and at such moments they dozed.

The next day was like the one before. Widdicombe was now sunk in deepest dejection. Morgan laughed, cried, shouted and sang, practically continuously. He varied this with demands for his mother. This, particularly, roused Widdicombe to fury.

"Shut up!" he yelled at Morgan, unable to support more. "Do you think *you're* the only one that wants his mother?"

The insane man was quiet for several minutes. He gave no sign of understanding a word of what had been said to him, but something in the tone of Widdicombe's voice penetrated to that distant spot to which his intelligence had withdrawn.

In the afternoon Morgan seemed to be clearing up mentally. He was quiet and spoke almost normally. Encouraged, Tapscott and Widdicombe put him at the steering oar and tried to get some of the sleep they had lost the night before. They had just dozed off when the boat swung wildly and took a big sea, drenching Widdicombe to the skin. Widdicombe leaped up. Morgan was on his feet, too, the boat left to the vagaries of the swell. Widdicombe threw himself on Morgan. In the struggle that followed the cook went overboard. Tapscott, always a heavy sleeper, awoke in time to see the cook disappear. Flinging himself over the gunwale he seized him by the hair, and, after a desperate effort, managed to get him back into the boat.

They drifted and sailed aimlessly until sundown and then went through the familiar and weary ritual of lowering the sail, putting out the sea anchor, and lying to. They pulled the boat cover over them and longed for sleep—anything to get away from the slow fire that was consuming them inwardly. But Morgan's dementia would not let them rest. What was torture by day became nightmare at night. The peak came toward early morning; then he subsided into coma, broken now and then by muttering and groaning.

The sun rose in a sky bright and clear. With scorched and bloodshot eyes they searched the heavens for signs of rain. The air was heavier and more humid than it had been, but there were only a few thin, high clouds and a steady breeze. With leaden hands they got in the sea anchor and set sail again west, resigning themselves to another day of suffering.

Morgan lay in the bow quietly, his eyes closed. Tapscott nodded at the steering oar; Widdicombe was stretched out on the port seat, the side that shipped the least water. They would go on this way until midday, when the sun, they knew, would be unendurable and they would have to bail water over one another.

Morgan pushed away the boat cover and got up. His expression was normal and his voice firm, clear and without the detached quality of insanity.

"I think," he said, as casually as if they had all been at home in a Newport house, "I'll go down the street for a drink." He climbed up on the seat, walked aft rapidly, and before they could rouse themselves, or even realize what was afoot, stepped over the side. He went down like a shot. When his body reappeared it was being carried away by the swell. He made no more movement, no outcry. They stood staring stupidly after him. Then they sat down and stared at each other. Of the seven men of the *Anglo-Saxon* they were all that was left.

They had no idea of their whereabouts, or even in what direction they were drifting. They had failed to put out the sea anchor in their orgy of sleep; but, luckily, the sea was smooth and windless. They got the anchor over and stretched out on their seats.

Sometime toward morning, Tapscott, who had dozed off into a catnap, was roused by a terrific peal of thunder. Lightning flashed on the horizon, throwing the clouds into livid relief. The surface of the sea showed a ghastly green for a moment; then all was dark again. The rumbling and muttering of thunder drew nearer. Balls of fire, a variety of lightning he had never seen before, flamed in the heavens. More clouds closed over them and a darkness so close it was impossible to see on the boat.

Tapscott peered uneasily ahead, wondering if squalls were bearing down on them. With a terrifying crash a tongue of lightning flickered down from the cloud mass and hissed into the sea. A moment later there was a splatter of drops on the boat cover.

They rolled themselves out from under the cover and stretched it across the thwarts. Rain! Now that it was here they disbelieved the fact of it; they had looked for it so long in vain. The drops became a shower and a puddle formed in the hollow of the canvas. They could not wait, but dipped their tins into it, scraping the tin edges frantically into the grain of the canvas in their eagerness to drink. At the first swallow, they spat the water out. It was saltier than seawater. The boat cover was so impregnated with salt from the gallons of spray that had fallen on it, the water was spoiled. Regretfully they drained the canvas overside and sat waiting for it to fill again.

They had collected a few mouthfuls when the shower ceased as suddenly as it had started. They threw themselves down in disgust, but did not despair. Surely there would be more rain. The very air smelt of it.

Toward dawn the rain came, a cloudburst of it. The skies opened and it sluiced down in steady, heavy sheets. It plastered their long hair to their skulls and their rags to their bodies, washing the salt out of them and filling the boat with almost fresh water.

With the cover spread again they soon had a good puddle in the middle of it. This time it was fresh. The first rain had washed the boat cover clean. They poured water down their throats by the canful, spilling it out of the corners of their mouths, down their chins and chests, with joyful, gluttonous, animal noises. Tapscott had drunk three canfuls when his stomach, constricted and unconditioned by the long drought, revolted and sent it all up again. After that he was cautious and took the water by sips. No man ever held an old wine in his mouth, savoring its bouquet, as Tapscott did each mouthful of rainwater. He let it roll voluptuously round the root of his tongue, and, tilting back his head with infinite caution, let it trickle down his damaged throat. Never before had he known such pleasure in drink.

Widdicombe, who had not drunk as much as Tapscott at first, had no trouble keeping his water down.

Using the boat hook for a tool, Tapscott pried out the bow airtight tank from its fastening. He cut a hole in the soft copper with the Mate's knife, making a bung in the top of it. They rigged a series of creases and runoffs and let the water drain off the canvas into the tank. Tapscott fashioned a plug for it from the loom of an oar. They caught about six gallons of water.

Their thirst quenched, Tapscott and Widdicombe were aware of hunger as a sensation apart from their general misery. It was the first recognizable hunger they had felt in days. They soaked sea biscuit in water and ate it.

By early afternoon the storm had passed and the rain ceased. A light breeze sprang up. Life flowed back into them. They were very weak, but the tide, definitely, had changed. Widdicombe was jubilant.

"I knew we'd make it," he declared. "I knew it the moment we got back into the boat. If we couldn't go then, it stands to reason that we're going to be O.K."

On the morning of September 18, they were becalmed. Worse, they had reached the bottom of the water tank again.

For two days they drifted this way. It did not seem so bad as before. They had learned a technique of suffering. They were unable to eat dry biscuit, and the horrible dryness was throttling them again. But they held on hopefully, confident that they would get rain.

It came early on the morning of the twentieth. It was a good rain. They rigged the cover and runoffs. They drank copiously. Tapscott, having learned his lesson, took his water slowly. He had no trouble keeping it down.

While the tank was filling they soaked six biscuits each in rainwater. When they were soft they ate them. Their supply was getting low, but they had been without food for two days. The rain did not last as long as they would have liked. Still, they had enough water for several days.

"By the time that's gone we'll have reached land," Widdicombe said confidently.

The biscuit tank was nearly empty now, so they decided to limit themselves to one biscuit a day. But they drank all the water they wanted.

Their stomachs swelled ludicrously with the food and water. They had sores on their hips from lying on the hard thwarts. In spite of life belts as cushions these sores grew worse. They noted with some surprise that their bowels had started functioning again. They had a decent night's rest, which helped their morale enormously.

Widdicombe got out the log and wrote:

Sept. 20th. Rain again for four days. Getting very weak but trusting in God to pull us through.
W. R. Widdicombe
R. Tapscott.

They had no thought of sailing that night. If they were so near land, why hurry? They had no suspicion that miles and miles of Atlantic lay between them and the nearest land.

"Keep your eye peeled, Bobby," Widdicombe said. "We may see it any minute now."

Toward sunset on September 24, they were sure that they had made landfall, a low, blue-black mass on the horizon. But as they drew nearer it shifted. Even then they were hopeful; a landmass gives the appearance of shifting sometimes with a boat's change of position. But when they had sailed a while longer they saw that it was cloud.

Several times they had arguments over this: a cloud mass that looked like land. It always revealed itself finally as mirage. They began to wonder what had gone wrong. They had held a course generally west. Even allowing for the aimless drifting they had done at times, wind and current could not have carried them anywhere but in the direction they wanted to go.

The next morning they upended the tank and dribbled the last of the water into their cans. They fumbled in the biscuit tank, but it yielded only broken bits and crumbs. They were without food and water.

Widdicombe fell into the deepest despondency. Fate had done him in the eye again! Water, he felt, they would get; but where would they get food?

No use giving up now, Tapscott said. They could take it. It couldn't go on this way much longer. He was hungry, it was true, very hungry, and both of them looked like scarecrows, but being without food was easy compared to being without water.

Widdicombe made a final entry in the log:

Sept. 24th. All water and biscuits gone. Still hoping to make land.
W. R. W.

During the muggy, stifling night the tension cracked and rain fell again. They had all they wanted to drink and collected a good tankful. The rain soaked them through and through, blanching and wrinkling their hands. It gathered in the boat and they were forced to bail.

When the sun rose, they stripped off their rags and put everything out to dry. The breeze lifted and they set sail. Had it not been for that gnawing vacuity in their middles they would have been gay.

Widdicombe was purposeful again.

"We'll have to sail nights," he said. "Something's wrong with our figuring. We should have made land by now."

They decided, too, that they had best ration the water. They agreed that three dipperfuls a day was about right.

They made good progress that day. When darkness came they did not lie to, but held their course. They took regular watches.

The boat sailed steadily in the starlit night, carrying them westward. As Tapscott sat in the stern sheets, holding the oar, giving an occasional glance at Arcturus or brilliant Jupiter and his satellite in their traverse of the sky, he thought of beef—thick, red, juicy, dripping slices of beef. He dozed off and then awoke with a guilty start. He must stay awake now. It helped to think of beef. What went best with it, a pint of bitter or a tankard of Irish ale?

The five weeks that followed their reprieve from death—the last lap—were like a long, bad dream to Tapscott and Widdicombe. They remembered certain days, the one when a flying fish flew into the boat, for example, but there were stretches when one day followed another in such an unvarying pattern of hunger, sun and sea that they ran together, an indistinguishable blur in the continuity of their suffering.

There were periods of great clarity, under the stress of extreme danger, and long periods of stupor from heat and starvation. All of this time the rhythm of physical existence was slowing down. The subtle debility of slow starvation mounted in unmarked stages until it reached and sapped the very faculty of memory. Their last week in the boat was almost a blank to them.

The day and night following their decision to sail at night were distinguished by nothing but hunger. They were new to a total lack of food. The water they drank revealed as a special craving what had before been an indistinguishable element in their general sufferings.

They cast about the boat for something to eat, anything. There was nothing, nothing they could even think of chewing.

Tapscott had an idea.

"Why not seaweed?" he asked. They had passed clumps of it in considerable number and he remembered the succulent variety of it sold and eaten in Wales under the name of rock laver, which went very well, indeed, particularly when fried with the breakfast bacon.

They kept sharp watch for the next seaweed they should encounter. They were not long in finding it. But far from resembling the long, black, edible laver, which, soft as it is, had, at home, to be boiled in huge pots before being sold for further cooking, this seaweed was tough, rubbery and salty. It was covered with small, hard bulbs resembling berries. They snared a large bunch of it with the boat hook and stowed it in the bow-sheets. It gave them hours of chewing, but very little nourishment. It was impossible to reduce it to a pulp they could swallow without prolonged mastication. The salt in it, even when they had rinsed it in rainwater, gave them intolerable thirst.

The seaweed was not very successful as food; but it was better than nothing.

Tapscott could not sleep. Sometime later he thought he heard a thud against the sail, another on the boat cover over him, and a desperate flapping in the boat. They had seen flying fish in schools but none had come very near them. He was sure, now, that one of them had barged into the sail and was somewhere in the boat. He fumbled for the Mate's torch, which still gave forth a sickly glow, and looked for his quarry. He could find no trace of it. He decided, regretfully, that it had flopped overboard. He went back under the boat cover to sleep.

The next morning, remembering the fish, Tapscott made a thorough search for it. To his incredulous joy he found it, wedged between two battens at the bottom of the boat. He got out Sparks' razor and cut it in two. He took the head half. Widdicombe had the other. They ate it all, every scrap, eyes, bones and fins.

What maddened them was that there were fish all about now. Small ones swam alongside them for hours. They saw dorsal fins. One large fish, which they were convinced was a shark, came up boldly alongside. Widdicombe thrust at it with an oar.

Widdicombe dabbled his fingers overside. The larger fish came to this dangerous bait. He stabbed at them with the Mate's knife. He spent fruitless hours at this and was never able to do more than wound one of them. They became an obsession with him. When they reappeared near the boat he cursed and swore at them, defying them to come within fair stroke of his knife.

The next morning they saw an impressive sight. A whole gam of whales appeared off to the starboard, ten or twelve of them. They cruised along serenely, apparently unaware of the boat, or, if aware of it, completely undisturbed. Tapscott and Widdicombe watched them with respect and apprehension. Suppose one of these huge creatures should take it into his head to charge them? They said nothing until the whole shoal had safely distanced the boat. Then Widdicombe apologized for having doubted Tapscott's story of the other night. He was overcome with belated awe that they had got off as easily as they had when they grounded on one.

Neither Tapscott nor Widdicombe knew enough about whales to identify the species. All that they could report was that they were long-headed, about twenty feet long over all, and that they did not spout.

The next day was without incident. Their initial supply of seaweed had dried out and they saw none that day. They chewed the hardened, leathery strings for hours; but, chew as they might, hunger was now an active torture.

"I wonder what became of that little fish," Tapscott said.

Several days before they grounded on the whale they had seen a small, pinkish object come over the gunwale in a sea.

"It must be somewhere about," Tapscott said, groping on his knees.

He searched the boat systematically, coiling rope, folding the boat cover, stacking the sodden life belts, stowing the sea anchor and generally tidying up. He bailed the boat laboriously, finally finding what he was looking for. The fish was small, soft and rotten; but they ate it, gladly.

"An odd taste it had," Tapscott said, "rather coppery."

After eating the spoiled fish they feared they had poisoned themselves. They waited for the symptoms to appear. Tapscott did feel some qualms in his stomach, but they passed. Widdicombe was unaffected.

Now they were encountering great patches of seaweed. They got a large supply of it aboard and were delighted to find a tiny variety of crab in its meshes. There were, also, some small shellfish, rather like the winkles they got at the seaside resorts at home, which one ate with the aid of a pin. They winnowed out a large number of these, but it took handfuls to make a decent mouthful.

In searching Sparks' attaché case for an implement with which to extract the meat from their shellfish, Tapscott found a safety pin, which gave him another idea. He bent it into a hook, fixed it to a length of spun yarn he found in the boat, sacrificed half a crab for bait and put it over the side. One of the big fish struck it almost immediately. He jerked the line, hooked his fish and let out a howl of joy.

"Play him!" Widdicombe yelled, wild with excitement at the prospect of a real meal. "Play him up to the boat and I'll get him with the knife!"

But the metal of the pin was too soft. The fish gave an outraged leap, plunged, and the hook straightened out, releasing him. Furious, they bent the pin back into shape and tried again. They had another strike. Again they lost the fish; this time he wriggled off the barbless point. They tried over and over. They had no trouble getting strikes. But, always, the hook was too soft and their fish got away. Disgusted, they gave it up in the end.

Seaweed was their sole source of food. The patches of it were growing larger in area daily. They scorned the small detached clumps now, waiting until they sighted a floating field of it. Sometimes there were leads through it, like open water in an ice floe. When they found one of these they steered the boat into it. Moving slowly, they picked crabs, winkles and anything that seemed edible out of it.

The seaweed patches they were now encountering contained a small shrimp as well as crabs and winkles. These were a most welcome addition to their diet—if such it could be called—but, like the crabs, were too small to supply much substance. Hours of work were required to furnish a meal.

Unsatisfied after such labor, and after dark, they picked over their supply of seaweed in the boat for the most tender morsels and chewed on that.

The weather held generally fair until October 8. Except for their side excursions into kelp fields and the extra mileage on tacks they made good progress westward. Late that day, however, squalls blew up, and rain. They lay to, spreading the boat cover and the sail over them in an attempt to keep dry. They passed a damp but, by comparison with some others during the trip, comfortable night.

Day broke overcast and drizzling. They decided to stay as they were until the weather lifted. They had already collected all the water they needed. There was nothing to do but sleep. Widdicombe was still snoring when Tapscott wakened. Rain was drumming on the canvas over them. Tapscott lifted the canvas, sat up and looked about. The sky was leaden and the visibility poor. There was some swell on the sea. He checked the sea anchor and found it in order. He was about to pull the canvas over him again when his glance, roving aft, fixed on a sight that riveted his eyes. Not more than a half mile away, off the port bow, bearing southerly, was a large steamer.

"Roy! Roy!" he yelled, shaking Widdicombe savagely. "A ship!"

Widdicombe sat up sleepily. He did not take it in for a minute. Tapscott was already heaving in the sea anchor. Together they got it in, grabbed oars and rowed frantically toward her.

Pulling as hard as they could, the steamer was distancing them. They rowed until they could go on no longer. They stood up in the boat, waving their arms and shouting. The steamer showed no signs of seeing them. They swung their oars, semaphore fashion, and Tapscott, finding the Mate's whistle, stood up in the bow and blew it until he was breathless. The liner steamed steadily ahead.

They picked up their oars again and tried to row to it. They were so weak and winded they achieved only a few strokes. Tapscott seized the whistle and blew it as hard and as long as he could. The liner kept her course. Then, turning sharply, she went off east.

Tapscott and Widdicombe collapsed on their oars, completely spent. Their hearts were beating as if to burst; their lungs heaved and they gulped down air in sobbing spasms. When they had recovered enough to handle the boat, they put it about and hoisted sail. Sick with disappointment and fatigue, they resumed their course west.

For four days after losing the passenger liner the weather was unsettled. The wind shifted about the compass uneasily. Rain squalls struck Tapscott and Widdicombe from unexpected quarters and the sea lost its reliable northeasterly swell. Confused winds and choppy cross waves buffeted them about, making steering difficult and exhausting. They shipped a great deal of water and had to bail at all hours. They noticed when bailing how much weaker they had become. They tired quickly and had to take more frequent rests.

On the morning of October 27, just after having started for the day, Widdicombe, whose turn it was, complained of dizziness and called to Tapscott to relieve him. Tapscott studied Widdicombe intently and decided he was speaking the truth. He took the oar and Widdicombe stretched himself out on one of the side seats. In a few minutes he was snoring.

After three hours at the helm, or thereabouts, as near as he could judge it, Tapscott called for relief. Widdicombe stirred, opened his eyes and heard Tapscott repeat his request. He rolled over again and paid no attention to it.

"All right, then," Tapscott said, shipping the oar. "Let the bloody boat sail itself. I'm through."

He left the stern sheets and made his way to the middle of the boat, where he sat down, braced against a thwart. Widdicombe, alongside him, watched him with narrowed eyes. He sat up slowly, his jaw jutted out. Tapscott had seen that expression before—the night Widdicombe had slugged Elliott. He was certain Widdicombe was about to hit. Before he could, Tapscott, gathering up all his remaining strength, punched Widdicombe flush on the jaw. Widdicombe went down on the seat, but was up a moment later flinging himself upon Tapscott. They rolled about in the bottom of the boat weakly pummeling each other. Suddenly, Widdicombe quit.

"I'm too weak," he said.

Tapscott pulled himself up on a thwart and waited. He did not relax his guard until Widdicombe had crawled aft and manned the steering oar.

They sailed and drifted for a long time without moving or speaking. Tapscott was feeling sorry now. He had not wanted to hit Widdicombe, but he was certain that it had been self-defense. Still, they were absolutely dependent upon each other. And when Tapscott thought of what they had been through and of the chaps who were gone, he was sorrier still.

"I'm sorry, Roy," he said, finally. "I'm sorry I hit you. It's crazy for us to fight."

Widdicombe grunted but said nothing. His lips were puffed and discolored from Tapscott's blow.

All that day, part of the night and until midnight the next day, they made fair progress. They said little or nothing, communicating when necessary by signs and grunts. It was an effort to talk and in spite of Tapscott's apology, feeling between them was strained.

To Tapscott it seemed as if they were moving in a child's dream of impotence, when he wants desperately to run, jump, hit or cry out and his body refuses to obey the command of his brain.

At midnight the wind fell away completely. They let the boat drift with the current and slept, not troubling even to lower the sail. Sometime between then and dawn Tapscott thought he heard a fish flapping in the boat. The night was dark, the Mate's torch had gone dead and he was too weak to look for it. He decided to wait until daylight.

With the first light of dawn Tapscott was in the bottom of the boat, looking for the fish. He found it; what he called a gar. Actually it was a Bahamian houndfish, a long needlelike creature, almost transparent, which is considered inedible by the natives. Houndfish lie near the surface of the sea and when frightened leap clear out of it. An enemy had chased it into the boat.

"I've found it," Tapscott said.

Widdicombe said nothing.

"I've found the fish," Tapscott repeated, looking up to see why Widdicombe received this important news so apathetically. Widdicombe was staring straight ahead, his eyes straining from the sockets. "Look," he said, pointing.

Tapscott, holding the fish firmly, raised himself on a thwart to see. Dead ahead lay a long line of lowland and beach, stretching north and south, apparently, as far as they could see.

They had been deceived so many times before, they did not dare to believe it.

"Land?" said Tapscott.

Widdicombe nodded.

"You're sure we're not seeing things?"

Widdicombe shook his head. The breeze was rising and the boat picked up way. As they drew nearer, they could see a line of reef with the sea breaking over it. Those rocks and the spray they threw up were no mirage.

"It *is* land, Bobby," Widdicombe said, sounding as if he were about to cry. "It must be the Leeward Islands."

Tapscott stared and stared at the reef and the beach beyond. There was no doubt in his mind now. Had the night lasted longer or the wind held the night through, they would have sailed right into it. Suddenly a wrenching pain racked his bowels. Still staring at the land, he grabbed for the bucket that served them as latrine.

A line of reef and broken water separated them from the land. They could see bush in back of the beach, and, in places, clumps of higher bush or trees, but no sign of human habitation.

"Land or no land," Tapscott said, "I'm going to eat this fish."

He cut it in half with Sparks' razor and together they ate it, staring at the land.

When they had finished the fish, they stood up unsteadily and studied the water ahead.

"I think I see a place to get through," Tapscott said, indicating a patch of smooth water. They got in the sea anchor, set sail and steered for it. It was a channel right enough, but extremely narrow. Tapscott lay in the bow and directed their course.

They threaded their way through patches of shoal and sharp, rocky heads. It was easy to see them; the water was the clearest Tapscott had ever seen. It was the most brilliantly colored he had ever seen, too, ranging from ultramarine in the depths to aquamarine in the shallows. Below him, around rocky drops and coral-encrusted banks, brilliantly colored fish swam and long, purple sea fans waved with the movement of the water. Here and there were patches of grass, and white sand between the rocks. He saw reticulated coral mounds like gargantuan brains. White trees of the same substance grew in this sea garden.

Twenty minutes later the bow of their boat grounded on the beach. Tapscott clambered over the bow, surprised at his strength. Widdicombe followed with the boat hook. He had some idea of mooring the boat to it, driven in the beach. The tide was ebbing, but they did not know it at the time. They were on land!

The sun beat down on the white sand. In the lee of the bush there was shade. Like drunken men they staggered up the beach to it and collapsed. The effort of walking was too much for them.

They lay in the shade until Widdicombe was feeling better. He proposed that they start northward up the beach. He felt that they might find human beings there. Tapscott got to his feet with infinite effort. Now that they were actually on land, all his remaining strength seemed to have gone from him. Laboriously they started up the beach. Thirty or forty feet of walking and Tapscott collapsed. The job he had been carrying on by sheer willpower and momentum was through.

How long Tapscott and Widdicombe lay on the edge of the bush they could not say. They were roused by the sound of blows somewhere in the bush in back of them. Someone was cutting a way through. Then they heard voices. They saw no one, but they knew someone was here, someone who retreated precipitously.

"They speak English whoever they are," Widdicombe said. "I heard them say 'fetch.'"

Tapscott was beyond answering.

"We'd better get back to the boat. They'll be coming back and might miss us," Widdicombe said. "Can you make it?"

Tapscott indicated that he would try.

They staggered and crawled back to a point on the edge of the bush opposite the boat. The tide had left it stranded. They lay there for a long time; then they heard voices again. The voices spoke English, an English such as they had never heard before, but, indubitably, English. A moment later, a man, a woman and several more men emerged from the bush and stood over them.

"Who you are?" one of them asked.

"English," Widdicombe said. "Off the *Anglo-Saxon*. Our ship was sunk by a German raider. We got away in the boat."

"When dat?" the man asked, dubiously.

"August twenty-first," Widdicombe said. "We were sixty-five days in the boat. We're starving."

A chorus of exclamations went up.

"Save me, Lawd!"

"Hey, man?"

"Today's the twenty-fifth, isn't it?" Widdicombe said.

"Today's the thirtieth," one of the men said.

"Then it's seventy days."

The group seemed suspicious. Nobody stirred.

"Look," said Widdicombe, taking Sparks' wallet from his pocket and handing it to the nearest man. "Papers."

The man took the wallet and extracted the log sheets and other papers from it. He studied them a long time and handed them to the others to look at.

Tapscott only half heard all this. He lay with closed eyes.

The spokesman was satisfied with what he read. He said something to the others. Neither Tapscott nor Widdicombe understood. The group broke into fresh exclamations of wonder and commiseration.

The seamen knew they were safe.

Sources

"The Loss of the *Indianapolis*," from *The Tragic Fate of the U.S.S.* Indianapolis. Raymond B. Lech. New York: Cooper Square Press, a division of the Rowman & Littlefield Publishing Group. 1982.

"The *Karluk*'s Last Voyage," from *The* Karluk's *Last Voyage*. Robert Bartlett. New York: Small, Maynard & Company. 1916. Lanham, MD: Cooper Square Press, a division of the Rowman & Littlefield Publishing Group. 2001.

"The Savage Sea," from *Survive the Savage Sea*. Dougal Robertson. Lanham, MD: Sheridan House, a division of the Rowman & Littlefield Publishing Group. 1994.

"Loss of the Whaleship *Essex*," from *Loss of the Whaleship* Essex. Owen Chase. 1821.

"The Shetland Bus," from *The Shetland Bus*. David Howarth. Guilford, CT: The Lyons Press, a division of the Rowman & Littlefield Publishing Group. 2001.

"The Wreck of the *Medusa*," from *Perils and Captivity*. Charlotte-Adélaïde Dard. Edinburgh: Constable and Co. 1827.

"The Last Cruise of the *Saginaw*," from *The Last Cruise of the* Saginaw. George H. Read. Boston and New York: Houghton Mifflin Company. 1912.

"Treacherous Passage," from *Eight Survived: The Harrowing Story of the USS* Flier. Douglas A. Campbell. Guilford, CT: The Lyons Press, a division of the Rowman & Littlefield Publishing Group. 2010.

"Seventy Days in an Open Boat," from *Two Survived: The Timeless WWII Epic of Seventy Days at Sea in an Open Boat.* Guy Pearce Jones. Guilford, CT: The Lyons Press, a division of the Rowman & Littlefield Publishing Group. 2001.